Linus Parker

Bishop Linus Parker

His Life and Writings

Linus Parker

Bishop Linus Parker
His Life and Writings

ISBN/EAN: 9783743373280

Manufactured in Europe, USA, Canada, Australia, Japa

Cover: Foto ©Lupo / pixelio.de

Manufactured and distributed by brebook publishing software (www.brebook.com)

Linus Parker

Bishop Linus Parker

THE EDITOR-BISHOP:
LINUS PARKER.

HIS LIFE AND WRITINGS

BY REV. CHAS. B. GALLOWAY, D.D.,
Editor of the New Orleans Christian Advocate.

WITH AN INTRODUCTION BY BISHOP McTYEIRE.

NASHVILLE, TENN.:
SOUTHERN METHODIST PUBLISHING HOUSE.
1886.

Entered, according to Act of Congress, in the year 1886,
By the Book Agents of the Methodist Episcopal Church, South,
in the Office of the Librarian of Congress, at Washington.

CONTENTS.

INTRODUCTION (by Bishop McTyeire) 7

HIS LIFE.

CHAPTER I.
Birth and Boyhood.. 17

CHAPTER II.
Early Religious History................................. 23

CHAPTER III.
Call to the Ministry.................................... 27

CHAPTER IV.
His First Circuit....................................... 31

CHAPTER V.
Two Years at Shreveport................................. 36

CHAPTER VI.
First Year in New Orleans............................... 43

CHAPTER VII.
First Year in New Orleans (Continued)................... 57

CHAPTER VIII.
The Diligent City Pastor................................ 62

CHAPTER IX.
Correspondence Up the River............................. 70

CHAPTER X.
Second Marriage—John C. Burruss......................... 87

CHAPTER XI.
Again in the Country.................................... 95

CHAPTER XII.
Twelve Years an Editor.................................. 99

CHAPTER XIII.
Three Years a Bishop.................................... 103

CHAPTER XIV.
Personal Traits and Characteristics..................... 107

CHAPTER XV.
Last Hours and Burial................................... 113

(3)

HIS WRITINGS.

THE PREACHER CALLED.
Call to the Ministry 123
The Ministerial Woe 126

THE PREACHER AT WORK.
Godly Craft 131
Comforting God's People 134
What and How to Preach 137
Cumulative Preaching 141

THE PREACHER IN METHODISM.
The Itinerant School 144
One Advantage of Itinerancy 148

THE PREACHER, YOUNG AND OLD.
The Young Preacher 151
The Old Preacher 155

THE CHURCH IN THE WORLD.
Added to the Church 161
Church Pillars 164
Counting the Cost 167
Garments not Defiled 171

THE WORLD IN THE CHURCH.
Forbidden Diversions 175
Loose Notions 179
Recreation in Religion 181
Peril to Methodist Experience 184

FAMILY RELIGION.
Children at Home 187
The Bible at Home 190
Prayer in the Family 192
The Son of Thine Handmaid 195

SOUL EDUCATION.
Training for the Life to Come 199
At the Feet of Jesus 202
Waiting for the Lord 205

CHRISTIAN DUTIES.
The Duty of Pleasing 209
Helping One Another 213
Serving the Will of God 215

CHRISTIAN GRACES.

Contentment	219
Love in Religion	222
The Denial of Self	225
The Grace of Gentleness	228
The Edifying Grace	231
The Surprises of Grace	235

THE BELIEVER'S POSSESSIONS.

"All Things are Yours"	240
The Secret of the Lord	243
Christ's Sympathy	246
Melody in the Heart	250
Divine Companionship	253

PRAYER.

Learning to Pray	257
Christ's Example in Prayer	260
Prayer and the Holy Spirit	264
Prayer Ended	267

MISSIONS.

Loosing from Troas	272
Jonah and Foreign Missions	276
The Appeal of Missions	280
An Old Objection to Missions	284
Dead and Buried	287

THE MISSION OF GOLD.

Christ Over Against the Treasury	289
Cost of Souls	292
Economizing for God	296
Sowing Money	299

FROM GRACE TO GRACE.

The Birth of the Spirit	303
After Conversion	306
The Spiritual Face	310
The Glory in Us	313
Shining More and More	317

THE LIKES OF THE KINGDOM.

Inspired Comparisons	320
Like Passions	323
Child-likeness	326

PLANTING AND TRANSPLANTING.

	PAGE
Planted in the House of the Lord	330
Transplanting	333

TEACHINGS OF THE CLOUDS.

Clouds Without Water	337
Clouds After the Rain	340
The Wind and the Clouds	343

DAYS AND SEASONS.

Thanksgiving	348
Christmas Greetings	350
New-year	353
The Gospel of Spring	356
The Fall of the Leaves	361
Birthdays	363

LIGHT OUT OF DARKNESS.

Out of a Dark Room	367
Not Orphans	370
God's Chastisements	373
The Discipline of Failure	376

THE LIFE THAT NOW IS.

As a Tale that is Told	379
"I Would not Live Alway"	382
The Duty of Living	384
Nothing to Live For	388

THE GRAVE AND BEYOND.

The Death of Friends	393
Dying as a Little Child	397
What We shall Take with Us	400
Heaven a Character	403

MISCELLANEOUS.

One Office of the Spirit	406
Golden Vials Full of Odors	409
The Heated Term	413
The two Marvels of Jesus	415
Old and New Methodism	419
Elijah's Mantle	422
The Cake and the Cruse	425
Lenten Cook-books	429
Revival Expedients	432
An Effectual Quarantine	435

INTRODUCTION.

Such a life as Linus Parker's ought to be lived over again many times. A character like his deserves to be perpetuated by a memorial. The world was the better for his presence, and this benefit may be prolonged and extended by a suitable portrait, now that he has left it.

There was a healthful Christian influence emanating from Linus Parker, as a man and a minister. His virtues were real and imitable. There was no quality abnormal, eccentric, or of doubtful import about him; no precocious growth; no moral rebate; nothing strained or sensational. A sound mental constitution; a genial, but not excessive, social temper; a taste for the true and beautiful as natural as is an ear for music; and a generous heart—these formed in him a basis upon which the purifying and consecrating Spirit wrought a model character and a useful life.

It is allowable here to describe my first impressions of him, and the beginning of our acquaintance.

The colonizing policy of New Orleans Methodism had been carried to excess. Three weak stations (or missions)—Steele Chapel, Andrew Chapel, and St. Mary's—occupied ground in the upper part of the city, which one commodious and central church could supply. Each had its own Quarterly Conference and officers, and claimed the privilege of enjoying its little autonomy, and of starving a preacher. William F. Brown, the pastor of the first, had died of yellow fever the year before the time of which I write; and Henry B. Page, on his way from Conference to take charge of the second, had been lost in the burning of the Yallobusha steamer, on the Mississippi River.

Bishop Paine decided to unite these three charges into one, and in

December, 1848, sent me from the Alabama Conference to effect this reorganization; and with the consolidated congregations and their assets—small indeed, two of the three structures being built of "flat-boat" lumber—to build a good church somewhere near the corner of Magazine and Felicity streets. This task was not accomplished without friction; the majorities were willing, but there were unwilling minorities. The situation suggested a text—Psalm cxxii., last four verses; and one Sunday, early in 1849, while preaching on this text in one of the three conventicles, my attention was attracted by a young man in the congregation: jet-black hair, and fine eyes of that shade; slender, and of full height. Possibly I had *seen* him before, but now for the first time I *perceived* him. He had about him the earnest, abstracted air of one who was revolving a great and devout question. He was such a listener as the pulpit feels. Well do I remember how his responsive attention caused the preacher to expand a certain part of the sermon beyond the original plan. Linus Parker was at that time hearing the voice, "Son, go work to-day in my vineyard." And he answered and said, "I go, sir;" and went.

After that day the parsonage was often favored with his company. From the way he quietly walked into the heart of every member of the household and took his seat there, and was ever at home, I understood the mystery of those friendships, tender and strong, which he formed elsewhere through life. There was no mannerism, no wordiness, no set effort to make himself agreeable; but a modest consciousness of truth in the inward parts that seemed to say: "I am in no hurry; I like you, and when you come to know me you will like me."

He succeeded me at Felicity Street Church, and my family fell heir to that nourishing discourse and gentle pastoral care which never can be forgotten. My wife insisted he had but one fault: Whenever you quoted any sentiment or told him of any thing that had occurred which he did not like, his dissent was so abruptly expressed as to leave on you an uncomfortable feeling, as though you were responsible for the sentiment or the occurrence.

It was in that pulpit, and over that congregation, I witnessed with deepest approval his pastoral methods. For though he was not a revivalist, as some understand the term, seldom did a year pass under his ministry without a revival. There were special seasons of refreshing; souls were converted and added to the Church. He honored the preaching of THE WORD, and looked for the Spirit to use it for conviction and quickening and salvation. Nice though his taste was, he would listen without weariness and with unaffected pleasure to the humblest embassador of God who had something to say based on God's word. I can never forget his criticism—to which he was little given—upon hearing a popular preacher. In reply to my question, "How did you like him?" his hand was lifted to his face and impatiently waved off—a characteristic gesture: "No ideas. *Vox, et præterea nihil.*" He loved diggers into the mine of truth, however rough their tools.

Linus Parker would have been an acceptable contributor to the *Spectator* in Addison's day. The *nom de plume* under which he wrote for the New Orleans *Christian Advocate* was taken from the steam-boat on which he ascended Red River, "Woodsman." It required no keenness of editorial instinct to discern, by his first paper, that he had a gift. The manuscript needed correction in one particular only: it had no paragraphs—from beginning to end it was run together in an unbroken whole. And this was the style of his sermons. The divisions were in his own mind, and the occult, logical processes were evolved and thrown off without any breaks. There were no "firstlys" and "thirdlys" and "finallys." The effect of his sermons remained with you, but it was hard to reproduce them.

As a Church officer, in any capacity, he had these excellent qualities: intense admiration for truth and honesty, great love of justice, proneness to take the side of the weak, and, without being suspicious, he was so judicious that no "ring" could capture him.

The Christian experience of Linus Parker—by no means a solitary case—presents a problem which I could wish to solve, or so to present it that others, more capable, might furnish the solution. His acquaintances might suppose that his religious life began when the young man attended the meeting at old Poydras Street Church, in New Orleans, went up to be prayed for, joined the Church, and attached himself to the Sunday-school and the class-meeting there. But, in fact, he was converted years before that—even when he was a little child. How can we make the most of childhood religion, conserve it, develop it? What can be done for those who are in the perplexed, perilous, lamentable condition of backsliders from that blessed estate? How can that dropped stitch be picked up, or connection be made over that missing link? Or, rather, how can this too often occurring lapse be prevented? As a tree when rived up sometimes shows signs of violence that was done to the twig, so these signs of arrested moral development frequently meet us in the analysis of noble lives.

I have heard his missionary speeches highly commended by good judges; but the best platform addresses I ever heard from him were in favor of the temperance cause. He went, from the first, very heartily into that reform movement; but was a modest and moderate smoker. "Brother S——," he remarked, on lighting one of a fragrant bunch of Havanas which a friend had presented him, "I do like a good cigar. It is such an antidote to fanaticism." I never saw him perpetrate the clerical vulgarism of smoking along the streets, or around the doors of a church. Well has it been said: "There are practices so unbecoming the ministerial vocation as to be inexpedient, and so inexpedient as to be unlawful. Christian ministers are, among other men, like statues upon a high pedestal, which must be larger than life to appear of life-size."

There was somewhat worth studying in his friendships. Not quick to ingratiate himself into favor, and never a seeker after popularity, he nevertheless numbered friends among the most different and even opposite classes of people; and, though not compromising in his disposition, I doubt if he ever lost a friend after once gaining him. In penetration of character he was not lacking; but he abounded in the charity of common sense as well as of piety. He looked not for perfection, and the presence of certain sterling and well-ascertained qualities atoned for much that was not according to his own mind. He enjoyed the prayer of the negro exhorter: "Lord, help us to put up with people you puts up with, and to bear with them you bears with." With felicitous tact he seized the right point of view from which to develop a text. To unravel a tangled subject, he began at the right place, wherever that was. And so he would, without any taint of moral indifferentism or the least affectation, look upon the best side of character; or, may be, make the most of the one virtue that hid a multitude of faults.

Of the various positions filled by him in the Church of God—pastor of a congregation, presiding elder of a district, editor of an ecclesiastical organ, General Superintendent—I make no question but that the first was most congenial to his taste. Personal convenience and social and spiritual comforts all lay in this direction, and along this line of duties. To have "a people;" to be in close contact with them, and enjoy the intimate relations and sympathy of a pastor's life; to watch the growth of individual religion, and minister to it; to know every one of his flock by name, and be known and loved by them—this is a rare delight. No one, with his fine temperament, ever passed beyond this sacred sphere into wider cares without looking back to it with regretful longings. Whatever of honor is implied by the summons of the Church to serve in more public places, and to bear heavier burdens, finds its offset in this separation from the throbbing heart of a spiritual family, and in the details of administration.

The election of Linus Parker to the office of Bishop in the Methodist Episcopal Church, South, by the General Conference of 1882, was at once a surprise to him, and a gratification to those who knew his abilities and his worth. At the first question propounded in his consecration to the office, he naturally hesitated. The Ritual has it:

"*Ques.* Are you persuaded that you are truly called to this ministration, according to the will of our Lord Jesus Christ?

"*Ans.* I am so persuaded."

But, while he conscientiously pondered the matter, before standing before the congregation to take vows, light was thrown upon the question by an ordination service that occurred several years before:

"*Ques.* Do you think in your heart that you are truly called, according to the will of our Lord Jesus Christ, to the order of elders?

"*Ans.* I think so."

The call of the Head of the Church was, in both cases, providentially indicated to him by the free suffrages of his brethren, in a representative capacity.

Dr. Summers, in his learned Commentary on the Ritual—a book that might be studied to profit by preachers—has this note:

"*Are you persuaded that you are truly called to this ministration, according to the will of our Lord Jesus Christ?*—He may answer in the affirmative if he has been chosen by the free suffrages of his brethren, feels that he has reasonable qualifications for it, and that he is influenced to it by pure motives."

It is possible that the history of simony, and of the corrupt practices of State Churches, might disclose the origin of that question in the past. It remains a proper question still, for the possible evils it suggests or guards against.

A preacher of excellent standing thus addressed another, in whose friendship and judgment he confided: "I have been written and spoken to by several persons about my election to the episcopacy. What shall I do?" The answer was: "Do nothing. As you fear God, and love the Church, and seek the path of safety—which is the path of duty—go right along as though no General Conference were approaching; doing nothing, of purpose, to promote your election; and, on the other hand, doing nothing, of purpose, to prevent it. A soldier may not maim himself to keep from being detailed or drafted for any service. Ambition, self-seeking, and intrigue are entitled to no position in the Church. Hold an even scale; and then you can conscientiously accept the result of the balances and of the ballots. If you are thus elected, expect official grace for official usefulness; and, without scruple, answer the question that meets you on the threshold: 'Are you persuaded that you are truly called to this ministration, according to the will of our Lord Jesus Christ?'"

Unreservedly might Linus Parker say, "I am so persuaded." Brief, but full and faithful, was his term of episcopal service. The first two years were given to the Texas Conferences, where it was my lot to follow him the next two—just closed. Everywhere his name, among people and preachers, was as ointment poured forth. Another year's labor in a different part of the Connectional field showed the same painstaking and wise administration, edifying preaching, and blameless example. Then, with portfolio full of appointments for District Conferences and special occasions, and the eyes of the Church turned on him with loving hope and large expectation, it pleased the Master to dismiss his servant from labor, and to call him to the exceeding great reward.

The following pages, by a most competent and appreciative hand, set forth the life and character of my beloved and lamented friend and colleague. I approved the design, and am thankful for the privilege of making the least contribution toward its fulfillment.

H. N. McTYEIRE.

February 24, 1880.

His Life.

CHAPTER I.
BIRTH AND BOYHOOD.

LINUS PARKER was born on the 23d of April, 1829, near the town of Vienna, in Oneida county, State of New York. His parents—John and Alvira Parker—were natives of Connecticut, and of the finest New England blood. To their sturdy virtues, strong characters, and pure, evangelical Christianity Linus was indebted, by the law of heredity, for the characteristics that gave him greatness. "Monica is better known by the branch of her issue than the root of her parentage," said the eloquent Fuller of the pious mother of St. Augustine. And so, however honorably descended, the names of John and Alvira Parker will be best remembered as having borne, trained, and given to the Lord a son of seraphic spirit and apostolic labors.

His father was born in Watertown, Litchfield county, Connecticut, August 12, 1788; but in the fifth year of his age removed with his parents to what was then called "the far West." As was the custom in that day, the entire household was packed on board a large sled, drawn by four oxen, and in ten days safely reached their new home in Greenfield, Saratoga county, New York, "a lonely wilderness scarcely inhabited except by savages and wild beasts." Thence, after a time, they moved into Montgomery county, and subsequently to Camden, in the picturesque and fertile county of Oneida. At the age of twenty-four he returned to his native Connecticut for a life-companion, and on the 7th of September, 1814, married Miss Alvira Wadham in the town of Goshen. They at once returned to New York State and settled on a farm in the vicinity of Vienna, where they lived comfortably and happily, and reared for the Lord a large family of sons and daughters. John Parker was a man of great intelligence, firmness, vigor of mind and body, and of large influence. He commanded universal respect. His opinions were almost the common law of his neighborhood, and his counsel was sought as confidently as the ancients inquired of their oracles and patron saints. With strong domestic affections, he preferred the quiet of his home and farm to the responsibilities of public office. But no doubt, had his tastes permitted, he would have occupied an honorable place in the councils of his countrymen. And withal he was a consistent and devoted member of the Methodist Episcopal Church. He was a veritable and typical pillar of the Church, durable as granite and transparent as light. At the advanced age of eighty-eight years he fell on sleep at Johnston, Wisconsin, on the 31st of January, 1866.

Alvira Wadham belonged to an old and numerous New England family. She was a woman of considerable culture and of rare loveliness of character and piety. Reared a stanch Congregationalist, she united the systematic training of that communion with the fervor and evangelism of "the people called Methodists." She had an exalted idea of the responsibilities and *honor* of motherhood. Her children were not a tax or a burden, but with old Jewish pride each was hailed as a special gift of God and token of his abundant favor. Rightly to train them for the highest usefulness was her constant study and earnest prayer. After a long pilgrimage of full threescore years and ten, she finished her course with joy at Johnston, Wisconsin, September 20, 1869. On the occasion of her death the Bishop made this modest mention of his model mother: "Though very infirm for the past two years, and at death her faculties were almost gone, her tender love for me and all the children never abated."

Milton's oft-quoted words, "Childhood shows the man as morning shows the day," were strikingly illustrated in the life of Linus Parker. The quiet, observant, thoughtful boy prophesied the modest, dignified, massive-brained man. His mind was cast in a large and serious mold. Genial and kindly in manner, and not lacking in warm, boyish friendships, he was yet far removed from the ordinary follies and frivolities of youth. From the beginning he was regarded as a mature child, having little affinity for childhood's recreations. He had a reflective disposition that readily analyzed and assimilated the gathered treasures of his eager observation. Together with this he possessed a chaste, exuberant imagination, and a gentle under-tone of humor that sometimes rippled out in school-boy rhyme. His class of reading was of the highest order—quite beyond his years. Histories like Gibbon's "Decline and Fall of the Roman Empire" indicate the character of his thirst for literature. At eleven years of age he read D'Aubigné's "History of the Reformation," and his young heart was stirred to the depths by that graphic story of the struggle and triumph of divine principle. His father, who was fond of reading, and a man of large information, used to remark, "That boy reads understandingly.' When the merest child he attended a "General Training" in the county-town, which was quite an event in that day, and, while others brought away memories of sports and revelries, he returned with a copy of the "Life of Sir Walter Raleigh." On such food his young mind fed and throve.

The habits of farm-life and the charming scenery of Oneida were well calculated to wing a young imagination and nurse his genius for books. The county bore the name of a famous, war-like tribe of Indians, which, being interpreted, was "tribe of the granite rock." Traditions of their daring deeds were connected with many spots familiar to the thoughtful youth, and intensified his thirst for historic reading. The beautiful valley of the Mohawk, with its poetic and Revolutionary associations; the great Erie and Chenango canals, crowded with every curious craft; the mountain-range that towered away to the northward, and the rugged hills sloping to the south, were the scenes amid which his boyhood days were spent.

The picture of his paternal home is best drawn by his own skillful hand. He describes it after an absence of more than ten years. He went away a beardless boy and returned a promising young preacher, stationed in one of the leading churches in the great metropolis of the South. The reader will notice his avoidance of the perpendicular pronoun. He writes:

"From these emotions and scenes let such a one as we have imagined pass to the very roof-tree under which he was born, and let him stroll over the fields and woods of the old farm. Every spot and thing is a remembrance, and fruitful of associations. With a heart wild with excitement, he explores the old house from cellar to garret; examines barns, stables, and sheds minutely; climbs the apple-trees whose fruit he ate and whose sprouts were terrible; until wearied, he throws himself upon the grass and reposes in the ample shade of trees which his own hands have planted. It seems a desecration to find strangers in the old home, and the loved ones gone, all gone. The noble dog that chased the cars when we went away, and pined for weeks when his young master did not return, is dead; the ancient geese "that gabbled o'er the pool," and the ducks that quacked in chorus with them, are no more. The weather-cock on the barn's gable looks the wind in the face, and the petit wind-mill beneath it plays as briskly as it played in days of yore. There is the trout-brook running quickly, clearly, and as young as ever. The changes are in living things, all living things; but inanimate nature maintains its wonted aspect, and even art withstands the tooth of time better than the hand which executes it."

And then he passes out into the family burying-ground and gives himself to meditation. His tenderly, beautiful reflections among the mounds that cover his precious dead, and especially at the grave of his little twin brother—"another self under the sod"—are as exquisitely delicate and discriminating as any thing in the English language:

"Here in one plot is a row of little graves—four in all—with little head and foot stones to mark them. Of the last one but a single memory is left. The babe that seemed asleep, the tiny coffin, the gentleness and care with which its occupant was put in, the wringing hands and sobs of one who wept more than any of us, the crowd of people who came and took the coffin and the baby, and their return no more—this is a picture which time has not effaced. The next one is of peculiar interest to just one other. He was one of two who saw the light at once, and was rocked in the same cradle. One was taken and the other was left. It is like another self under the sod, and strange, strong yearnings were excited to see one so doubly near and yet so totally unknown. More than a score of years he has spent in the silent land—long and weary years to his cradle-mate, but bright and all-glorious to him. Of the other two maternal story says that they were blue-eyed children, who, like buds in sweetness and beauty, dropped into the grave. Connected with their names are treasured mementos of auburn hair, nicely curled and carefully kept, and other memorials, besides the mounds which are here. Dear, dear dust! Thankful for the life and immortality revealed in the gospel, the sad heart turns away and rejoices in the light which it sheds upon the graves of those who engross its affections."

His opportunities for scholastic training were quite meager. Methodism had not then developed her splendid system of education. So, like many another leader in the Church, Bishop Parker attained unto respectable scholarship by dint of his own unaided toil. The common schools of the country furnished his only educational advantages, and they were attended not more than six months in the twelve from his sixth to his sixteenth year. One year he attended a somewhat better school at Binghampton, New York, and for four months, shortly after his arrival in New Orleans, he was a student in old Mandeville College, across the lake. But by patient and well-directed private study he became an accurate classical scholar, including a considerable acquaintance with Hebrew, and was a master in the department of belles-lettres.

CHAPTER II.
EARLY RELIGIOUS HISTORY.

HIS parents were Christians in fact as well as in name, and their religion shed its aroma over their home-life. The children were not unused to the voice of prayer, and were early trained in the paths of righteousness. So carefully and watchfully was Linus Parker reared at the altar of Methodism that he said, "As a child I hardly knew that any other Church existed." In the shelter of that Christian home and in the neighboring church, whose pulpit, to his young imagination, was "like the throne of Jupiter Tonans," indelible impressions were made that in after years flowered out in his symmetrically beautiful character. Writing from that old roof-tree, he said: "Amongst the multiform instruments which work out the soul's regeneration, those which bear upon its earliest consciousness are most effectual. Not that these consummate the work, nor that they are more powerful, but that without them all after influences would be impotent."

A sister thus refers to his early religious life: "To us he appeared like unto Timothy of old, knowing the Scriptures from a child. Surely they made him wise unto salvation." But the story of his first divine impressions, of his falling through the ice on the Chenango River and its influence upon his religious life, and all the circumstances attending his joyous espousal to the Lord Christ at eleven years of age, must be told in his own words:

"My first serious impressions were received when six or

seven years of age. At church there was a protracted meeting. An old class-leader, passing near where I sat, asked me if I wanted religion. I knew not what he meant, but I began to inquire and think about it from that time. In 1840 —the year I spent in Binghampton in the family of my brother-in-law, Dr. N. S. Davis—I was brought to seek the salvation of my soul. Dr. Davis was a most exemplary Christian and Methodist, and my sister, Mrs. Davis, was also a pious member of the Church. Dr. Joseph Cross, afterward a resident of the South, was the stationed preacher that year. In the early spring, while playing and running on the ice in the canal, the ice, having been weakened by a thaw, suddenly gave way, and I came near being drowned. I was rescued by several of my companions joining hands and forming a line from the bank to the hole into which I had fallen. While struggling in the water all my past life and sins came vividly before me as in a moment, and I promised God, while sinking beneath the water, that if my life should be spared I would serve him. From that day I took a deeper interest in my Sunday-school, and in preaching, and began at once earnestly to pray and seek salvation. I made known my purposes to no one, and I suppose no human being ever knew of my religious awakening. I told no one, but continued to pray in secret probably for two or three months. One night in the summer, after praying as usual, I went to bed, but felt so much concern that I got up and knelt again by the side of my bed, and began to pray with more than ordinary feeling. There and then the blessing was received. 'Precious Jesus!' was the first and almost continuous expression of the joy of my newborn soul. I felt melted and completely transfused with the heavenly baptism. I seemed to be in a cloud of light, and the plan of salvation—but a moment before so dark—seemed now perfectly clear. My soul was filled with love. The Spirit was sent into my heart crying, 'Abba, Father!' Thus God revealed himself to my poor heart in my *eleventh year*. My faith has never been shaken in the truth and reality of the gospel since that clear and wonderful demonstration. In times of temptation to skepticism my mind recurs to that powerful and supernatural experience, and is convinced and confirmed. For the space of a year I enjoyed uninterrupted religious assurance, but afterward fell into sin and condemnation. The rock on which I came near making shipwreck was my unwillingness to make public confession and unite with the people of God. This was partly from natural timidity, and a good deal from pride. From 1841 to 1846 I was a backslider, all the time resisting the Spirit and refusing to confess Christ."

And so Linus Parker will rank with many others of the Lord's apostolic chieftains who came to Christ in tender childhood. Polycarp, the martyr, was converted at nine years of age, President Edwards at seven, Dr. Watts at nine, Matthew Henry at eleven, Bishop Hall and Robert Hall at eleven or twelve, and scores in our American Methodism at a like early period of life. Thus God is pleased to perfect praise out of the mouths of babes and sucklings.

The first of July, 1845, when about sixteen years of age, Linus Parker left his father's house for the far South, which was henceforth to be his adopted home. He came to New Orleans an adventurous youth in quest of fortune. Little then did he know what a history he was to make, and what a memory Providence would bequeath to the world. But his ways are not as our ways. He who converted a dreaming shepherd-boy into the prime-minister of a great empire, and made him the princely benefactor of his people Israel, guided the steps of this lad into a pathway that grew brighter and brighter with the luster of a holy purpose and consecrated zeal. He found not riches, but the pearl of great price. He became not a merchant prince, but a prince and leader in Israel. Forsaking the counter and ledger, he entered the pulpit and pastorate, and, with tongue and pen, became a messenger of life and peace to multiplied thousands. The Exchange lost a conspicuous figure, but the Church gained a hero and martyr.

Immediately after reaching New Orleans he went across the lake to Mandeville College, and remained there prosecuting a course of study for about three months. Returning, he became an employé in his brother's store—first as a salesman and afterward as book-keeper. From the very first Sabbath he was a regular attendant at service, and joined the Bible-class in the old Poydras Street Church. The Hon. William H. Foster, the Robert Raikes of the Southwest, was the superintendent of the Sunday-school, and the sainted William Sherry, the Carvosso of New Orleans, was the teacher and also his class-leader. These two at once discerned the fine spirit of the young man, and each became a trusted friend like unto David and Jonathan. In the winter of 1846 he united with the church which was at that time served by his old Binghampton pastor, the Rev. Dr. Joseph Cross. Of that event he speaks as follows: "At the time I became a probationer there was a protracted meeting in progress, and I felt, when constrained to yield, that perhaps I was experiencing the last call of the Spirit. Here in the discharge of a long-neglected duty my religious enjoyment gradually returned. I began by taking up every cross, going to the altar for prayer as a seeker, attending class-meeting, and praying and speaking whenever called upon."

CHAPTER III.

CALL TO THE MINISTRY.

FROM the hour he united with the Church, Linus Parker felt renewed convictions of a divine call to the ministry in greater power. From his earliest religious consciousness such impressions had vaguely pursued him, alternating in vividness and urgency with the mutations of his religious experience; but, as was his wont, the momentous question was only settled after the most thorough conviction and the calmest deliberation. He hated shams and dreaded mistakes. Not until the clear trumpet-voice of the Holy Spirit was distinctly recognized, and became too authoritative for resistance, would he assume the sacred responsibilities of the gospel ministry. There had to be the distinct assurance of a *divine* commission. But amid all his hesitation and plannings he was being equipped of God as a wise winner of souls. While diligently engaged in his clerkship the Spirit was preparing him for a higher calling and nobler destiny. That thirst for knowledge which compelled him to rise early before business hours and sit up till the high noon of night studying so unweariedly was used by Providence in developing one of the ablest expounders of the gospel known in the history of our Methodism. Even then, under the tuition of the Holy Ghost, he was strengthening and disciplining mental muscle and fiber which in after years made him a master of great thoughts and a masterful defender of the truth. He enlisted as a young soldier, and went to the Mexican war; but camp-life and force-march failed to hush the voice within calling him to a higher commission and a nobler warfare. He began the study of law, and pursued his course with characteristic diligence, at the same time serving at night as book-keeper in his brother's store; but the conviction remained that his mission was to practice in a superior court, and that Blackstone, Kent, and Greenleaf were to be laid aside for Moses, Isaiah, Paul, and other canonical writers. About this time the Mississippi Annual Conference held a session in the Poydras Street Church, and young Parker was an interested visitor. During that Conference Dr. William Winans, the great leader and logician of South-western Methodism, preached a sermon that fastened the convictions of this duty most strongly upon him.

One office of the presiding elder is to discern spirits and recruit the Lord's ministry. And in nothing does he demonstrate eminent fitness for his office more clearly than in discovering and presenting to Conference promising young men with gifts and graces. Richard Deering was such a one. His unfailing eye rested upon that young man, and God chose him to be the Elijah to clothe another Elisha with the mantle of the prophetic office. But the full history, detailing conflicting emotions and yet growing convictions, is given from the Bishop's own pen:

"During the month of March, 1849, I preached my first sermon in the little Methodist Church at Algiers, called Good Hope Chapel. At this time I was studying law in the office of T. K. Durant and Charles Horner, and had not made up my mind to devote myself *exclusively* to the ministry. Rev. R. Deering was presiding elder of the New Orleans District, and through his persuasion, greatly aided by my own convictions, I was induced to try a single appointment. There were not more than fifty or sixty persons present, and my effort was better to my own mind than I expected. My hearers seemed well pleased, and the leading members—having no regular preacher—invited me to come as often as possible. The text was First Timothy, first chapter, and a fragment of the eleventh verse: 'According to the glorious gospel of the blessed God.' This text was suggested to my mind by hearing the first sermon of Rev. William R. Nicholson after he was reördained in the Protestant Episcopal Church. The subject was unsuitable for such a tyro as I was, but it pleased my fancy. The skeleton covered the half of a letter-sheet page. My position was: God is the source of all glory; ergo, a thing is glorious in so far as it exhibits the divine attributes—(1) the gospel exhibits God's justice, (2) his power, (3) his love.

"I continued from this time to preach regularly at Good Hope Chapel every Sabbath for several weeks, pursuing my law studies the meanwhile, and debating the question of my call to the ministry. At one time my mind was so far made up against preaching that I refused to apply for license of the McGehee Quarterly Conference, and continued to preach for two months or thereabouts with only verbal license from Brother Deering. At last my mind was decided. I determined to preach, and apply myself exclusively thereto. I received license of the Quarterly Conference May 15th, 1849, left the law-office forever, removed to Algiers, and took charge of Good Hope Chapel. My charge consisted of one appointment of about thirty members. These were nearly all mechanics—mostly ship-carpenters and their wives and children. They were poor and pious. The average of spirituality was greater than any of my subsequent charges. From May until December of this year I resided in Algiers, applying myself to study, pastoral duties, and preaching; and I can truly say I never spent so many months as pleasantly and happily. I continued to prosecute the study of Greek and Latin, devoted a good part of every morning to the Scriptures, and before the end of the year read Watson's Institutes, Wesley's Sermons, Dr. Chalmers's Select Works, and Fletcher's Appeal, besides some historical, philosophical, and light reading. Much time was then spent—as ever since—in preparing sermons. I should be almost ashamed to confess how much time these indifferent efforts cost me. I wrote but little, only the most meager skeletons—a single letter-page was usually all. But the arrangement of subjects, the careful premeditation of every point, and the study of the whole theme occupied at least two whole days of each week—so divided, however, as usually to give a portion to each day. My labor in this respect was most arduous, because of my ignorance—especially of theological matters—and the want of a library for purposes of reference. My remembrance of Good Hope Chapel is exceedingly pleasant. I was much attached to the few humble, pious souls there, and I left them in tears. These few months of ministerial life were rich in profit to me. They were to my mind a trial and a self-probation which confirmed me in the course I had chosen."

Thus the great question was settled, and for all time. That was a *willing* sacrifice, without reservation or subsequent regret. He kept back no part of the price, but for all time gave himself *entirely* to his divine and diligent calling. With the spirit and the understanding he could and did sing:

"To *taste* this love our only joy,
To *tell* this love our best employ."

And from that fresh, hopeful young morning of life, through a varied ministry of thirty-six years, to the gathering twilight of the evening, when he "ceased at once to work and live," he never turned aside for a single moment to lay an offering upon any other altar. There were no other gods before him. A life of more perfect consecration it is rarely the privilege of any one to know.

CHAPTER IV.
HIS FIRST CIRCUIT.

A YOUNG preacher's first Conference is a time of visions and revelations, of sights and insights, of appointments and disappointments. Every face is a study, every item of business an observation, and every discussion a new disclosure of the economy of Methodism. The presiding Bishop seems so apostolic, the older preachers so heroic and grand, and the younger ones so brave and full of faith. How he covets similar gifts, and prays to be worthy of such companionship! The intimate friendships and associated trials of subsequent years never obscure the romance and halo of the first Conference. How it impressed the calm, philosophical young novitiate he has told us with his own pen:

"A Methodist Conference is not like any other deliberative body in the world. It is perfectly unique. A Methodist preacher is a decided character, and an assembly made up of decided characters is of course full of decided characteristics. These peculiarities do not now, as of yore, consist—either in whole or in part—of the hat-brim or coat-tail. Whatever is distinctive of them as a class can no longer be located in their costume; but it is rather found in their mental and devotional habits, and in their general fondness for bonhomie. The Conference floor affords opportunity for the display of all these qualities. For a specimen of mental acumen just witness the examination of a single character. With all the skill of anatomists they dissect their subject from crown to sole; every fact is brought out, and every feature of the case is examined and discussed at length. This ordeal, in some instances, reminded me of those Indians who improved their archery by making targets of their captives, and seeing how nearly they could throw the shaft and not pierce the victim."

The Louisiana Conference met December 25, 1849, in the city of Shreveport, then and now the largest and most prosperous town in the northern part of the State. Bishop Capers presided, and Philo M. Goodwyn was Secretary. The Bishop was in the zenith of his power. His gentle spirit, benignant appearance, and eloquent preaching and speaking profoundly stirred the young preacher and rebuked every lingering fear of failure. The trip up the river was unpleasant and uneventful to all save one. The Bishop, the New Orleans preachers, and a number of other members of the Conference were crowded with all sorts of passengers, to the number of five hundred, on a small, miserable boat called the "St. Anthony," and were nearly a week in reaching their destination. There were two eager ears that caught every incident, anecdote, and observation of the venerable Bishop and other preachers, and from the boat's deck two thoughtful eyes studied the country that was to be the field of his ministerial labor.

Four young men were admitted on trial—Linus Parker, John Pauley, Elisha Waller, and Henderson A. Morse. Elisha Waller ceased to travel after one year, and the name of Henderson A. Morse soon disappears from the roll of Conference; but the memory of John Pauley and his heroic labors in behalf of German Methodism in New Orleans is an abiding and an inspiring heritage. From a "rag-picker on the streets" he became a consecrated apostle, worthy of the land of Luther. He had a genius for self-denying labor that knew no flagging, and a lofty Teutonic courage that feared neither the threat of ruffian nor the tread of wasting pestilence. His triumphant death two years ago in Houston, Texas, was the fitting close of a heroic, apostolic career. He went up from the field of battle the veteran victor of many a struggle.

> His sword was in his hand,
> *Still warm with recent fight.*

Of his appointment to Lake Providence, Carroll parish, Louisiana, and his first year of itinerant service, Linus Parker will speak for himself:

"My solicitude on the evening the appointments were read out was very great. I rather expected to be returned to Algiers, and this was the wish of the people there, but it was not the order of Providence, and it proved for me far better. I had prayed over the matter often as the time of Conference approached, and I had, at the time of my appointment, the full conviction that God had ordained it aright. Subsequently I clearly saw the wisdom and goodness of it. To me and to others it was an eventful evening when we assembled to hear our appointments. These times have always been affecting to me. There is in them, with all the hopes, fears, anxieties, and solicitudes that agitate every breast, such an exhibition of the spirit of sacrifice, such a heroic, missionary spirit, and such a strength of faith, that I must pronounce the scene presented by a Methodist Conference receiving appointments from the lips of a venerable Bishop amongst the most sublime that history has recorded or that the mind can conceive of. The impression made upon me on hearing my name read in connection with Lake Providence was one of perfect complacency. I knew nothing of its character, *I knew not where it was.* I had no recollection of having heard of it before; indeed, its mention was a positive enlargement of my geographical knowledge. How much I had gained or lost, therefore, could not enter my mind under these circumstances. I found out its position on the map before I slept, and from intercourse with the preachers was tolerably acquainted with its character and history before we reached New Orleans on our return.

"I went to my work some time in January, and found that it consisted of two appointments—one in the town of Providence, the other about sixteen miles below on the river at Pecan Grove. Providence at this time was made up of a court-house, one hotel, and one church—the Methodist—quite a number of business houses, a Masonic hall, and several pleasant residences. The place was a village, and small for such a designation, not more than five hundred inhabitants in all—white and colored, children and adults. I landed in the night and slept at the hotel, and in the morning looked for the first time upon the head-quarters of my first real labors as a preacher. I did not know an individual in the place, but Dr. Speer, my presiding elder, had furnished me with a letter to a prominent member—Dr. Larchè. I walked from the hotel (tavern?) around to the Doctor's before breakfast, introduced myself to the family, and never left them during the year. It was my pleasant and welcome home as long as I remained in the country.

"The year passed away pleasantly and quickly. My services were more appreciated than they deserved to be. I was well provided for, and left for Conference with the wish of all that I should be returned for another year. In estimating the fruits of the year's labors I felt humiliated and dissatisfied. A very few had been added to the Church, all of whom, I think, remain faithful to their profession. The church was well attended, and the members were in better spiritual condition than when I commenced my labors. This was all the *visible* result. If other good was done, eternity will reveal it."

Lake Providence first appears on the Minutes of Conference in 1828, served by A. Hewett as a supply, and through all the intervening years has enjoyed the ministrations of faithful, devoted men. But the frequent and destructive overflows of the Mississippi River have arrested the development of the country and the progress of the Church. More than once our pastors have had to escape from the floods with all of their household goods on a speedily constructed and insecure raft. Yet the little vine, long planted, still lives and bears fruit unto God.

CHAPTER V.
TWO YEARS AT SHREVEPORT.

THE Louisiana Conference met December 25, 1850, in the Felicity Street Church, New Orleans. Bishop Capers again presided, and on the first day of the session formally dedicated the handsome new church in which the Conference was held to the worship of Almighty God. His sermon on that occasion was from Matthew xxiii. 17: "For whether is greater, the gold, or the temple that sanctifieth the gold?" and never did that silver tongue preach a gospel of greater sweetness or more spiritual power. He talked like one having authority, but it was the majesty of love. That church had been built under the wise administration of Dr. J. C. Keener, presiding elder of the New Orleans District, and by the active labors of the young pastor, Holland N. McTyeire. It was the consolidation of two or more smaller chapels, and has been for all the years a strong center of evangelical influence in the city. The cornerstone of that church has a history, related by Bishop Keener in the New Orleans *Christian Advocate* of March 22, 1851, and is worth preserving. Its reproduction here seems appropriate:

"There is a corner-stone under the Felicity Street Church out of which the devil was fairly cheated. It has been twice dedicated—once for a theater and once for a church. It lay out to the weather for a long time, until the Lord had need for it; and then, with prayer and thanksgiving, it was put into the ground, and a church built upon it.

It is not often that Satan is allowed to furnish a carriage for the Lord's cannon. I am not quite sure that he has even in this case. The history of this elect cornerstone is about this: In the year 1837 it was resolved to build a theater at the corner of De Lord and Foucher streets. With due flourish of trumpets a great crowd of people was assembled, a stand erected, an oration delivered to suit the occasion, and the corner-stone was laid. At that time J. N. Maffitt was in the city and in the zenith of his fame, and on the afternoon of that day walked out in company with Mr. Fontaine in the direction of the celebration. Mr. Maffitt saw the crowd, asked what it meant, and soon they were both standing listening to the orator. Presently a messenger came from one on the stand to Mr. Maffitt, inviting him to come up. Mr. Maffitt declined. He was again sent for very pressingly, when they both went up, and were seated among the distinguished of the day. When the orator had finished, strange to say, the master of ceremonies asked Mr. Maffitt if he would 'conclude' the exercises with a blessing. Sure enough, Mr. Maffitt arose, stretched out his hands, and fairly went at it —half oration and half prayer—for some thirty minutes, in which he quite eclipsed the orator. Spoke of Isthmian, Olympic, Pythian; of the design and influence of the stage; and prayed that He who is greater than him of Ida might mark and bring his own mysterious and wonder-working power to overrule for good the scene of the day and the intentions of the hour; and, after having prayed with great eloquence and fervor, concluded. Now let the reader mark: the theater was never built, and that corner-stone is the identical one of the Felicity Street Church."

At this Conference the young preacher of only one year's experience was assigned to Shreveport, the most important station outside the city of New Orleans. It was quite unusual in that day to appoint young, unordained men to the full charge of a pastorate, and never to a prominent *station*. But so conspicuous were his gifts, and so marked his success, that no fear was entertained in intrusting the Methodism of the growing and wealthy city of Shreveport to the hands of Linus Parker. Nor did he disappoint expectation. It was there he developed his peculiar methods in the pulpit, and established his reputation as an able, instructive expositor of the word of God. Many of the sweetest memories of his beautiful life and helpful ministry linger around that place. Old friends and parishioners yet live who relate stories of his pastoral and pulpit experiences, and their children will keep in perennial freshness the traditions of those happy years. The influence of that young man abides, a heritage of radiant virtues and an inspiration to higher aims and deeds. His pulpit became a throne of light, whose ever-widening circles of mellow radiance were seen and felt even beyond the confines of his State. He now took rank as a popular preacher and eminently wise pastor.

At this Conference a measure was inaugurated which, under Providence, largely determined the sphere and fame of Linus Parker. Unconsciously to himself and unsuspected by all, it became the most potential factor in his history as a Methodist preacher. Though the matter had been long and much considered, it was at this Conference the first authoritative action was taken which established the New Orleans *Christian Advocate*. A publishing committee was appointed, consisting of J. C. Keener, W. E. Doty, and R. H. Rivers, and the first number of the paper appeared February 8, 1851, with H. N. McTyeire as editor. A similar committee of publication was appointed by the Alabama Conference, but, on account of some difference of opinion as to details of management, the Mississippi Conference did not *officially* become a patron of the paper until several years later. In this enterprise the young pastor became greatly interested, and, encouraged by the quickly discerning and proverbially discriminating editor, began a correspondence that soon demonstrated journalistic genius. Over the *nom de plume* of "Woodsman" he wrote many articles for that *Advocate* in 1851-2—then almost a boy-preacher —that displayed the graces of style and vigor of thought which in maturer years gave him Connectional fame. We cannot but wonder how a quiet, unobtrusive boy, scarcely beyond his majority, and with few educational advantages, so thoroughly disciplined and richly stored his mind, and what models he studied to give his pen such variety and classic elegance. During the summer of 1851 he attended his first camp-meeting not far from Shreveport, and wrote a charming description of what he saw and heard. The following were his closing reflections, and illustrate the purity and flexibility of his style at that early age:

"The rural pulpit is the light artillery of gospel warfare. Readily brought into action and admirably adapting itself to circumstances, it tells with lasting effect upon points which could not be reached through the instrumentality of church and chapel ministrations. Here I saw the peculiar adaptation of Christianity to man, as the religion of the world. It finds a rostrum and an altar everywhere. Christ taught upon a mountain, a well-curb, the sea-shore, and the deck of a fisher's boat. With the same felicitous independence evangelists of every age have occupied the field of the world, and have sown beside all waters."

During that year he conducted a controversy with Dr. Clapp, of New Orleans, a somewhat celebrated Unitarian preacher, on the subject of future punishment, and demonstrated undoubted polemic skill and logical power. But that was the one exception in his entire ministry. His was a gospel of peace. In that controversy he showed large acquaintance with ecclesiastical science, and evidenced the breadth and grasp of real statesmanship. The following, on the most vital principle in our Methodist economy, displayed a maturity of judgment far beyond his years:

"The Connectional principle, which is to some extent retained in most of our sister denominations, and eminently and fully illustrated in our own, is really the great conservator of an evangelical ministry. It is not difficult to see how this principle guards against errors by placing mutual checks upon the idiosyncrasies of different minds, and by throwing wholesome restraints around the erratic tendencies of wayward thinkers. This is what makes Methodism everywhere the same. It is this which preserves her economy intact and saves her doctrines from corruption. Pure Congregationalism is without these restraints, and the results which we have noticed legitimately and necessarily follow. It is the embodiment of doctrinal liberty and independence, where 'every one hath a psalm, hath a doctrine, hath a tongue, hath a revelation, hath an interpretation.' What wonder that in such an element of liberty a master-mind should sometimes shake off the thralldom of creeds? What wonder that genius should shed its sanctity and its orthodoxy and indulge in the wildest heretical pranks?"

The next Conference was held at Thibodeaux, December, 1851, and Bishop Paine presided. From Shreveport to Thibodeaux the trip was made almost entirely by private conveyance, which gave the young station preacher a real itinerating experience such as he had never before enjoyed. The fertile valleys, beautiful streams, broad prairies, and curious people along the way, awakened an intense interest. He was completely fascinated with the country. The New Yorker became a zealous, loyal Louisianian, and remained so to the day of his death. Writing of that trip, he says:

"Louisiana, with all her alligators and agues and swamps, is surpassingly rich in history and beautiful in geography. He who has merely seen her from the deck of a steamboat can have no correct or adequate notion of what she really is. To such an observer she presents a monotonous, funereal aspect, through which there scarcely gleams a suggestion of the wealth and interest that lie hidden behind her cypress boughs and palls of moss. Louisiana, of all the States, claims the Father of Waters as her sire; and though she sometimes feels his rage, she is more largely enriched by his munificence. Right proud is she of her parentage, and right royally she wears in one the names of consort sovereigns. The sole heir of the Mississippi, her soil and geology are the hoarded sums of more than a thousand annuities. It was due to such a land that the proudest and the bravest chivalry alone should achieve its discovery; and hence Providence has allowed the names of La Salle and De Soto to stand foremost and almost alone upon the pages of her earliest annals."

At that Conference he was returned to Shreveport, and labored with increasing diligence and growing popularity. Of his pastorate there he only made this modest entry in his journal: "Two years they were of great enjoyment and of some usefulness."

It is a striking coincidence that three members of the Conference at Thibodeaux afterward sat with Bishop Paine on the episcopal bench—Holland N. McTyeire, John C. Keener, and Linus Parker, whom he then ordained a deacon. Bishop Paine also officiated when he was ordained an elder, and when he was consecrated to the high and holy office of a Bishop in 1882. For his venerable chief pastor the young preacher had the profoundest reverence, which ripened into increasing personal admiration; while on the other hand the Bishop watched with pride the development of his son in the gospel, and rejoiced at his election as one of his colleagues. Of the intimate relations between the three Conference co-laborers and episcopal colleagues we shall learn more hereafter.

CHAPTER VI.
FIRST YEAR IN NEW ORLEANS.

THE seventh session of the Louisiana Conference was held in the city of Baton Rouge, the capital of the State, beginning January 5th, 1853. Bishop James O. Andrew was present and presided for the first time over this Conference. The session was pleasant and profitable, and became historic by adopting a tentative measure in the interest of lay delegation, the first movement of the sort in Southern Methodism. Having completed a full pastoral term of two years at Shreveport, Linus Parker was appointed to Felicity Street Church, New Orleans, as the successor of H. N. McTyeire. His former residence in the city and thorough acquaintance with its spiritual condition, together with a calm, philosophical appreciation of the *character* of work needed to be done, gave a specially providential expression to his appointment. Evangelical religion in Louisiana, and especially in New Orleans, has won its way against "a sea of difficulties," and has demanded men of peculiar gifts and graces. Years ago in his admirable sketch of Richmond Nolley, the first pioneer preacher to die in that field, Bishop McTyeire said: "The gospel plowshare never struck into harder soil than South-western Louisiana." The mass of population intensely Roman Catholic and speaking a foreign language, the country subject to epidemics of yellow fever and overflows of the Mississippi River, there were few conditions favorable to evangelical religion. Methods successful in other fields were fruitless there. Great revivals that swept over entire communities and counted converts by hundreds were impossible in a section dominated by priestcraft, ignorance, and infidelity. In a letter to the Nashville *Christian Advocate* the young pastor thus discerned the difficulties with the eye of a philosopher, and unintentionally outlined his own pastoral history:

"Owing to various circumstances the aggressive movements of the gospel in Louisiana are slow. The laborer here must have *long patience;* casting his bread upon the waters, the faith that ventures and the patience that waits must be his. The character of the people, their employments, wealth, descent, and sparseness of white population, conspire to make the progress of the gospel slow. The country cannot be taken by storm. Rather, it must be conquered by the labored parallels and gradual approaches of a siege. In the older States—in your own Tennessee—your revivals sweep whole communities; you have the denser population, numerous village communities for centers of operations, hereditary Protestantism and nurtured Methodism, which we have not. . . . In communities (of which there are more in Louisiana than elsewhere) where Methodism is not understood, and where there is little or no sympathy for the preacher, the preacher becomes the sole exponent of the Church, and the planting of the gospel depends greatly upon the personal fitness of the man. The harmlessness of the dove must be blended with the wisdom of the serpent; intelligence and education must be combined with the purest flame of piety. There are two sides to instrumentalities—the human and the divine. The fishermen of Galilee were not specially chosen for the Gentiles. For this work regard was had for human fitness, and Saul of Tarsus was set apart to expound the gospel to the Greek and the Roman."

And to New Orleans those words had emphatic application. Christian evangelism there, from the days of Elisha Bowman to the present, has contended against peculiar and stubborn evils. Nowhere else in the United States have embarrassments been so great and opposition so intense. With Romanism comprising one-half of the entire population, wealthy, well organized, and enjoying the powerful protection and liberal support of the French and Spanish governments until Louisiana was ceded to the United States, the growth of Protestantism has been a ceaseless struggle. As far back as the year of Linus Parker's first appointment to New Orleans, there were in the city and vicinity not less than twenty-five Roman Catholic churches, fifty or more priests, four orphan asylums, two convents, and five free schools. There were also an ecclesiastical seminary and numerous institutions and organizations connected with their Church-machinery—monks, nuns, Sisters of Charity, Brothers of the Christian Schools, two weekly papers—one in French and one in English—and multitudinous buildings of varied architecture and for multifarious purposes. Studying the difficult problem and estimating the immense outlay of men, time, talent, patience, courage, and prayer to achieve even the meager results of Methodism at that time, the young Felicity pastor said:

"The history of the planting of these churches in an early day and a dark day, the persecutions which they sustained, and the sufferings endured, may never be written; but should it be, there will be chapters of heroism, Christian faithfulness, and devotion to God such as the annals of Christianity might covet to enroll upon its pages."

The first adventurous Methodist preacher to visit New Orleans for the purpose of planting our standard there was Elisha W. Bowman. He came by appointment of Bishop Asbury, and reached the little city of less than fifteen thousand souls about the 1st of December, 1805. He found the place "as filthy as a hog-sty," but few American people, no house of entertainment except at an expense of two dollars a day, with his money "pretty well spent," and no place in which to preach. Failing elsewhere, he called on the Governor, told his business, and secured from him the promise of protection and the use of the capitol for Sunday service. But when Sunday came he found the door locked, and his only chance of preaching was to "a few drunken sailors and Frenchmen" in front of the building. Though assured of more hospitable treatment the next Sabbath by both the Governor and Mayor, he again found the house securely fastened, and preached "to ten or twelve persons in the open air." As the lonely missionary passed along the street in the evening he heard loud curses against himself and the Methodists, and was told by one of the officers that the Methodists were a dangerous people and ought to be discouraged. But, nothing daunted, he preached the next Sunday "to a few straggling people in the open street." Without a friend to advise him, without money to rent a preaching-place, and unable to sell his faithful horse for the small sum of forty dollars, his situation was becoming desperate. Learner Blackman, the nearest Methodist preacher, was three hundred miles away; to remain was impossible, and to leave his appointment, "without Mr. Asbury's direction, was like death." So he concluded to make his way into the Opelousas country, and said: "I accordingly, on the 17th of December, shook off the dirt from my feet against this ungodly city of Orleans, and resolved to try the watery waste and pathless desert."

Those three weeks of reconnoissance and the three open-air sermons of Elisha Bowman were the first and only services of a Methodist preacher in New Orleans until 1812, when Miles Harper came as a missionary. Though a man full of zeal, of great unction and power, and at times "surpassingly eloquent," his year's labors were without visible results. The next year Lewis Hobbs, the "weeping prophet," a most devout but delicate young man, spent his last strength toiling and praying, in a vain endeavor to gather a small congregation. He became "deeply consumptive," and in a lingering, dying condition traveled a thousand miles to his home in Georgia, to finish his course.

The first provisional session of the Mississippi Conference met November 1, 1813, at the residence of Rev. Newit Vick, with Samuel Sellers as President, and William Winans, Secretary. William Winans, who afterward became the greatest pulpit orator and most distinguished ecclesiastical leader in the South-west, was appointed to succeed the sainted Lewis Hobbs. Of the thirty-nine dollars and eighteen cents in the Conference treasury, thirty dollars "was voted to Brother Winans to enable him to fill the Orleans Station." The missionary found shelter in the hospitable home of Jacob Knobb, the ground-floor of whose house he used for a school-room and chapel. That house, a two-story brick, as we learn from the historian of South-western Methodism—the Rev. John G. Jones—was located on Bienville, between Chartres and Royal streets. Persons yet living remember to have seen the old, faded sign over the door—"*William Winans, Teacher.*" Here he taught school for his daily bread and preached for the glory of God. But so unimpressible were the mixed multitudes, and so intense the war excitement, that the zealous missionary was forced to go up to Conference with a very meager report. He had spied out the land, however, and ever thereafter was zealously devoted to the interests of New Orleans Methodism. As presiding elder of the district, as agent, with the eloquent John Newland Maffitt, "to raise funds for the Methodist Church in New Orleans," and in every possible way, he contributed to the firm establishment of our cause in that "Paris of America."

For five years after the retirement of William Winans no Methodist preaching was heard in the city, but in 1819 New Orleans again appeared in the minutes, with Mark Moore as missionary. With the coming and ministry of that brave evangelist two interesting historic facts are connected. The first Bishop McTyeire thus relates in his "History of Methodism:" "An effort to assist the Rev. Mark Moore in establishing the Church in New Orleans suggested to Joshua Soule, Nathan Bangs, Laban Clark, and Freeborn Garretson the grand movement of the period—the formation of a missionary society." The other was securing the first local habitation for Methodism in the city, and is related by Bishop Keener in his eloquent memorial-sermon in honor of Judge Edward McGehee:

"Judge McGehee's connection with Methodism in New Orleans began in 1819. In that year Dr. Winans, Mark Moore, and Judge McGehee came to this city, and a preaching-place was secured in the loft of a flour-inspector's office at the corner of Poydras and Carondelet streets. The Judge gave the bagging which was used to cover the rafters and to form the sides of the room. Those were the days of Sisters Skinner, Canu, and Coleman, and Mark Moore was the preacher in charge. Out of this beginning grew the church, a frame building on Gravier street, between Baronne and Carondelet. Afterward, in 1838, a very imposing brick church was built on the original site of the loft at the corner of Poydras and Carondelet."

Another fact that year distinguished the annals of New Orleans Methodism—the first visit of a Methodist Bishop. In the month of March Bishop McKendree reached the city, and on Sabbath preached to "a large and attentive congregation." It must have been a great day with the little flock. "Two young men joined the society, a lady of about thirty years of age was baptized, and the sacrament

administered to about *one hundred and thirty* persons."
Mark Moore was abundant in labors, and the fruits appeared.
He had large congregations and "about sixty members in society."

In 1820 John Menifee succeeded the indefatigable Mark Moore, but the society did not prosper, and the next year was quite disorganized by a dreadful epidemic of yellow fever. Among other victims was John Menifee himself, the first of a long list of martyrs who have fallen by that scourge while preaching the gospel in New Orleans. In 1824 Daniel Hall was appointed to reöccupy the abandoned field and shepherd the scattered flock. Of his work little is known. But the next year marked a new era and the real beginning of Methodism in that city. Benjamin M. Drake was then in the vigor of a splendid young manhood and the freshness of a zeal that never flagged to the end of a laborious life. He united the little band, built the first Methodist church in New Orleans, and gave to Methodism there its first permanent organization. His labors were phenomenal. He preached to the spirits in prison, had stated appointments for the garrison of United States troops, visited the hospitals, held service with the seamen, sold Bibles and Testaments, distributed tracts, and ministered to the sick and dying. He was returned the next year, and again in 1832. In the completeness of his consecration and the moral grandeur of his life there is no more conspicuous figure in the Pantheon of our illustrious dead than Dr. Benjamin M. Drake.

Under the pastoral care successively of Peyton S. Greaves, William M. Curtiss, and William V. Douglass, the little company so throve and multiplied that in 1832 New Orleans appeared as the head of a district, with Barnabas Pipkin as presiding elder and O. L. Nash as preacher in charge. In 1835 a special mission to the people of color was inaugurated, and to this work the eloquent, eccentric S. L. L. Scott was appointed. This became one of the special and prominent features of Methodism in the city, and it prospered greatly. The sixty-three colored members in 1826 increased to one thousand two hundred and thirty-four in 1860. For their careful spiritual instruction all the preachers zealously labored, and none more joyously than Bishops McTyeire, Keener, and Parker. In that year the name of William M. Curtiss appears as "Book Agent," with John C. Burruss in charge of the station. Of this gifted man— the Chrysostom of early Methodism in the South-west—we shall see more hereafter.

About this time a handsome, brilliant young man of business was attracted by the joyous services of the Methodists; was converted and became one of their number. He at once engaged zealously in all good works—holding prayer-meetings, distributing tracts, and visiting the hospitals. Obeying the call to preach, he desired to go North and complete his education; but so popular were his ministrations and so imperative the demands for his services that he entered the itinerancy at once, and has been known to continental fame as the eloquent Dr. Charles K. Marshall.

Another name intimately and honorably connected with the Church in New Orleans was that of William Hamilton Watkins, who came first in 1838 as the colleague of the ardent, strong-willed Lewell Campbell. He remained in the city nearly ten consecutive years, and left his impress deeply graven in the history of that time. It was by his efforts mainly that the Moreau Street Church was built, and he became its first pastor. With the elegant manners of a Chesterfield and the gentle spirit of John Fletcher, he was a model gentleman, and an affable, able, loyal Methodist itinerant preacher. When the Louisiana Conference was organized in 1847, he returned to his native Mississippi and remained in effective service until his peaceful death in the capital of the State on the 5th of February, 1881.

At the Conference which met in Vicksburg in December, 1840, Elijah Steele was appointed to the Poydras Street Church, New Orleans, with W. H. Watkins and P. Dieffinwerth as his colleagues in the city. It has been the privilege of very few on earth to make such a history as this young man. He was the Summerfield of the South-west. Though not so widely known as that prodigy of pulpit eloquence, and with fewer literary advantages, he had a mind of equal grasp, an imagination of like imperial sweep, a voice as richly musical, and a piety as divinely beautiful. Dr. Winans said that the gifted Summerfield was the only person he ever met "who could compare with Elijah Steele in richness of thought, extensiveness of range, clearness of presentation, dignity of manner, and effectiveness." The year before his appointment to Poydras Street he visited the city by invitation to preach a special sermon. Of that effort his biographer, Dr. Drake, said: "It is doubtful whether a single sermon has ever made so strong an impression in that city." One of the city papers pronounced him the equal of the blind preacher described by the eloquent William Wirt. This led to his appointment the following year—the scene of his closing labors and place of his martyrdom and translation. The young preacher was soon an extraordinary sensation. He attracted crowds to every service—not by clerical buffoonery or dramatic sacrilege, but by the fervor and splendor of his sacred eloquence. But alas! the gracious work so auspiciously begun must soon come to an end. With summer came a fatal epidemic of yellow fever. Hundreds and thousands fled at the first note of alarm, but the brave young pastor remained. When urged to leave by anxious friends he replied: "I feel not the least sensation of fear; if I live, it will be to glorify

God; if I die, it will be in glorious triumph." From house to house, day and night, he moved like an angel of mercy amid the sick and dying, carrying to all the glad tidings of great joy. On the 6th of September, while conducting a prayer-meeting, he was seized with the fatal fever, and was borne to the house of his friend James Ross, where he died after four days of suffering, a willing sacrifice to duty. To his mother and special friends in the ministry he sent this confident message: "Tell them I am gone straight to heaven." His last articulate words were, "I am safe." The annals of heroism have preserved no incidents more thrilling, no courage more daring, and no sacrifices more unsparing than an epidemic of yellow fever in the South. And among the earliest and bravest of its martyrs was the amiable, eloquent, gifted Elijah Steele. A chapel was erected a few years later near the present Felicity Street Church which bore his name and perpetuated his seraphic ministry.

The Poydras Street Church—an imposing structure, the corner-stone of which was laid by Rev. John Newland Maffitt, and the dedicatory sermon preached by Bishop Andrew—was begun in 1835, and was built mainly by the munificence of Judge Edward McGehee. When completed it remained indebted to him over and above his gifts some forty thousand dollars. Of this amount he would only receive two thousand dollars, and used it in building a Methodist Church in Wilkinson county, Mississippi. The present spacious temple on Carondelet street—the successor of old Poydras—is also a monument of his princely liberality, and in his honor it was properly and imposingly dedicated as the McGehee Church. He was the father of church extension in New Orleans—the Sir Frances Lycett of the South-west. Of his other royal doings—the establishment of Woodville Female Seminary, giving seventy thousand dollars or more to Centenary College, supporting his local church, educating poor young men, etc.—are they not written in the chronicles of the skies? Noble, kingly soul! his name will ever be conspicuous in the annals of American Methodism, and in the firmament of God will shine as the stars forever and ever.

In 1842 the Rev. William R. Nicholson, a cultured, scholarly young man, and eloquent withal, was stationed in New Orleans. He was quite popular, and his ministry was attended with marked success; but he became impatient with the inexorable law of our itinerancy, and in 1848 connected himself with the Protestant Episcopal Church. When the Reformed Episcopal Church was organized in 1871 he became an early and ardent adherent, and was elected one of its Bishops.

In that year another movement was projected which has been one of the chief glories of New Orleans Methodism— the establishment of its first German mission. The Rev. Charles Bremer was the first missionary, who emigrated to the United States in 1837. He was awakened in the old country, but came to America for a knowledge of full salvation by faith only. He had fine talents and a consuming zeal. Entering the Conference in 1843 or 1844, he devoted his toilsome life to mission work in the city, and had many seals to his ministry. In the year 1845 he received an assistant in Rev. Nicholas Brekwedel, when work was begun in Carrollton, where Judge Preston donated a lot to the mission, and built a small chapel upon it. The work went on prosperously until at length five excellent congregations had been organized and substantial brick churches were built on Dryades, Soroparou, and Craps streets. Though somewhat disintegrated by the war between the States, and the establishment of German missions in the city by the Methodist Episcopal Church, it is yet among the most important missionary achievements of the Church. For some years the work in the city has been under the immediate superintendence of Rev. Dr. J. B. A. Ahrens, who is also the accomplished editor of our German books and periodicals. In these missions Bishop Parker was much interested, and his ministrations to them were greatly enjoyed. A few days after his death Dr. Ahrens published a beautiful tribute, entitled "A Floweret on Bishop Parker's Grave," in which he said:

"I have often admired the richness of the departed Bishop's vocabulary and the expressive sweetness of his style, so entirely devoid of pedantic ornateness. This very much endeared him to our German congregations. Though many were not very familiar with the English tongue, they could nevertheless understand him. Invariably were exegesis and application instructive and edifying. No wonder that on the Sabbath succeeding his death our three German churches in New Orleans were draped in mourning, and that memorial-services were held in each. When three years ago he was elevated to the episcopacy, our German sisters presented him a valuable cane and umbrella. Acknowledging the receipt, he addressed an exquisitely affectionate epistle to Mrs. Ahrens. Among other things, he said that the cane pointed him to the divine support which David enjoyed, declaring, 'Thy rod and thy staff, they comfort me.' The umbrella eloquently referred him to the 'secret place of the Most High.' 'Pray for me,' he concluded, 'that I may abide under the shadow of his wing as long as life endures.'"

Of other laborers, who braved the perils of yellow fever epidemics and wrought nobly in that difficult field, we cannot speak in detail. Time would fail us to tell of Deering, Nixon, Langard, Whitall, Cross, Brown, Trippett, Thweatt, and other honored names not a few. But in 1848 a then comparatively young man, whose acknowledged leadership was destined to give new and nobler direction to our cause in the great South-west, was transferred to New Orleans. He became the warmly attached and life-long friend of Linus Parker, and had much to do in shaping his successful career. He yet lives as one of our honored chief pastors, and unites in himself an apostolic zeal worthy of Francis Asbury and "a genius for government not inferior to Richelieu." Of his work in the city, Bishop McTyeire thus speaks in his "History of Methodism:"

"The minister is yet living—and we trust the day is far off when his name can be more freely spoken to—whose pulpit and pastoral fidelity and administrative power crowned the work which others began. The systematic and comprehensive plans laid and carried out by Rev. John Christian Keener, D.D. (now Bishop), date the epoch of the present New Orleans Methodism. He was appointed by Bishop Paine pastor of Poydras Street Church in 1848, met the yellow fever and outlived it in 1849, and has since resided in the city a witness and, under God, the chief director of the prosperous condition of its Methodism."

Of the heroic men and devout women not a few who composed the membership of the church—who "tarried by the stuff" and nobly sustained the reproach of "the people called Methodists"—we cannot speak at length. Conspicuous among those "who stood firmly by the feeble and despised cause when friends were few" was Madame Theresa Canu, who came to New Orleans as early as 1816. She was of French birth, and from St. Domingo, fleeing from the horrors of a bloody insurrection. She landed at Wilmington, North Carolina, where she became acquainted with the Methodists, and where, at a camp-meeting, she was soundly converted. Her home was ever open to the brave missionaries, and her presence "in the little conventicles where

Methodism took shelter for many humble years" was an unfailing inspiration to the toiling itinerant. Her little house, with its small, round columns and one dormer window, still stands on the north side of De Lord street, near the Lee monument. And around that stately column, surmounted by a bronze statue of the great military chieftain, possibly more tragic, but less sacred, memories gather than about the humble little home of the Methodist saint whose joy was to shelter the prophets of the Lord, and whose life was an unceasing prayer for the bloodless triumphs of the Redeemer's kingdom. But all the labors of Keene, the beloved disciple; of William H. Foster, the princely gentleman and model Sunday-school superintendent; of R. W. Rayne, whose large liberality almost alone erected the handsome church on St. Charles Avenue; of J. D. Parker, the tireless toiler for the Master and Israelite in whom is no guile; of Dr. Moss, the St. Luke of New Orleans Methodism; and of Price, Dameron, Palmer, Tully, Sutton, Howell, Robertson, Werlein, and others—will they not appear in "that day?"

CHAPTER VII.
FIRST YEAR IN NEW ORLEANS (CONTINUED).

THE young pastor of Felicity entered upon his duties at once, and preached his first sermon from the very appropriate text in 1 Cor. ii. 2: "For I determined not to know any thing among you, save Jesus Christ and him crucified." And never was the apostle's declaration and purpose more sincerely and faithfully illustrated by any son in the gospel. No other ambition distracted his thoughts or divided his energies. He was a man of one work. The zeal of that house consumed him. His pastoral and pulpit labors were according to a definite, well-matured plan, requiring singleness of aim and "long patience." He well understood how difficult it was to gather and train a Protestant congregation in the pure faith in the gayest and most pleasure-loving city in America. The boulevards and theaters of Paris were not more frequented, according to population, than the promenades and operas of New Orleans. The Sabbath then, as now, was grossly desecrated. Saloons, banks, and dry goods emporiums were as much astir with business on the Lord's-day as any other. In the midst of such scenes he often felt himself to be but a feeble voice crying in the wilderness, and that he was never to see an end to the day of small things. The weariness of his faith in watching for the dawn of a brighter morning was well expressed in another letter to the Nashville *Christian Advocate:*

"Think of Paul in Athens! how his spirit was stirred there! Were he to rise up in this century and take a walk through this metropolis, would there be nothing to stir his spirit? Let him go about of a Sunday night. The few churches tolerably full to be sure, but room for more. There is Fowler, the phrenologist, giving the religion of bumps at Odd-fellow's Hall; Christie's or Campbell's Minstrels, laughing and singing in burnt cork at the Armory; grand opera at the Orleans—perhaps 'Les Huguenots' on the bill; horse-riding at the Amphitheater by Miss Somebody; St. Charles full from pit to gallery; Varieties ditto; and so on for a page full. The world is not saved yet. These civilized heathen are hard to pluck from the burning; easier to save Chinese or Mexicans. But shall they be left without a trial?"

The difficulties were great, but God's grace was all-sufficient. During that year, though the city was scourged with the most terrible epidemic of yellow fever ever known in its entire history, and the young pastor suffered the sorest trial of his life, his ministry was blessed with most gracious results. About twenty were converted and added to the Church, and the whole membership renewed their baptismal vows. One characteristic of his pastoral history is worthy of all emulation—the care with which he instructed and trained young converts. The manner and spirit in which his revival-meetings were conducted are best indicated by his own mild criticism upon a service he once attended:

"Young penitents, and old ones too, need more instruction, more prayer, and less excitement-making. I may be heterodox—and if so, it is not desirable to be otherwise—in condemning the kind of hymnology which pervades these meetings. These fanciful, *ad captandum* songs should be purged from the Church and banished the sacred precincts of our altars. No Church has produced so rich and beautiful a collection of spiritual and evangelical hymns, adapted to all occasions and states, as our own. The best of these are neatly compiled, selected with taste and judgment, and probably for the very purpose, in part, of excluding the pernicious doggerel of which I speak from the pale of worship. Such a result would be creditable to religion, and any thing but detrimental to enlightened and scriptural piety."

On the 7th of June of this year Linus Parker was married to his first wife, Miss Sallie F. Sale. She was the daughter of Rev. Alexander Sale; and the ceremony was performed by Rev. Thomas Stringfield, at Mr. Sale's residence, near Courtland, Lawrence county, Alabama. The father of this young itinerant bride was for many years a great leader in the Church. Entering the Virginia Conference in 1808, he soon ranked among the strongest men in that historic body. After some years he located, but having removed to North Alabama he reëntered the itinerancy in 1823, and remained in active service until 1827. His noble and dignified bearing, his robust intellect, his large liberality and profound piety, united in making him a prince and leader in Israel. From such a father descended the bride of Linus Parker. She was a rarely gifted woman and of remarkable loveliness of character. Her piety was radiant and intelligent. At the age of fifteen she was converted at a revival-meeting in Aberdeen, Mississippi, and to the end of life kept inviolate her covenant with God. But their happy wedded life was of short duration. The flower had scarcely been transplanted to its Southern home before it withered and died. In the early summer a fatal pestilence visited the city. It was the most appalling epidemic of yellow fever that ever ravaged the State of Louisiana. It raged during summer and autumn, extended in various directions into the interior, and subsided only after its victims could be counted by the thousands. Hundreds and thousands fled at the first note of alarm,

The crowded, noisy, busy city lapsed into the painful quietude of a deserted village. The young wife was urged to leave the city and find refuge near Mandeville, across the lake, while her heroic husband remained at his post ministering to the sick and dying. But the scourge reached her there, and on the morning of the 13th of September she passed peacefully away. Tidings of her critical illness were dispatched to the city, but her husband only arrived in time to receive her loving farewell message. Her last words were: "Linus, God will do right. Trust in God, love!" This was a great sorrow to the gentle, affectionate young pastor. In three short months he was wedded and widowed, and the most of that time he was separated from the wife of his youth, hoping to save her precious life from the raging pestilence. That memory he tenderly cherished, and under God, it sanctified to his people a gospel of sweeter comfort. As a revelation of his gentle, chastened spirit, and an example of his rare gift of beautiful composition, an extract from a letter to the New Orleans *Christian Advocate*, written in the summer of 1857, is given. It is descriptive of old Mandeville College, and the place near by where his sainted young wife was buried:

"There is a later, sadder vision of the past. Farther up the coast, about two miles as the crow flies, is another summer village, whose cottage roofs are shaded by giant trees, and whose open porches are sure to catch the freshest and sweetest of the newborn zephyrs. There was a time when the pestilence came with fearful power upon the city. In all its years it had known no such a visitation—so terrible, so utterly appalling. Brooding over the larger prey, the destroyer's wing threw its deadly shadow across the water and upon the air of this salubrious retreat; nor was it lifted away till the sound of woe-stricken souls wailed out upon the lake breeze, and retreating through the moss-hung live-oaks, finally lost itself among those requiem-singers of nature, the grieving pines. And now, as our boat skims along and away, the telescope of memory pierces yonder dim and wooded shore, and fixes the eye upon a single grave, over which a sheltering oak stretches its moss-craped arms. The very mound seems to borrow grace from the form it covers; the violets on it grow more lovely and breathe their fragrance more softly than elsewhere, and the moss-rose and spotless jessamine keep their vigils of odors at the head and foot of the slumbering dust. Between the buoyant school-scenes of the Quondam College and this heart-trial there is but two miles, and little more than thrice that many years."

CHAPTER VIII.
THE DILIGENT CITY PASTOR.

THE most delicate and difficult work of a preacher is outside the pulpit; and there is the true test of his power. He may have all the gifts and graces of a peerless oratory, and enrapture a congregation with the splendor of a genius, and yet be a humiliating failure in pastoral administration. The eloquence of Apollos may dwell on his tongue, while his soul is cast down with the thought of a barren, unfruitful ministry. Pulpit preparation and power are imperative. It is an offense to God and a sin against souls to bring unbeaten oil into the sanctuary. But the training, edifying function of the pastoral office is best emphasized in personal, private, and social contact with the flock. Speaking of this important work aimed at by the Church, the great Dr. Robert South said: "To expect that this should be done by preaching or force of lungs is much as if a smith or artist who works in metal should expect to form and shape out his work only with his bellows." The itinerancy of Methodism, however, is perhaps unfavorable to the most effective pastoral influence. There are adequate compensations elsewhere, but this inefficiency has somewhat affected the growth of the Church in the larger towns and cities. Our preachers have been evangelists—voices crying in the wilderness. Like moving battalions upon the field of battle, they have hurried to places of greatest danger, and have found but little time for the quiet, delicate, wise work of the pastorate. But in the cities it cannot be neglected without serious loss. And in no place is large sagacity and patient industry more demanded than in New Orleans. To make full proof of his ministry in that city Linus Parker sought to combine the methods of Paul and Apollos. His plans were carefully matured and wrought out with the patience of an unfaltering purpose. The embarrassments of his work, occasioned especially by the annual dread of an epidemic of yellow fever, are best told by himself in a letter to the Nashville *Christian Advocate*, while filling the Felicity pulpit:

"Our churches are sad losers by the annual hegira. Immanuel's armies are much reduced, and some congregations are nearly broken up. All of our social and religious institutions suffer; Sunday-schools are partially disorganized by the absence of teachers and by departure of scholars; class-meetings and prayer-meetings are apt to languish; and the attenuated congregations in their endeavors at keeping cool present the appearance of animated wind-mills. In the sphere of the pastorate—which is the right arm of the ministerial functions in cities—the evil is sorely felt. The flock is scarcely gathered before it is scattered; and the pastoral relation, with its vital ties and manifold benefits, is rent asunder. The autumnal avalanche of traveled Christians, besides baffling the pastor's vigilance and overtaxing his industry, partakes but imperfectly of the communion of saints, and contributes little to the religious influence and material strength of the Church. Nowhere are faithful pastors harder worked, and nowhere are their labors more exhaustive to mind and body.

" In the fall comes the reörganization, when the scattered fragments come together, 'bone to his bone,' and the knitting body, with the drawback of a summer's disintegration, enters upon a new growth. These winter overflows, however, leave behind them a certain sediment of progress which the careful culture of our resident people turns to account. Thus the growth of religion in New Orleans has been like the growth of a tree—the full sap is in the trunk but half of the year, and the development is marked by the concentric circles of periodic advance and stagnation."

Into the homes of his people he went an evangel of love and a trusted, honored friend and counselor. Revered by the children, admired by the cultured, confided in by the troubled, caressed by the aged, and loved by all, he was an admirable city pastor. Cheerful without jocularity in the social circle, and instructive without brilliancy in the pulpit, he was popular everywhere. He had the successful pastor's rarest endowment, TACT—that "delicate and subtle gift almost like a sixth sense, which enables its possessor to grasp a situation and say and do the best thing in the best manner at the right moment." And this he displayed without compromise of manly dignity or religious conviction. He pleased not for pleasure's sake, but to gain influence and win souls. He felt—and truly—that gruffness is not grace, nor is grossness the badge of holiest zeal or grandest fidelity.

A like cordial welcome awaited him, whether at the hovel door of squalid poverty on a back street, or in the mansion of the rich on the most popular thoroughfare. And to each he carried the same message. Through every epidemic of yellow fever he remained courageously at the post of duty, and feared not to follow with a gospel of comfort wherever the wing of the death-angel had flown. Many beautiful stories of his sympathizing pastoral labors during these dark periods might be related. They belong to the sacred, unwritten history of Christian heroism. Many an aching head was soothed by the touch of his gentle hand. Sad hearts were cheered by his radiant face. When death is entering every door, baffling all scientific skill, defying the tenderest vigils, and the sense of utter helplessness is so oppressive as during an epidemic of yellow fever, no visit is so grateful, and no countenance so hope-inspiring, as a loving pastor's. By the works he wrought, by the homes he brightened, the doubting he strengthened, and the dying he comforted, Linus Parker wrote his name in letters of living light in the annals of New Orleans Methodism.

There was another popular young Methodist pastor in the city at this time who attracted large congregations to Carondelet Street, and became a pulpit orator of Connectional fame. He came to New Orleans the same year with Linus Parker, as a transfer from the Mississippi Conference, and for over thirty years they were intimate friends and co-laborers. It was fitting, therefore, that at the burial of the Bishop his life-long companion in toil, Dr. Joseph B. Walker, should deliver the memorial address. He yet lives in active itinerant service, an attractive preacher and the charm of every social circle he enters.

For three years—from 1853 to 1856—Linus Parker was pastor of Felicity Street Church, and each year reported a revival and a large ingathering of new members. The Conference which met at Mansfield December 14, 1853, became historic because of the offer of a two-hundred-dollar prize for the best essay on the support of the Methodist ministry, which led to the writing of "Post Oak Circuit" by Dr. J. C. Keener. It is a Methodist classic, and will long hold a chief place in our denominational literature. In 1856 Mr. Parker was stationed at Carondelet, and remained there three years also, with growing pastoral success. In 1859 he was made presiding elder of the New Orleans District, and also had pastoral charge of the colored work of the city, embracing three large churches and about fourteen hundred members. The next year he was returned to his beloved flock at Felicity, and continued to serve them until forced to leave in 1862, when the city was surrendered to the Federal forces.

During the earlier years of his city pastorate Linus Parker's reputation as a preacher spread abroad. He was in demand for college commencements and great public occasions; but his shrinking modesty and exacting home duties allowed him rarely to accept urgent invitations. In the early summer of 1854 he attended the Commencement of Centenary College at Jackson, Louisiana, and extended his visit to Woodville, Mississippi. Of the visitor, and his characteristics and career, the Rev. W. P. Barton, then pastor at Woodville, and yet an honored member of the North Mississippi Conference in regular service, thus writes:

"My personal acquaintance with Rev. Linus Parker began in Woodville in 1854. From mutual friends I had heard much of him before our meeting. My expectations were high; they suffered none in the acquaintance. Woodville in those days, though a small village of a thousand or twelve hundred inhabitants, the seat of justice for Wilkinson county, was a place of great social importance. It was in a fertile country, surrounded by rich planters of intellect and culture. Methodism was in the ascendency. The McGehees, Hoards, Burrusses, Waileses, Lewises, Angells, and many other cultured families, made up a congregation rarely equaled in the elements that compose the highest qualities of mind and heart. They had been ministered to by Drs. Winans, Drake, Marshall, Watkins, Light, the seraphic Elijah Steele, the silver-tongued John C. Burruss, and others. That the young preacher gave the fullest satisfaction, and met the highest expectations of such a community in his brief visit among us, prepared us to expect much of him in the future.

"More than thirty years have passed, in which our acquaintance ripened into friendship and intimacy. That choice circle at Woodville is broken—gone. The young preacher grew on, ascending step by step, steadily, gracefully, by the application of a well-poised mind and sanctified heart, filling well and profitably the circuit, station, district, and editor's chair, and finally the episcopal office, whence he ascended to our Father's house. While he was fully equal to any place to which he was called by the Church of God, his best and most lasting work was with his pen. He was not a newsmonger, nor did he excel as a paragraphist, but he was a devotional writer of rare gifts and graces. His editorials, like the gospel, created their own demand, and then fed the hungry soul with the marrow of the gospel. They had the grace and sweetness, freshness and polish of Jay's "Exercises." His episcopal career, full of promise, was cut short by death before the Church had tasted the ripe fruit. The promise, well assured by a successful past, was all the Church could ask. He would doubtless have diffused the spirit of holiness on his episcopal tours as he had so well done with his pen."

The young pastor's own account of that visit is as cheery as the balmy breath of morning in the summer mountains. An extract will be given, as it graphically describes one of the pioneer railroad enterprises in the United States, and displays the writer's genius for newspaper correspondence:

"Two and a half o'clock precisely we are at the Feliciana depot (Bayou Sara), and off on the cars for Woodville. One passenger-car and two for freight make the train. Five hours of time and twenty-seven miles of space, through a country of surpassing beauty; hill and dale, grassy lawns, shady groves, and cultivated fields we see by the way—the pleasantest rural scenes to be met this side of Mason and Dixon's line; English, I imagine, in some respects, but in a freer country. To eight miles of Woodville it is West Feliciana, a parish abounding in wealth and comfort, and in a high state of cultivation. We have but one passenger besides myself, a gentlemanly conductor, and Mr. Hoard, the superintendent, a planter of Wilkinson. This road is the best in the world in some respects, and the worst in others. It is the most varied rail that a man ever rode on —the old flat, the modern T, and sometimes none at all. Rather more than five miles an hour is the speed we average. This gives opportunity to breathe and look about. At times we are slowly moving at a perilous height over ravines and creeks; then again creeping through deep places, the bluffs looking down upon the train and seeming to ask, 'Why do n't you go faster?' Now we are stuck in the mud. The little superannuated locomotive plunges and blows like a corpulent horse in a quagmire. At length we drag our slow length along, 'and we are escaped.' This road was built some time between 1830 and 1840, in what is familiarly known as 'the flush times of Mississippi,' by a company having for its style 'The West Feliciana and Woodville Railroad Company.' The road has never been remunerative, the stock seldom, if ever, at par; but it still exists as a relic of the past, kept up by the money and enterprise of the chief stockholder, Judge McGehee. The cars do not run on Sunday, preachers are always franked through, and not a single life was ever lost by accident. This is more than can be said of any other railroad in the world probably. Our time and space are accomplished, and here is Woodville, and here too is Brother Barton to greet us. The greeting of one such man is worth more than that of a joint board of aldermen."

While on that trip he rode out nine miles south-east of Woodville to see the Bethel camp-ground, a place of consecrated celebrity, and for forty years before the scene of a yearly revival. There the great men of early Methodism had preached and prayed. After examining the hallowed ground, the devout young man sat down to meditate, and the following were his tenderly beautiful reflections:

"This is a sacred spot, hallowed by many, many sacred associations. In the stillness of this August noon we sit in the old rustic altar and meditate. Thousands of souls have been converted just here where we are; and what men of God and how many have poured out burning words of gospel truth! These grand old woods have rung and rung again with song and shout. Here mourners have agonized, have found peace, have gone to their earthly homes telling what great things the Lord had done, and from thence have gone to their heavenly homes to prolong the strains of praise born here. The throng is not here; the tents which face us on every side are forsaken; but association enables us to

> Find tongues in trees, books in the running brooks,
> Sermons in stones, and good in every thing."

CHAPTER IX.
CORRESPONDENCE UP THE RIVER.

IN the summer of 1856, from June 1st to August 21st, Mr. Parker was absent from his pastorate at Carondelet on a trip to the North and East. This was his first visit home since coming South. The account of his return to the old family roof-tree near Vienna has already been given, and will be omitted from this chapter. This tour was in every way enjoyable and profitable. He had for traveling companions his life-long friends the Hon. W. H. Foster and wife, Mrs. Thomas, and others, making up a refined and cultivated company. While on board river steamers the days were spent on deck making observations, and the evenings in the cabin for literary and social entertainment; and among the most favored of the party was the modest, refined, companionable young pastor. His letters written to the New Orleans *Christian Advocate,* under the general title of "Correspondence up the River," descriptive of the sights and insights of that trip, are among the choicest gems of his graphic pen. As they are so characteristic of the author's style, and contain so much information concerning scenes and places visited that now seem strange after the progress of thirty years, extracts from some of them must be inserted in this memorial. None of them have ever appeared in book form:

High Water and its Advantages—Signs Northward—Cliffs and Rocks.

"The advantages of a full river to the seeing voyager are

manifold. The Mississippi itself is more majestic in high water; it is most itself and most natural; it seems to be the state it was born to. High water becomes its dignity, it sets well, it gives a fullness and rotundity to its grandeur, and seems to tell us that all subordinates have paid their tribute. This circumstance makes a vast difference in the notes and enjoyment of a traveler. The scenery of the river—that which made up its islands, points, and bends—is enhanced. It is then to be counted a particular felicity to find ourselves on this great water when it rolls its greatest volumes, when it rejoices as a young man to run a race.

"The monotony of the great river is in everybody's mouth, but it is the monotony of the sublime, from which there is no descent. As we proceed northward there are some noticeable changes. The cypress and the moss are left behind in Louisiana, and the live-oak and the magnolia. As we near the mouth of the Ohio cotton disappears, and on the river corn is the main object of cultivation. I left the corn in Louisiana in gleeful tassel, looking over the tops of the fences; up here it is yet in the blade, and not large enough to make the field look green.

"Another indication of our northing is the protracted evening twilight. With good company we hasten to the hurricane roof to see the sunset and its effects upon the scenery. In Louisiana the sun goes down quickly—you can see him drop below the horizon, and presently it is dark; here, with such dignity as becomes a king, he retires slowly, and his motion is as difficult for the eye to mark as it is to detect the movements of the hour-hand of your watch. For a space he lingers behind the trees, and his beams play and dart amongst their tops like laughter in the face of humor. At last

>The evening sun hath made a golden set,
>And by the bright track of his burning car
>Gives token of the goodly day to-morrow.

And now nature mixes her dyes and paints the world. The clouds, the woods, the waters, all take up the colors of the parting day and reflect them variously. Gradually the features of all mingle and the tints mix. The scene dissolves, and the rent mantle of the setting sun in twilight patches fades and is lost in the night. Then the stars come out one by one, until the milky-way, like a Mississippi of light, a river of stars, flows overhead, and the young moon, with its thread-like horns, like a silver mantle, is suspended just above the dip of the western horizon.

"Where the Ohio debouches into the Mississippi we witness a magnificent confluence. Cairo is on the narrow and sharp point made by the meeting of the waters. Illinois literally comes to a point here. The place has about six good houses in it, and a substantial wharf-boat on the Ohio River side.

"From Cairo to St. Louis we have two hundred miles of more pleasant western travel than is afforded by the eight hundred miles we have left behind us. We touch at Cape Girardeau after tea. All we can say of it is that it is a city on a hill, and that most of the adult population is at the landing.

The Upper Mississippi.

"Before attempting to give a pen-glimpse of the Upper Mississippi, let us look at ourselves and our fare. At our first breakfast we had a rare dish—it smacked of Paris, China, or the Gallic epicureanism of New Orleans. It was a broil of nether extremities. They had a look of life, a living, jumping attitude. Doubtless the cook had spitted them in the very act. I thought of Æsop, the boys, and the frogs—'sport to you, but death to us.' Nobody but an old croaker could object to the flavor; it was so nice to see, and so delicate and squab-like to taste. The company in cabin is unusually various—more than a fair complement of children, all mindful of their right to make as much noise as possible. There are men and women of course, young people and old people, invalids going to St. Paul for better lungs and improved digestion, Eastern men bent on land speculations, and parties of pleasure, raftsmen returning to the lumber regions, and wanderers seeking homes and fortunes where they may best find them.

"Between St. Louis and Rock Island the scenery is worthy of note, though not comparable with what awaits us farther up. There are a number of cities which have sprung up in an incredibly short time. Alton, Quincy, Keokuk, Nauvoo, and Burlington are all beautiful and flourishing places. Nauvoo, the quondam capital of the Mormons, is more beautiful for situation than any. A hill rises in long and graceful slopes from the water; around it the river makes a spacious bend, so that we seem to nearly circumnavigate the place; the houses are built on the slopes of this three-sided hill in circular order, and looking toward the river. On the summit and facing up stream stands the unfinished temple; two winged turrets, and a center wall which connects them, are all that we see. The town is now occupied by a company of French Socialists, who are making an experiment in political economy, not as demoralizing but quite as absurd as that of their Mormon predecessors. A peculiarity of city building on the river is that there are usually two, one on each side. A spirit of rivalry and emulation inspires them, and looking each other in the face they are pushed forward in enterprise. Rock Island and Davenport are opposite, the former in Illinois and the latter in Iowa. The approach to these towns from below is fine, indiscribably so. As we steam along within four or five miles we find ourselves inclosed in a vast amphitheater having a diameter of at least ten miles. We are surrounded by hills which rise gradually from the basin, and whose distant summits are robed in azure. The river is dotted with islands, amongst which we make our way. The towns grow upon our vision, stretching up and down on both sides and climbing the heights. Rock Island, from which one of the cities takes its name, rises in the channel between and nearer the left bank. Its face to the south is steep and rocky. From either shore to this island there is a railroad bridge, not suspension, but with arches and abutments. This and the suspension bridge at the Falls of St. Anthony, are the only bridges which have spanned the Mississippi. Its entire length is five thousand eight hundred and thirty feet, consisting of six spans of two hundred and fifty feet each.

"From this point our progress is one of uninterrupted interest. The hills, the everlasting hills, are most prominent. At times their tops are in the blue distance, everywhere surrounding like the mountains round about Jerusalem. Then they rise directly from the water to a height of four hundred feet, and the castle-like rocks at the summit look as if they would topple over and fall upon us. Frequently these hills are all around us, and the clear river with its islands looks like a placid lake embosomed amongst them, or like a prisoner hemmed on every side and taken unawares. Very often they stand in groups, peaked and grotesque, and then again they assume the attitude of regular mountain ranges, with every imaginable beauty of outline. Lake Pepin, an enlargement of the river, is celebrated for its scenery, but we were so unfortunate as to pass through it in a dark and rainy night. One object we saw through the gloom, the Maiden's Rock, which has a perpendicular of four hundred and fifty feet. Tradition says that years and years ago an Indian maiden, daughter of a chief, being thwarted in love, threw herself from the top of this promontory. This was a very romantic way for a young red lady to rebel against paternal authority and to die for love.

Minnesota and Minnehaha.

"Minnesota, which being interpreted is 'sky-tinted water,' is the first territory I have visited. Every thing goes on here just as in the States. The Territory was organized by act of Congress March 3, 1849. It is seven years old, and by the census is already entitled to the dignity of Statehood. . . . What nature does here she must do quickly. There are but three growing months—cold spring, chilly autumn, and freezing winter embracing the remainder of the year. The ice thaws and begins its southward journey in the last of April, and by the first or middle of November the rivers and lakes are frozen. The atmosphere in summer and winter has the dryness, electricity, and high salubrity of the Mexican table-lands. You can sleep with open windows, or even in the open air with impunity. Invalids with pulmonary diseases spend the winter here and are benefited.

"Our first excursion is to White Bear Lake, twelve miles from St. Paul. Fine horses, but a slow and perverse driver, bring us to it in time for a dinner of fish and game—the best dinner we have found in the Territory. The lake is twelve or fifteen miles in circumference, a large island of several hundred acres is in the center, and both island and main-land are crowded with a munificent growth of sugarmaple and oak. The water is as clear as light, is the best in the world to drink, and deep enough to look blue. We are rowed over its surface and circumnavigate the island. The water sparkles like wine twenty feet below the surface; we see fish and shells, and every sort of submarine thing. Each passenger has hook, spoon, and line, and dancing over the waves trolls for such fish as he has just eaten for dinner. On the pebbly shore of the island our little fleet is moored, and all fall to work seeking for chameleons and other curious and precious stones. Of these many fine specimens are found which jewelers would prize. Once more aboard with hook and line, we linger in the shadow of the island till the sun gets low, and then return to port.

"This lake is supplied by a spring which bursts up from the center and bottom, and always keeps the lake at a uniform height. White Bear is the largest lake we saw, but there are many others smaller and not less beautiful, which we passed and saw at a distance. They are supplied by gushing, powerful springs, and their outlets are the source of several large rivers. The Red River of the North and the Mississippi take their rise in these spring-lakes. Minnesota has been styled with truth the artesian-fountain of the continent. No country in the world equals it in the number, beauty, and purity of its lakes.

"Our next excursion, and the one of greatest distance and interest, is to the Falls of St. Anthony, and other noticeable places. There is an observatory below the falls and near the bank of the river, called 'Cheever's Tower,' as high as the tower of St. Patrick's, and built like the fine tower on Washington Avenue. Over the entrance somebody has perpetrated the following distich:

> Pay your dime
> Before you climb.

After fulfilling the truth of this poetry (?) we ascended to the dizzy, buzzy top, and luxuriated in the magnificent *coup d'œil*. We look upon the Mississippi at least two thousand miles from its mouth. The channel is visible in its windings for miles above and below St. Anthony. The prairies, with their varied woods, grasses, and grains, stretch away like the dead swells from the mast of a ship. As we stand and contemplate we are filled with regret that we could not have looked upon the falls before the utilitarian pale-faces came and haggled and ruined what must have been one of the loveliest scenes on the continent. Half a mile above the falls is a suspension bridge, built like the bridge at Niagara, but not of equal size or cost. Crossing on this bridge we drive to the Falls of Minnehaha, six miles below Minneapolis. The outlet of Lake Minnetonka here makes a perpendicular leap of eighty feet. It is a small stream, between a brook and a creek, twenty or thirty feet wide, and half-knee deep. Crossing it above we wind around, and in a deep gorge or dell, shut in by precipitous banks, and overhung with trees and vines, we see the 'laughing-water' face to face. It is a thing of beauty, or rather of marvelous prettiness. With the trees and shrubs—which from some points partially hide it—and with the sparkling, dimpling, cachinnating look and sound of the water, we feel that Minnehaha alone expresses what is heard and seen. Some wretch has attempted to change the name to perpetuate his own—'Brown's Falls.' 'Shades of the Dakotahs! The man that would be guilty of such an impious thing ought to be scalped!'"

[The party returned to Chicago and went eastward by way of Niagara.]

Niagara.

"After what has been said and written for a hundred years, and after the world's suffrage has accorded to Niagara the first place amongst the wonders of nature, it is impossible to approach the first view without emotion. We tremble lest the introduction shall overpower, and then are fearful lest it shall fall below excited and extravagant expectation. Either of these alternatives was obviated to some extent by the twilight, and by the very partial view which the bridge affords. The effect was unexpectedly passive and tranquil. There were no interjective heart-throbs, no breathless awe, nothing overwhelming. Every thing, the river beneath us, and the falls—of which we had but a side-face glimpse—were less grand; they were smaller than we expected. Tupper did not think Niagara sublime, and said so. For the first time I began to think well of Tupper, who could be heterodox that he might be true. But with this sense of disappointment there was a consciousness of illusion, and a conviction that the first impression was deceptive. Like the chef-d'œuvre of painting and sculpture, this great work of God must be studied in all lights and views, and in connection with many accessory features. The idea of magnitude is derived from comparison and analysis.

"A stranger is struck with the points of difference between the descriptions he has seen and read and the scenes as he sees them himself. Descriptive writers and artists, in their word and pencil pictures, give accurate expression of lions, elephants, and landscapes, and we are surprised, when we see the originals, at their truthful delineations. But with Niagara it is all the other way. The traveler feels that he has never had any adequate and accurate idea at all. The half has neither been described nor painted, and never will be. The following features had escaped my attention: First, the outline of the falls and their relative position. Instead of making a curve or semi-circle, the extremes of which are opposite, the trend of rock and the direct line of the comb of water extend diagonally across, far up and down the river, so that the falls present a nearly front face to the Canada shore. Goat Island is the second feature of which I had no right conception. The pictures are mostly profiles, and this island, like people's noses in such cases, is higher and sharper, and not relatively as broad as it really is. The front face gives its proportions better, and causes it to fill one-third of the entire span. Its area is greater, not a mere foot-hold for goats, but broad, covered with magnificent forest-trees, and of ample dimensions for the site of a city. In the next place the greater breadth above the falls and the rapids had escaped my attention. It is more like a lake than a river, converging like the mouth of a bay, and becoming a river proper not till it tumbles over the precipice. The rapids, to my mind, dispute with the falls for the palm of sublimity. From the calm, deep lake the waters commence their mad race, and for miles above they come in giant strides to the final and fearful leap. Like a troop of horse rushing to the charge, they come in a gallop; with manes of foam and tread of thunder they come. The foremost waves are baffled and broken by the rocks and islands, but with conscious invincibility they deploy to right and left, reform below, and in massive grandeur hurl themselves into the smoking abyss. It is impossible not to feel that these waves are animated, and the illusion clothes them with life and individuality when they disappear in the depths; and then again when they come out of the spray and creamy foam and flow lazily away, as if stunned by the shock or subdued by the terrible experience of their recent revel. . . .

"Niagara by moonlight would startle the dullest prose into poetry. Not for our accommodation, but because it was the right time of the month, the moon shone on us and enhanced the scene by her charms. Goat Island is quiet now. Only a few are moving among the trees, or standing like specter sentinels on the points of interest. The moonbeams mingle with the shade and give a wild solemnity to the scene. The roar of Niagara is terrible at such a time, and its sullen, awful voice speaks of eternity and of God. The ground trembles beneath its weight, and the leaves sparkle like aspen in the breezeless air. In the mists which rise slowly and heavily in the night atmosphere are lunar bows, sometimes in perfect arches, at other times broken into fragments, or turning on their axes and changing the plane from arch to circle. They looked like the ethereal drapery and flitting forms of the spirit world; almost colorless, and almost eluding the sharpest eye, it was not unnatural to think that those bows indicated the presence of disembodied spirits.

"Divested of our usual apparel and clothed in submarine style, we descend to the foot of Table Rock, more than one hundred and fifty feet of stairs, and tread the narrow foot-path which leads under the falls and to Termination Rock. Here the roar and crash is deafening, and the spray is blinding and suffocating. Besides having the sublimest shower-bath in the world, the adventurer obtains the only full conception of Niagara's power. This, unlike all others, is not a superficial view, for we stand under and behind it, and are overwhelmed. Ascending and resting from the fatigue of our adventure, we drive to the Clifton House and witness the finest of all our sight-seeing. The moon rises directly over Goat Island and gradually bathes rocks, trees, and water in light. We see the falls in all their breadth and majesty, and the rapids have put on brazen helmets.

"While at Niagara we visit the celebrated battle-field of Lundy's Lane. There are two towers erected on the battle-ground, from which the view is wide and charming. Our guide—the man of the tower—was in the battle, and by our leave fought it over again. There is a quiet burial-place near the tower, in which some of the officers who fell are interred. Where the greatest slaughter was, and where scores are buried, corn and wheat are growing luxuriantly. All is peace now. The din of battle, the marshaling of armed men, and the groans of wounded and dying have given place to peace. The dead sleep well, and war has left no trace of its bloody march. In the distance to the south-east the spires of Buffalo are perceptible, to the north-east Brock's Monument lifts its head from Queenstown Heights, and to the north-west the surface of Ontario glistens in the evening sun. Nearer, and yet distant, the falls, the villages, the river, the islands, and Lake Erie are spread out as if at our feet.

Wilbraham.

"Eight miles from Springfield is Wilbraham, a picturesque village situated at the foot of a range of mountains and ornamented by some of New England's most ancient and stately elms. These elms are to New England what the live-oak is to Louisiana—the pride of her forests. A chapter might be written about them, for they are of storied interest, and witnesses of events that are most thrilling. Apart from the fact that they are useful and ornamental adjuncts to scenery, they are monumental. They constitute, to my mind, a decided feature of what is beautiful and revered; and the care with which they are cherished is evidence of taste and patriotism. These, with her old homesteads and her hoary and honored grave-stones, live in relief upon the tablets of memory. Dr. Raymond, President of Wilbraham Academy, showed us through the buildings of the institution. . . . The name of Fisk, the first president, is still remembered and revered; and his portrait is suspended over the desk of the chapel and over the seats of the presiding officers of each of the societies. The influence which such men exert after they are dead is wonderful. The people here, if they were Romanists, would cross themselves at the mention of his name. Such a deep, abiding heart-worship is secured by few, and the secret of it is worth investigation. I do not find that it was peerless intellect, nor that it was the urbanity and goodness of a Christian gentleman. Some or all of these qualities Fisk may have possessed, but they do not disclose the cause of that deathless love which his friends and disciples cherish. . . . Wilbraham is honored in her graduates, many of whom are amongst the most useful and distinguished men and women of the country. You know it is an academy for both sexes. They are classed together, and eat at the same table. Dr. Raymond thinks the policy good, and that the system works well; that young people who are educated for society are better educated in it, and that a mutually good and healthful influence is exerted. The experiment has been long and fairly tried in this institution, and as a fact is worthy of consideration.

Boston.

"On the first Sunday morning of August the sun rose upon us in Boston, the city of notions and the metropolis of "Down East." On our way to church, and on our way back again, the crookedness and irregularity of the streets are both striking and troublesome. The streets are scrupulously clean, and the buildings, for uniformity and elegance, are not excelled by any of our American cities. But the heat was terrible—as near the roasting point as weather could be. It subdued, it melted; even Southerners became fusionists. For two days and two long nights the thermometer stood at or near a hundred degrees; and far more oppressive than the same temperature in New Orleans.

"At six o'clock in the evening there was preaching on the Common. Services were held under an immense awning, and attended by a large concourse. The sermon was on that delightful text, "God so loved the world," and came from the preacher's lips with sweet and refreshing unction. I could not help turning from this demonstration —indorsed by all denominations—to the old elm under which Jesse Lee stood half or a quarter of a century ago and preached alone, without an escort or a friend. It was an unmeant acknowledgment, the triumph of a policy which Methodism has illustrated, and for which she has been abused.

"The packet which plies between Boston and Portland

leaves 'Long Wharf' at seven o'clock in the evening. The railway is direct and more expeditious, but by boat the traveler gets a view of Boston Harbor, snuffs the salt breeze which steals over the deep, and is rocked soundly asleep by the gentle waves of the Atlantic. If these considerations have due weight, he goes on board and spends the long twilight on the bay, whose surface is calm and unrippled. Standing out from the wharf are vessels at anchor, others moving out to sea and spreading sail for distant shores, and others still, with press of canvas, have come from foreign lands, and are at the end of their voyage. A ship tied up and stripped of her canvas and colors always looks crestfallen and melancholy. Her black hull crouches in sullen submission in the dock, and her naked spars are like skeleton wings divested of plumage and wasted to bone. But when under sail a ship is a beautiful and glorious thing. See yonder three-master as the tug swings her around and conducts her seaward. At first she moves heavily, and with sluggish unwillingness the sails are gradually unfurled. From the top-gallants down, one by one they are shaken out; cat's-paw breezes play hide-and-seek in their flapping folds, and the ponderous vessel treats them with unperturbed disdain. But now the wind awakes her slumbering power, the cordage creaks, the spars bend, the timbers groan. Dropping her steamer deliverer, she spreads her winged arms to embrace the breeze, and with wild delight courts the kisses of the free and buoyant waves. She is clothed with the grandeur of the element with which she contends. Neither depth nor expanse nor agitation deter. She hurries onward to meet all that is terrible in danger and all that is sublime in safety.

White Mountains.

"The steamer enters Portland harbor between day-break and sunrise. We breakfast in the city, and take the cars for Gorham, the nearest approach to the mountains by railroad. Taking stage at Gorham, an up-hill road of eight miles, through wild and rugged scenery, brings the coach and its contents to the 'Glen House.' It is in a *glen*, deep and secluded, around which the mountains rise in indescribable grandeur.

"And here one might sit forever unwearied with gazing, looking at nature in her loftiest mood, and feeling all the time a fullness of satisfaction that never surfeits. If all of God's works are means of education and development, the mountain is the last lesson in the school of nature. Its awful form is most godlike, and most akin to eternity. It has the functions of an educator, whose mighty lessons have been going out 'since the mountains were brought forth or ever God had formed the earth and the world.' They have taught men liberty, and they have helped men to survey the heavens above and the earth around. They have been consecrated to learning and religion; and history, romance, and superstition have clothed them with the attributes of immortality. In Scripture they are symbols of the unchangeable and the everlasting.

"Few visitors go away without making the ascent. Eight of the clock in the morning is the hour to start. The distance is eight miles. Horses are kept for the purpose, and specially selected for their long experience and sure-footedness. Twenty-five in company—ladies and gentlemen—are in saddle and off at the hour. Two guides—one in front and one in the rear, and well provided with horseshoes—accompany the miscellaneous squadron.

"As we proceed, vegetable growth dwindles all at once, and but three or four miles from our point of departure we come to a forest literally *struck* with death. They are the corpses of trees—ghastly, leafless, and dead. It is the picture of all that is desolate. There is no living thing, neither quadruped, nor bird, nor even insect. Through this a half mile or more the road is at its end, and all timber disappears. Hence, to the top several miles ahead, we proceeded in single-file along the most perilous bridle-path the most of us ever ventured to pursue. It is worse than riding up a flight of stairs—sometimes at an angle of ninety degrees, and ever exceedingly rough and abrupt. . . . . We begin to be in cloud-land. They form at the top and come down upon us in avalanches of mist; then they sweep across through the gorges and intersect our path; and anon they creep up the acclivities and surround us, while rainbows play in their curly locks. Onward and upward, through clouds and amidst a world of granite, till at last in clear sunshine we halt upon the very top, seven thousand feet above the ocean, and the highest eminence in New Enland. . . . Strange to be a matter of record, but a fact, the only form of winged life is a mosquito—a real Lake Borgne gallinipper—and at *his* work sucking the life-blood out of me. Sublime insect, and welcome! The only form of vegetable life is moss, and a delicate moss-flower, as modest in its habits as the violet, and not very unlike the heliotrope in appearance.

"The scenes change constantly. Now, above the clouds and with the blue sky over us, nothing is visible below but thick fog-clouds, whose waves of mist wash the brow of the peak on which we are, and stretch in one unbroken gloomy expanse around as far as the eye can reach. Suddenly the great deep is broken up; a clear spot opens here and there, through which we see the lower world; then the mist condenses, and reaches down into the notches and gulfs; or, driven by opposing currents of wind, it boils and whirls in the vapory abyss like a mighty caldron. Now for a space all is clear in our immediate neighborhood, and the horizon is walled in by those towering cloud-structures whose snow-white heads rise in awful majesty. Lightnings dart from their inky bases, and the thunder comes from them pealing across the vale and echoing amongst the heights. It is the birth-hour of a thunder-storm. These monsters unite, their identity is lost in one huge dark mass, and this at length is broken and separated by contact with the mountains or by rapid condensation. But these aspects of nature as we saw her here must be dismissed. Difficult as is the ascent, the return is more so. It requires good horsemanship and firm nerves. The old gray that carried this writer and his fortunes deserves honorable mention; how he made not one false step in all the trip, carried his rider through storm and cloud and paths most appalling to look at, and looked glad when his day's work was done."

CHAPTER X.
SECOND MARRIAGE—JOHN C. BURRUSS.

THE twelfth session of the Louisiana Conference was held in Mansfield, De Soto Parish, beginning February 3, 1858. Bishop George F. Pierce presided, and greatly endeared himself to the brethren, who had only known him by reputation as a prince of pulpit orators. In his honor the educational enterprise there inaugurated was called the "Pierce and Paine College." At that session Linus Parker preached, by previous appointment, the Conference sermon, which added to his growing reputation as a lucid, spiritual expositor of the word of God.

Just before the Conference assembled, on the 20th of January, 1858, he was married to Miss Ellen K. Burruss, at the residence of her father, Rev. John C. Burruss, in the parish of Caddo, Louisiana. That union was in every way fitting and fortunate. Miss Burruss was a cousin of his first wife, and of royal Methodist stock. One of her sisters was the last wife of Judge Edward McGehee—a woman of marvelous gifts and magnificent character.

In those days a trip from New Orleans to that "most beautiful of North Louisiana homes," near Shreveport, was not made in a few hours, as now. It sometimes required weeks, and gave full opportunity to test the fiber of patience. On one of his visits, if not this last and most important, Mr. Parker spent three weeks on a steam-boat between the mouth of Red River and Shreveport. On account of low water the average progress was only about fifteen miles a day. But the time was not unemployed or idly employed. Becalmed at sea on one occasion, Mr. Wesley mastered the German language. Not less active was the brain or receptive the heart of Linus Parker. When not engaged in reading or Bible-study, he was making observations from the deck of the vessel on the scenery of the country or the geological formations displayed in the river-banks. An extract from a letter descriptive of a trip gives us one of his finest pen-pictures—that especially of the crane, "the Izaak Walton of the feathered tribe"—and further indicates the chastened maturity and poetic exuberance of his imagination:

"We became profoundly versed in the uses of yawls, hawsers, and capstans, and have the nomenclature of fresh-water sailors at our tongue's end. Amidst the continual jingle of bells in the engine-room we distinguish between one jingle and another jingle. Each bell is identified by its tone, and what had once the confusion of a French tête-à-tête becomes a clear and rapid utterance of words which we discriminate with the intuitive readiness of our own vernacular.

"Our observations are shut in from the outer world by banks from fifteen to twenty feet above the sky-lights. On one side the shore rises perpendicularly, displaying the various deposits which the floods of centuries have borne hither from the roots of the North American Andes. The age of the formations can be *guessed* at almost as accurately by these marks as the longevity of a steer by the circles on his horns, or of a tree by the concentric rings which mark its annual growth. At this stage of the water the geology of the valley is laid open to the lovers of natural science, and there are advantages of investigation that no other time affords. Agassiz, Nott, and Miller would do well to bring their lore in contact with this marvelous but not always opened book of nature. On the side opposite it rises gradually in beautiful slopes, presenting the same geological chapter, only in larger print. The scenery at times is most beautiful. The abrupt bank is thick with forest-trees, which stretch out their broad arms as if praying for a 'rise,' and fling their shadows half-way across to the other shore. Richly dressed in their own foliage, many of them wear bridal-veils of moss, laces of wild ivy and roses, while pendant from their boughs and reflected in the water beneath are luxurious tresses of wild-grape and muscadine. The slope just across, where it meets the water, is not a point, but a delicately rounded curve—Hogarth's line of beauty. Upon the extreme convex of this line stands a tall white crane, his long neck bending gracefully, his head so turned that one eye looks straight down into the water and one straight up into the sky; one foot and leg are lifted akimbo, as if to secure the greatest silence; the whole, in pantomime, proclaiming him the Izaak Walton of the feathered tribe. We look beyond these immediate surroundings, ahead and up the wild, romantic gorge, through which the emaciated river drags its slow length along, and lo! a southern sunset completes the picture. The warm and mellow horizon comes down to meet the gilded waters, banks of golden cloud continue the red and emerald walls which shut us in from the lower world, and the illusion steals upon the heart that we are entering the golden gate that opens into the splendors of the tearless land."

As the lives of Linus Parker and his father-in-law, the Rev. John C. Burruss, became so tenderly, intimately intertwined, this memorial would be incomplete without a sketch of that remarkable man. He received the gifted young husband of his daughter into the family as his own son, gave him a father's blessing, and felt more than parental pride in his apostolic labors and growing success, and in the hour of death committed family and estate into his hands. How far he impressed his own pure and noble spirit upon the son, and how much it affected the character of his ministry, the eternal years alone can reveal. A very prince and leader in Israel was John C. Burruss. He had the splendid bearing of a commanding general, the elegant manners of the highest refinement, and the gentle, seraphic spirit of "the beloved disciple." His voice was a marvel of compass and sweetness, and his eloquence was Ciceronian in the sublime sweep of his periods. Of large benevolence and ample fortune, he gave liberally and preached divinely. Whether as a zealous itinerant on an old-time circuit, presiding elder of a district embracing half of a State, agent of the American Bible Society, city pastor, college president, or local preacher, he worked the works of his Lord, and left a heritage of worth and achievement as imperishable as the everlasting hills. As president for some years of the Elizabeth Academy at Washington, Mississippi, he was a pioneer Methodist educator, and deserves to be remembered as the Wilbur Fisk of the South-west.

John C. Burruss was a native of Maryland and a child of the Church of England. He was born near Port Tobacco, October 7, 1788, but removed with his parents to Caroline county, Virginia, while yet a child, where he grew to man's estate. He was baptized in infancy by a clergyman of the Church of England, but never assumed the vows of confirmation. Though he became a worldly, irreligious young man, his clear perceptions of Christian piety and propriety aroused distaste, if not disgust, for the fun-loving, card-playing clergy of that day. Into that section came Bishop Asbury and those godly men of "the people called Methodists." A great religious awakening followed. Among those convicted of sin was John C. Burruss, a gay, godless young man of twenty-four years of age. He sought spiritual counsel of the only deeply pious woman whom he knew, and she was a Methodist. As one of her daughters had to lead the family devotions, the presence of the young stranger occasioned some little embarrassment.' But while the family were on their knees and the modest young daughter of Israel was offering the evening prayer, the visitor received a baptism of power—his sorrow was turned into joy, and he rejoiced aloud. With the ardor and enthusiasm which always characterized him, he mounted his horse the very next morning and rode ten or twelve miles through a blinding snow-storm to the nearest Methodist "society," and had his name recorded among that despised and then persecuted people. His family were grieved and astonished beyond measure; but the new life which animated him, and the divine zeal that consumed him, overcame all opposition, and converted hostility into sympathy. He very soon had the pleasure of seeing his widowed mother and two younger sisters received into the same communion with himself, and within a few years an elder sister and his two brothers. Six months after his conversion he was licensed to exhort, and at the end of twelve months—in 1814—was admitted on trial into the Virginia Conference. His first circuit was Gloucester, which he traveled for two years, and on it was everywhere a flame of fire. His winning address and gracious manners gave him access to the people, and his preaching was universally and exceedingly attractive. Endowed by nature with a handsome, classical face, and that best gift of an orator—a voice of great flexibility, compass, and sweetness, the young evangelist went forth preaching free salvation with the rare grace of Whitefield and the intrepid earnestness of John the Baptist. But a shadow fell across his itinerant path and stayed his imperial career. The prolonged ill health of his wife compelled him to locate and remove to the milder climate of North Alabama. That was a noble company of emigrants from Virginia, during that year and the following, which constituted the intelligent, cultivated community of Courtland, Alabama. Among them were the Rev. Alex. Sale, Rev. Jesse Butler (brothers-in-law of Mr. Burruss), Mrs. Le Vert, and her sons, John Poindexter and Richard Norment (brothers-in-law of Mrs. Burruss), and others.

In 1822 Mr. Burruss joined the Mississippi Conference, and was appointed to the Cahawba District. In 1824 he was stationed in Natchez, Mississippi, and the following year he became President of the Elizabeth Female Academy at Washington, Mississippi. In the minutes of the Mississippi Conference of 1826 there is this sentence in the list of appointments: "John C. Burruss, President of the Elizabeth Female Academy, to devote as much of his ministerial service as may be consistent with his other avocations to the village of Port Gibson." The same note appears in the minutes of 1827. In 1830 he located, but continued for some time at the head of the academy, and preached largely in the regions round about. In 1835 he again appeared in the regular work, and was appointed to New Orleans Station. There his great gifts as a pulpit orator shone forth in full-orbed splendor. The following admirable pen-picture of the man and his preaching, by an intelligent hearer, is found in an old newspaper. It graphically describes a scene worthy of the ministry of Wesley or Whitefield:

"It was at one of the early Conferences in Mississippi that I first saw John C. Burruss. He was in the prime of life, with a physiognomy decidedly classical, an eagle eye, a bold, high forehead; a nose prominent and aquiline; the mouth wide; lips thin, delicately chiseled and firmly compressed, throwing over the countenance a blended expression of benevolence and firmness. His hair was fair, and worn long, and his costume strictly clerical and scrupulously neat. Some eminent preacher had just concluded an impressive discourse, and a very solemn feeling, deep and intense, prevailed. Mr. Burruss, a stranger to the whole congregation, commenced to sing a revival hymn, and the feeling grew deeper and deeper. He read from the Epistle to the Hebrews, chapter tenth, and selected a text from verses twenty-five to thirty-nine, inclusive. Read the chapter, and you will find how appropriate it is for such an occasion and such a discourse as he delivered. He began in a very low tone—so low that it required the closest attention to hear him; and this was what he was aiming at, to concentrate the attention of the large and agitated congregation. His manner was extremely solemn, and at the same time so insinuating that each hearer seemed to feel that he himself was the object of special interest with the preacher. Gradually he pitched his voice to a higher key —not loud, but *vox argentea*, the silvery voice which Cicero praises so much. His manner grew animated, his gestures expressive, with such a flow of harmonious cadences, of beautiful words, of poetical imagery, and persuasive appeal, the whole congregation was enraptured—captives to the fascinations of elocution. Having made this favorable impression, he addressed himself to the feelings of his hearers; painted their errors, their sins, their ingratitude, and their crimes with colors so vivid that many hung down their heads in shame, and felt that they were the basest of criminals. Groans began to be heard; and when he described the perils of their position, the vengeance about to fall upon them, groans were followed by shrieks, and many involuntarily, terror-stricken, moved toward the altar as though for protection. Observing this, the skillful orator made a rapid transition, and with inimitable pathos dwelt on the sacrifice of our Saviour and the efficacy of his blood.

His own eyes filled with tears; his voice trembled. Unable to proceed, he descended from the pulpit, and the whole congregation wept with him. Sobs and cries were heard in every quarter. The revival had commenced, and it went on from day to day. The ministers caught the holy fire, and throughout the bounds of the Conference its influence was felt. Mr. Burruss became at once an established favorite. He found a way to every heart. The spirit-stricken sought him for the consolation which his gentle spirit well knew how to impart; the worldly admired his elegant manners; and the young and aspiring made his splendid eloquence their study. He was subsequently prevailed on to take charge of the Elizabeth Female Academy at Washington, Mississippi. It was the first institution in this section of the Union that the Methodists, as a denomination, established—the first step, it may be the suggestive step, in the grand system of education which they now have in operation everywhere."

In 1838 he again removed to Alabama, and remained there until 1845, when he removed to Aberdeen, Mississippi. In 1848 he settled in Caddo Parish, near Shreveport, and there spent the evening of life as a laborious local preacher and successful planter, and where he died on the 4th of September, 1863. The last two years of his life were saddened and clouded by the anxieties and sorrows of the civil war then in progress. The suffering and loss of life it brought upon the country seemed almost to crush his spirit. His tender, loving nature was utterly overwhelmed at the great national calamity.

Thus passed away one of the grandest men in South-western Methodism His life was a benediction to every community where he resided, his example stainless and beautiful, and his name never mentioned but in blessing.

CHAPTER XI.
-*'AGAIN IN THE COUNTRY.

LOUISIANA, and the city of New Orleans especially, early felt the wild excitement and stirring enthusiasm of the war between the States. It was a son of Louisiana that fired the first gun at Fort Sumter, whose echoes rang northward and southward, hurrying both sections to bloody conflict. A Bishop of that diocese, having had a military training at West Point, was induced to lay aside his episcopal robes and accept a major-general's commission. The streets of New Orleans echoed only to the rattle of wardrum and the tread of gayly-uniformed volunteers organizing and departing for the campaigns in Virginia and Tennessee. Nearly all lines of business were suspended and all vocations forsaken. The Church also suffered from the prevailing excitement, while many pastors enlisted either as soldiers or chaplains, and went to the front to preach and pray with the "boys in gray."

But Linus Parker remained at his post, preaching regularly to the little flock at Felicity, now composed mostly of women whose sons, husbands, and fathers were far away in camp and field. There he staid, doing all the work of a sympathizing, helpful pastor, until the latter part of April, 1862, when Farragut's fleet having dismantled and successfully passed Forts Jackson and St. Philip, anchored at the city's wharf, "black with men, heavy with deadly portent; the long-banished stars and stripes flying against the frowning sky." The city having surrendered to the Federal forces, he joined his family at Mr. Burruss's delightful home in Caddo, and there remained until the close of the war. Our churches in New Orleans were soon placed in charge of Northern preachers, who retained them under the famous "Stanton-Ames Order" for some time after peace was restored, and surrendered them at last only in obedience to a mandate from the President of the United States. Though exiled from his regular pastorate Mr. Parker was not at ease in Zion. The preacher at Shreveport having entered the Confederate army as a chaplain, he supplied that station for two and a half-years. He resided some twenty-three miles distant on a plantation, but filled his appointments regularly, and had a good degree of success. At the Conference held at Minden, beginning December 7, 1864— Rev. J. C. Keener, D.D., President—he was appointed to Caddo Circuit. There he labored with accustomed fidelity, but the disorganized state of the country, and necessary secular duties in order to obtain a support, rendered any upbuilding or ingathering quite impossible. After the death of his father-in-law he had charge of the large planting interests of the estate, and demonstrated no little aptitude for agricultural pursuits.

Though a native of the far North and reared in the valley of the Mohawk, Mr. Parker became intensely Southern in his convictions and sympathies. He admired the conservative spirit of the South, and rejoiced in her history and institutions. The uninformed and purblind are accustomed to speak of this people as passionate, hot-blooded, and fickle; quick in their impulses, unstable in their convictions, and fanatical in their preferences; but as a matter of fact they are calm in judgment, catholic in spirit, conservative in prinicple, and tenacious of their opinions. Wild political vagaries and theological heresies, that find ready advocates and apologists in other latitudes, never secure home and throne in the South. On this subject the observant, philosophical mind of Mr. Parker meditated as follows:

"Southern soil has not proved congenial to the growth of those morbid and wicked aberrations of mind and morals which have of late years sprung up and flourished in the temperature of the free States. There is in the South some healthful principle of conservatism which saves us, in the main, from those evils that are so rampant elsewhere. That principle must lie in the profoundest elements of the genius of the people and in those extraneous circumstances which are peculiar to them. The history of Church and State for the last half-century sufficiently establishes the position that ultraisms are mostly born and bred in the North, and that a wholesome and constitutional moderation has been maintained in the South."

And in the controversy and correspondence between the two branches of our American Episcopal Methodism he ably defended the Southern view. While desiring the establishment of ecclesiastical and Christian fraternity, he insisted that it should preserve the plighted faith of the Plan of Separation, which in substance affirmed and secured the complete equality of the Southern Church, and its unimpaired rights of name and property. With the conclusions of the "Cape May Commission" he was entirely satisfied, and rejoiced in the removal of all obstacles to honorable, cordial fraternity with the Methodist Episcopal Church.

In this connection it is proper to give Dr. Parker's matured and dispassionate views concerning the negro and slavery:

"If previous to their enslavement the American negroes had been civilized Christian people, there might be some reason in speaking of the unfavorable influence of slavery; but in fact, and in the order of a beneficent Providence, the ignorant and brutal savage of Africa has been immeasurably elevated and blessed. The hand of God was in it, and when the mission of slavery was accomplished, the institution was abolished. . . . By it they were brought in contact with the very best type of Anglo-Saxon character and with the purest form of the gospel, as preached by the Southern Methodists and others. The negro, thus enlightened and saved by means of slavery, has reason to be thankful that in this wonderful way he was brought up out of savagery and made a Christian man. Slavery is a thing of the past, but why may not fair-minded men review the matter calmly and concede that incalculable good has come out of it for the negro? The salvation of the African continent is likely to grow out of American slavery. God, who sees the end from the beginning, had a great and benevolent purpose in it, and in time that purpose will be made more and more clear. With all the evils connected with slavery, it is evident that the good greatly exceeded, and that the people enslaved were the chief beneficiaries. The English and Yankee slave-traders, we may well believe, had no humane object in view, but we cannot now shut our eyes to the fact that good to the negro and to Africa has come out of their sordid traffic."

CHAPTER XII.
TWELVE YEARS AN EDITOR.

THE New Orleans *Christian Advocate* began its existence in February, 1851, by the joint action of the Alabama and Louisiana Conferences. The Rev. H. N. McTyeire, then pastor of the Felicity Street Church, was made editor, and the paper at once took rank as one of the most influential journals in Southern Methodism. He presided over its columns with masterly skill and ability until 1858, when he was elected by the General Conference editor of the Nashville *Christian Advocate*. His successor in the office at New Orleans was the Rev. C. C. Gillespie, who for several years had been editor of the Texas *Christian Advocate* at Galveston. He had eminent literary gifts, and his polished editorials displayed wide versatility of genius. But with the outbreak of the civil war, and the early surrender of New Orleans to the Federal forces, the *Christian Advocate* suspended publication, and its brilliant editor went to the tented field as the gallant colonel of a fine regiment. In 1865, after the alarms of war had died away and the avocations of peace were resumed, Dr. J. C. Keener revived the *Christian Advocate*, and became its vigorous, versatile editor. Through this medium he rallied the scattered tribes of our Israel in the South-west, and largely aided in restoring their ecclesiastical autonomy. His editorship embraced that trying reconstruction period from 1865 to 1870, which witnessed the transference of war passions into party aggression. The times demanded an apostle of courage and self-confidence, and he was not found wanting. His editorials had the epigrammatic freshness of Prentice and the sturdy strength of Carlyle—that master of letters who has been facetiously denominated "a trip-hammer with an Æolian attachment."

When Dr. Keener was called to the episcopal office by the General Conference of 1870,.the Publishing Committee of the New Orleans *Christian Advocate* unanimously elected Dr. Linus Parker as his successor. In January, 1866, he had returned to the city and to the pulpit at Felicity. Of that pastoral year he writes:

"We were glad to see the city once more, and I was cordially welcomed back to my old pastorate. I opened my ministry with the text: 'As for me I will behold thy face in righteousness: I shall be satisfied when I awake in thy likeness.' (Ps. xxii. 15.) I was refreshed by the sight of old friends, but some were no more of earth.

"The General Conference met the first Wednesday in April, in Carondelet Street Church. The session, lasting about one month, was one of great interest and importance. My charge was moderately prosperous this year; a number of new members were added, and a good many wanderers were hunted up and reclaimed."

In that charge he remained until called to edit the paper to which he had contributed regularly from the days of his early ministry. His succession to that office was generally expected and universally applauded.

As a journalist Bishop Parker was best known to Connectional Methodism. For twelve years he presided over the columns of the *Christian Advocate* with such distinguished ability that he increased the high character it had already achieved under his illustrious predecessors. He was preëminently a *religious* journalist, and nearly all of his editorials were on strictly spiritual subjects. He eschewed both dogmatism and latitudinarianism, and aspired to be neither sensational nor partisan. He sought diligently the "old paths," and had no ambition to be an inventor or adventurer in ecclesiastical or theological science. His aim was to be neither sectional nor sectarian, but catholic and Connectional. "Food convenient" for spiritual nurture he prepared with anxious care and earnest prayer. His supreme thought in the conduct of his columns was to honor God and help his readers to a higher spiritual life. The divine purpose ever in view, as he sent forth the *Christian Advocate* on its weekly visit, is best told in his own words:

"Not what we would like, nor always what we think best for ourselves, but what will do our readers the most good, is the uppermost thought—something to meet their spiritual, mental, and social wants, and help them to holy and happy lives, is our constant study. Scholars and philosophers are comparatively few; the preachers are not numerous as compared with the people. A crumb now and then for them is well, but the mission of the *Christian Advocate* is to the people and their homes. We try to make it a wholesome, faithful, and acceptable visitor to them, putting into it just such matter and in such proportions as shall best serve this purpose. These years of care and labor would be well repaid if even in a few instances the *Christian Advocate* has led sinners to Christ, helped believers to a better and deeper experience, and brought comfort to the bereaved and stricken. As our thousands of readers come up before us we think of the time when God shall bring every secret thing into judgment, and when 'the fire shall try every man's work of what sort it is.' May those who read and those who write be clear in that day! In view of this responsibility, we would endeavor to build up the personal piety of our readers, to break up the fallow-ground, and to urge each one to repentance, faith, and holiness."

His "leaders" were models of pure English and elevated thought. No writer in American Methodism excelled him in finish and limpid purity of style. Dwelling himself among the higher spiritualities, his writings were eloquent and redolent with the voice and presence of the Holy Spirit. The following extract from the writer's salutatory as his successor in the editorship, expressed a hope that has found grateful fruition through the intervening years:

"The seeming embarrassment of immediately succeeding one so successful and distinguished is fully appreciated; but that embarrassment is only seeming; it is a help and not a hinderance, an inspiration and not a discouragement. The high character his great abilities gave this journal will conceal many deficiencies. The momentum he gave it will long keep the machinery in action with a less skillful hand at the wheel. On every page will be reflected the genial expression of his well-known face, and every damp sheet fresh from the press will infold the aroma of his kindly, generous spirit."

CHAPTER XIII.
THREE YEARS A BISHOP.

SOUTHERN Methodism has been singularly favored in the selection of her chief pastors. They have possessed every variety of talent—the widest diversity of gifts—but the same spirit. In one the genius and prescience of the ecclesiastical statesman was prominent; in another, the clear discernment and calm deliberation of the great jurist; in yet another, the magnetic orator and model preacher; and all these in great variety. But each had the same spirit of profound consecration to the office and work of the gospel ministry. Not one proved faithless to his high commission, and each went up to his reward without a blur on his name or a stain on his shield. Great in their consecrated gifts and culture, they were glorious in the peerless purity of their lives. In this Pantheon of apostolic chieftains must now be placed the name of Bishop Linus Parker. His episcopate was short, embracing just the period of our Lord's active earthly ministry, but was no less faithful and honorable than those of his illustrious predecessors and colleagues. Life cannot be measured by length of days.

> The dials of earth may show
> The length not the depth of years.

Dr. Parker's elevation to the episcopal office was not of his own seeking or consent. He kindly but emphatically declined to hear any suggestions on the subject from special friends, and assured them of his greater love for the quiet editorial chair or the work of a pastor. Nor was his election the result of some special or brilliant achievement of his—a sermon of thrilling power on some grand occasion, a General Conference speech on an important question, or some ringing paper evidencing the grasp and greatness of a parliamentary leader. It was the calm, deliberate judgment of his brethren, who knew him well and recognized his eminent fitness for the responsible office. So when the General Conference of 1882 met in the city of Nashville, it was generally understood by the Church at large that if the episcopacy was to be strengthened, Dr. Parker would be one of the elect.

Nor was the judgment of the Church misplaced. His qualifications for the office were evident and eminent. He was a loyal lover of Methodism both in doctrine and polity. He was hopeful for the Church. Though readily recognizing dangers and evils, and bravely warning and exhorting against them, he was no sour pessimist, idly lamenting that the former times were better than these. He was self-sacrificing. There was no desire or disposition to spare himself. He entered upon the duties of his office with an unreserved consecration of purpose and energy. To him the voice of the Church was the voice of God. He traveled much, preached frequently, and did all the work of a Methodist bishop. The burdens of the office oppressed him, and the care of the churches was a constant strain upon his sympathies. In the "stationing-room," where the laborers were distributed over the field, he earnestly sought divine guidance, and keenly felt the possible privations of each preacher. With an almost unerring intuition, he was a ready discerner of the spirits of men. He gauged the "gifts and graces" of his preachers with prayerful precision, and made their appointments in the immediate presence of God. Gentle and sympathetic, he was yet inflexible in purpose and courageous in the discharge of duty. He was dignified without austerity, and affable without familiarity. At the Conferences and elsewhere he was the same genial, modest, companionable man as a bishop that he was in the quiet pastorate or in the editorial chair. If long life had been granted, he would have grown upon the Church as a wise administrator and worthy successor of the apostolic men whose historic names are a precious, priceless heritage to American Methodism.

The first two years of his episcopate were spent in Texas, and to the Texans he became warmly attached. It was doubtless his purpose to secure a permanent residence in that State, though many other and flattering invitations were extended him. His letters to the New Orleans *Christian Advocate* from Texas indicated how thoroughly he had studied the necessities and possibilities of that vast field, and with what eager interest he marked its rapid development. He found especial pleasure in the work on the Mexican border, and talked delightfully of his experiences there. And it was a beautiful expression of their grateful regard when the members of the Mexican Border Mission Conference, at its last session, sent a free-will offering to the "Parker Memorial Church" in New Orleans, which is to bear the Bishop's name and perpetuate his fame. In a generous, eulogistic mention of his death, character, and public services, the Texas *Christian Advocate* concludes:

"His first two years of episcopal labor were spent in Texas, where by his courtesy, his faithfulness, his humility, his modesty, his firmness, his abounding charity, and his ability in the pulpit and on the platform, he proved himself well fitted for the office and work of bishop in the Church of God. His death after one year, more of such labor seems to us a strange providence. He was not worn by age nor enfeebled by disease. He was in the full possession of all his physical and mental powers. Why was he not spared to perform, for many years to come, the duties of that high office which he had thus far filled with such great usefulness and distinguished ability? It may be that God would teach us how little he needs the best human counsel and the strongest human arm. He buries his workmen but carries on the work."

His third episcopal tour embraced the Conferences in Missouri, and the North Carolina, Mississippi, and Baltimore Conferences. This round had been completed except the last, and he was about starting for that when the summons came, and he entered his Master's joy. Everywhere his labors gave the fullest satisfaction and left a fragrant memory. The Raleigh *Christian Advocate*, speaking for the brethren of the old North State, said: "No man ever impressed himself so favorably and so indelibly upon our Conference in so short a time as did Bishop Parker." At the Mississippi, one of the old patronizing Conferences of the New Orleans *Christian Advocate*, and to which he had sustained official and personal relations for so many years, he was enthusiastically welcomed and highly honored. That was the last Conference over which he presided, and the preachers who had been so long and faithfully fed and edified by his fruitful pen were the last to be recommissioned by his episcopal hand. From that Conference he returned to New Orleans to spend a rest season with his family until the meeting of the Baltimore Conference. It proved to be a rest from his loved employ—an eternal rest in the home of the glorified.

CHAPTER XIV.
PERSONAL TRAITS AND CHARACTERISTICS.

BISHOP PARKER was a man of commanding presence. Standing erect, six feet or more, with a large, well-knit frame, comfortably and handsomely cushioned with flesh, he was a fine specimen of manly beauty. The expression of his bright black eye blended at once the flash of intelligence and the glance of love. It evidenced keen, clear penetratior and a gentle, benignant disposition. His forehead was broad and massive, the seat of calm deliberation and ponderous thought. His movements were deliberate, an index to the smooth, even action of his mental machinery. There were no quick, jerky steps in his walk, nor was there any "lost motion" in the well-regulated enginery of his mind. It had not the action of a little "dummy," with its rapidly revolving wheels, but rather the majestic movement of a great Corliss engine, whose strides are like the tread of another fabled Jupiter, turning thousands of feet of shafting without apparent strain or effort. True poetry, it is said, is born, not made. It flows with scarcely more effort than a silvery stream sings along its pebbly channel borne by the fountain's exhaustless tide. And Ruskin has applied this thought to all mental operations. He says " no great intellectual thing was ever done by great effort." Though not accepting the truth of that statement, of Bishop Parker it may be said that his finest thoughts, both as preacher and journalist, *seemed* to be produced without labor. His most polished and powerful editorials were written rapidly and with apparently perfect ease. The first draft of an article was ready for the printer without revision or emendation.

Another distinguished characteristic was *his singular modesty and unaffected sincerity.* He coveted a quiet ministry, and shrunk from conspicuous position. His promotion resulted from the persistent power of great merit, though against his own sincere protest. He always thought more highly of others than of himself, and found pleasure in their success. He was perfectly transparent—the light shone through at every pore. He had no hidden motives, no ominous concealments, no diplomatic reserve. Envy and jealousy found no place to plant a foot in his generous bosom; hence the loving devotion of his old Conference comrades. He was beautifully innocent of ecclesiastical politics. He never projected plans nor abetted schemes for personal or ulterior reasons, for he neither had enemies to punish nor selfish friends to reward. His brethren honored him against his own judgment and desires. When Centenary College conferred upon him the honorary degree of Doctor of Divinity, he considered it more modest to accept than decline the flattering distinction. More than once, with characteristic humility, did he remark to friends that he feared the Church made a mistake in his election to the episcopacy. But her call was to him the will of God, and he obeyed with apostolic fervor and zeal.

Bishop Parker was an *humble, symmetrical Christian.* He was one of the finest products of Methodist culture. He had a rich experience and a ready testimony. In the class-meeting he loved to sit, and was generally the first to speak, though in few words and with becoming modesty. On his rounds of episcopal visitation he never failed to attend the Conference love-feast and witness to the regenerating and sanctifying power of the Holy Ghost. There were no gaps or chasms, no abrupt heights or dark gorges, in his religious life. Whatever were his inward conflicts, he seemed to be ascending a regular incline. There was no demonstration, no ostentation, but a calm, constant, blessed glorying in the cross. His light burned with a steady flame. To outward seeming there was no eclipse—no, not even an obscuring cloud. And in the grace of humility he had preëminence. It adorned and beautified his private life and public ministry.

Bishop Parker was conspicuous for his *generous, catholic spirit*. Every good cause found in him a helpful friend, and every Christian a brother beloved. No narrow inclosure of ecclesiasticism could confine the wealth of his fervent sympathies. Though well defined in his convictions—theological and ecclesiastical—and abundantly able to defend them, he was neither a partisan nor a sectarian. For controversy he had no taste, but a real aversion. Born of this broad catholicity were his generous judgments. He had a genius for discerning and commending the better elements in every character, and had an almost divine forgetfulness of deficiencies and unavoidable errors. Never condoning wrong, he loved to discover and applaud the right. In a long and intimate acquaintance I never heard from him an unkind criticism or an unsanctified judgment of another. And yet withal he had the fearless courage of a hero and the unflinching purpose of a martyr. Together with this, and of which it had birth, was a spirit of singular devoutness. It threw a strange charm over his life, and gave him peculiar power in personal intercourse. A distinguished minister thus writes:

"There was no conventional devoutness about the Bishop, but it came from a heart animated and warmed by the fires of the Holy Spirit, and there was a peculiar contagion about it that made one feel he was in the presence of a man that held kinship and communion with the Father."

He was *a man of much prayer.* He frequented the holy of holies, and understood what is meant by a "*sweet* hour of prayer." And he offered the prayer of faith. The following was related by Rev. Dr. J. B. Walker, presiding elder of the New Orleans District and the Bishop's life-long friend, in his eloquent funeral-address:

"I remember an incident that illustrates this characteristic of our beloved friend. It occurred during the fearful epidemic of 1878. Our esteemed Brother Mathews, as many of us well remember, was stricken with a second relapse of yellow fever. Brother Parker called on the morning of the critical day. He met the attending physician, who remarked: 'Brother Mathews will die, for I have never heard of a man recovering from a second relapse of yellow fever.' Brother Parker said to the doctor: 'Go back to his bedside and exert yourself to the utmost of your ability, and I will go to the parlor and pray God to spare his life.' For over two hours did Bishop Parker plead with God to grant this favor; and on his approaching the sick-chamber the physician met him and said: 'There is a marvelous change in Brother Mathews. It was not wrought by human skill; it is the hand of God.'"

Bishop Parker was *an eminently wise counselor.* He possessed an even poise of character that exempted him from partisan bias or prejudice. This enabled him to look at all sides of a question and render an unclouded, unprejudiced opinion. I have known no man whose counsel was more frequently sought, and whose judgments were so readily and entirely accepted.

He was an *able preacher.* As a sermonizer, he stood among the first in our pulpit. His style was expository and eminently practical. He opened the Scriptures to the people with a rare, luminous exegesis, and was peculiarly happy in discovering the hidden meaning of a text. He dwelt on great spiritual themes, and studiously eschewed all mere speculation and parade of learning in the pulpit. It was his profound conviction that the best cure for doubt and the surest corrective of scientific skepticism was positive gospel preaching. And all his ministrations had the aroma of the closet and the overshadowing of the Almighty. Living much and intimately with his Lord, he testified of that which he knew, and with a confidence that carried conviction. Without the talismanic gifts and graces of the orator, never soaring into the doubtful realm of popular eloquence, he was an instructive, analytical, suggestive, profound preacher, *rightly* dividing the word of truth. And the oftener he was heard the more he was appreciated. His was a vast treasury of spiritual knowledge, and out of it he always brought something fresh and savory—"food convenient" for the nourishment and enrichment of the people. In this aspect of his ministry he strikingly resembled Canon Liddon and Dr. Joseph Parker, of London. He was not what is technically known as a *revivalist*, but he emphasized the old Methodist methods and reported large ingatherings. Logic, learning, and unction beautifully blended in his amplification of a subject, and often with immediate, mighty results. Every year he conducted a long protracted meeting, doing most of the preaching himself, and had the gratification of seeing scores joyfully converted to God. At camp-meetings he was diligent in the altar, instructing penitents and rejoicing with the redeemed.

His home-life was beautiful. In that inner sacred circle his gentle virtues shed a fragance sweet as the breath of heaven. Of strong domestic attachments, he found the hearth-stone his earthly paradise. Among the hardest trials of the episcopacy were his necessary and long absences from home. An ideal husband and a fond, considerate father, he illustrated the harmony and consistency of faithful public service with the holiest domestic duty and happiness. His three sons—John Burruss, Fitzgerald Sale, and Frank Nutting—with their mother, treasure the sweetest memories of his amiable, beautiful life. The two younger sons have recently entered the Louisiana Conference, following the footsteps of their illustrious father. Through them, he being dead, will yet speak.

CHAPTER XV.
LAST HOURS AND BURIAL

ON Sunday morning, March 1, he preached to his beloved little flock at Louisiana Avenue, New Orleans, from the text, "I am not ashamed of the gospel of Christ; for it is the power of God unto salvation to every one that believeth: to the Jew first, and also to the Greek." After the sermon, which was characteristic in freshness and spiritual power, there was a most impressive and delightful communion-service. That was the Bishop's last sermon, and doubtless if his own desires had been expressed he would not have ordered it otherwise. He would have sought that modest little chapel to deliver his last will and testament. At night he attended service at St. Charles Avenue with his family, and was a helpful hearer of the sermon preached by the pastor, Rev. Beverly Carradine. And what a hearer he was! Not critical, not censorious, but prayerful, sympathetic, attentive, encouraging. On Monday he came down in the city, and spent two hours or more at the *Advocate* office. He was never more genial and companionable, and talked cheerfully of his work, the Baltimore Conference he was to attend in a few days, and his long line of District Conferences during the year. Again on Tuesday he came down to Camp street, and, as was his habit, walked all the way home, a distance of three miles. During the night he suffered great pain in one ear, but after the application of some simple remedies relief was given, and he fell asleep, resting comfortably till the afternoon of

Wednesday. There was no apprehension on his part or his family's that any serious illness would result; but as his symptoms seemed not to improve in the afternoon, a physician was summoned, who arrived about seven o'clock. Mrs. Parker met him in the parlor, and explained the case in a few words, her entire absence from the room occupying not more than five minutes; but a fatal congestion had seized him, and when they returned the Bishop was unconscious, and never again uttered a word or gave a sign of recognition. In that condition he lingered until Thursday afternoon at half-past six o'clock, when the silver cord was loosed, and the glorified spirit ascended to the house of many mansions. During the day the preachers in the city came and went, with softened step and anxious hearts, to inquire after their beloved co-laborer and revered chief pastor. Fervent prayers were offered that our Father might spare his precious life, but he chose to crown him early. When he ceased to breathe, for a moment there was a holy calm in the room. Not a word was spoken, not a sigh was heard. There seemed to be the vanishing sweep of wings and the faint, distant echo of an unearthly music. At length the silence was broken by Rev. T. B. White, who said, "The Lord gave, and the Lord hath taken away." Dr. John Mathews said, "He has fought a good fight, and kept the faith." Some one then observed, "It is a fitting time to pray;" and at once all knelt around the sleeping Bishop, and Dr. Mathews fervently led in the devotions. How strikingly descriptive of his own death-scene are the words of his pen in an editorial entitled "Our Friends in Heaven:"

"The death of one very dear to us seems to rend the veil that our faith had not hitherto quite penetrated, and the line of separation between earth and heaven, however narrow it was, becomes less now. . . . We cannot but follow the spirit, just now breathing in our ears the words of a loving good-by, as it moves out into the mysteries and sublimities of the better life. Surely heaven is not any more a bright abstraction, nor the subject of speculative thought nor of curious imaginings. It becomes as real as our own souls, and it is brought as near to us, and is as clearly discerned, as our own heart-throbs. . . . And thus it comes to pass that this ordeal of affliction, under the ministry of grace, gives the highest touches and finish to the heavenly-mindedness of the children of God. It sets the riches of grace with brilliants and gems of an incomparable luster."

There were no imposing scenes in his death. He was not privileged to talk with friends and loved ones at the hour of parting; but such a life needed no dying-testimony. No triumphant exclamation then uttered could have given so glorious and cloudless an assurance of his heavenly coronation as the stainless beauty of his daily walk and conversation. He did not have to secure a ticket of admission at the gates of the celestial city, because for more than thirty years he had carried a "title clear" to a fadeless crown and an incorruptible inheritance. Every day he caught "revealments of God's paradise," and lived in the conscious presence of the Invisible.

The manner of his death—so quiet, peaceful, and unimposing—was in accord with his modest, reticent disposition. Years before, he wrote as follows:

"There is something unhealthful and morbid in the love which people sometimes have for death-bed scenes. It is certain that the Scriptures do not countenance nor gratify any extravagant tendency in this direction. Neither the truth of religion nor the piety of the saint is made to depend upon these phenomenal manifestations. If the Christian dies in his senses, and the circumstances of his death admit of it, we expect to find peace and comfortable assurance. Christians die well, and there is sometimes what we call triumph—triumph uttered, dazzling light, wavy forms, and celestial melody. The end of the upright is peace; but the death-scene often testifies nothing, and we are thrown back upon the holy life and the promises for assurance that 'all is well.' Chalmers died alone, in the still watches of healthful repose. Fletcher and Toplady, whose polemic lances had often crossed, died almost seraphically. In the death of eminent saints something remarkable is often looked for and not realized. The chariot and horses of fire come, but not with observation. They are carried home, but they glide noiselessly away. The wind that fills the parting sail is not felt by those who linger on the shore. How we should choose to die is best left to God. It matters little, so we are ready. Happy dying may not be consciously for all, but substantially it is for every Christian. If death is a narrow stream, it grows narrower as we approach the brink, until what we supposed to be the turbid flood is left behind. We have looked for death, but have passed it without recognizing the fact. 'Verily, verily I say unto you, If a man keep my sayings he shall never see death.'"

He was buried from St. Charles Avenue Church, where his family worship, and which is but a square from their residence. The funeral-services were held at three o'clock on Friday afternoon. Long before the hour arrived hundreds came by every line of cars, and filled the spacious temple. The pall-bearers were representatives of the several Methodist churches in the city, and each had been a special friend of the Bishop. These men were preceded by all the ministers resident and visiting in the city. The church was heavily draped with crape, and just in the rear of the pulpit were the words, "Our Beloved Bishop." Within the chancel two tables were covered with flowers of beautiful designs. One was a magnificent arched gate-way, on

LAST HOURS AND BURIAL.

the top of which sat a white dove with wings spread for flight. The gates beneath swung back and stood open, ready for the triumphant entrance of the redeemed of the Lord. The other was a large cross of white flowers, with a heart and anchor on either side. After a beautifully rendered and appropriate voluntary by the choir, Dr. John Mathews read the ninetieth Psalm. Dr. C. W. Carter read the lesson from Corinthians, and Rev. S. H. Werlein offered prayer. Rev. Beverly Carradine then announced the seven hundred and thirty-ninth hymn,

> Servant of God, well done!
> Rest from thy loved employ,

which was sung with deep emotion. Dr. J. B. Walker, presiding elder of the New Orleans District, and the intimate friend and co-laborer of the Bishop, delivered the funeral-address. It was a pathetic portraiture of a spotless character and glorified comrade. At the conclusion of this address the seven hundred and sixteenth hymn was read by the author. At the cemetery the service was read by Dr. J. B. A. Ahrens, and the tomb was sealed forever from mortal eyes. Connectional Methodism wept over the untimely fall of a noble, heroic leader, and the churches in New Orleans, where his life was mostly spent, sorrowed for a personal friend and beloved pastor. In that narrower circle, where his rare virtues shone in full radiance, he was loved to devotion. Old and young, rich and poor, mingled their tears over his bier, and thanked God for his beautiful life.

His Writings.

PREFATORY NOTE.

REQUESTS for Bishop Parker's editorials to be collected in book form have been many and urgent, and from the chief men in the Church. Long before his death, admiring readers of his "leaders" in the New Orleans *Christian Advocate* pronounced them the choicest gems of our sacred literature, and worthy of permanent preservation. They were "food convenient" for the thousands who sat at his table week after week, and will be strengthening meat to those who may read these pages. It is hazarding nothing to say, no man in American Methodism wielded a more polished pen. As a writer he had the classic elegance of Addison perfumed with the devotional spirit of Jeremy Taylor. Some of his editorials were as stately as "Corinthian mold," and others as beautiful as "Doric chiseling."

In the following compilation the editor has been embarrassed most of all with wealth of material. Bishop Parker was a diligent editor for twelve consecutive years, and a regular correspondent of the religious press during his entire ministry. He left sufficient "copy" for several choice volumes. Those selected are in nowise superior to the vast number rejected. The plan of the compiler determined the selection and, not exceptional excellence. Doubtless some will be missed that were specially admired and remembered.

In these editorials the reader must not expect an elaborate treatise on any subject. The function of the weekly newspaper is suggestive, and not exhaustive. Its domain is distinct and apart from the magazine or review. But unless the critical judgment of hundreds is at fault, many will be regarded as almost perfect pieces of art. For lofty spiritual thought and literary elegance, they are scarcely equaled in their sphere.

THE PREACHER CALLED.

CALL TO THE MINISTRY.

THIS may, in a general way, be defined as an impression made upon the mind by the Holy Spirit that it is a man's duty to preach the gospel. It is a conviction that comes to him, a strong and persistent persuasion, that God would have him devote himself to this particular work. There may be in some instances an anticipation of this call before conversion. Especially may this be the case in young men who have been reared religiously. In their awakening and concern for their souls, the realization of peace has been consciously suspended upon a complete submission to the will of God in this regard. With them conversion carried along with it the vital qualification and the fully developed call to preach. We have known such cases. They may be more numerous than is generally supposed. The rule, however, is that some time after conversion the conviction comes gradually as a revelation speaking out of the depths of religious experience, and confirmed by the development of gifts and graces in the ordinary path of Christian life.

There are sudden conversions, and there are surprisingly sudden revivals of spiritual power in believers, but we imagine the call to preach is usually an impression of the Spirit that has a faint beginning, and that by slow degrees grows and expands until all doubt is dispelled. Those who have this impression are usually disposed to resist it, and to sift the matter with prayerful concern. It is well that they should put themselves upon a rigorous probation of self-imposed watchfulness and thorough self-examination, even when tried friends are forward to advise. In the midst of revival influences young men may sometimes, in their newly awakened fervor, conclude that they are called. They have never thought of the matter until then, and in their zeal the ministry seems to them to be the opening for their religious activity. In some instances they may be right; but before deciding let them wait until they have tested themselves. Perhaps when the excitement and the emotions enkindled at the camp or protracted meeting have subsided, and they once more encounter the ordinary conditions of the spiritual conflict, they will reach the conclusion that they are simply called to a more devoted religious life.

All that we insist upon is that young men move with deliberation and with the utmost prayerfulness in this direction. With them there can be no visible divine manifestation, nor any voice to the ear, as in the call of Moses and of Paul. The secret of the Lord, however, is with them that fear him, and there need be no mistake if we move slowly and prayerfully.

The judgment of the Church will always have its weight with those who have the right spirit. If the decision be adverse it may mean delay, or it may indicate that the individual has made an honest mistake. If the Church persists in its belief that a man is not called to preach, it is a strong presumption that God has not called him. On the other hand, neither Quarterly nor Annual Conferences are infallible. Their authorization will go far to confirm the applicant's conviction. Very justly it contributes much toward the settlement of the question. But after all, the Church is sometimes in error, and the young licentiate finds that there was a mistake all around. The man must be tried by the Church before it can decide. The probabilities arising from character, experience, and general qualifications are strong, but only actual preaching can determine the possession of gifts, grace, and usefulness. There can be no fruit as a preacher until the attempt to preach is made. Nor can a man be fully satisfied in his own mind until he tries to preach. The call, previously and honestly felt, becomes an assured and joyous certainty when souls are converted and when the baptism of love and power is poured upon him in his pulpit ministrations. The call to preach is often reviewed with zealous and searching rigor by preachers who have spent years in the ministry. In their earlier ministry, under temptations and discouragements, they have wrestled and agonized over this question.

The call thus has its various stages—a conviction in the mind of the young convert, the voice of the Church confirming and testing, and the ministerial experience of greater or less duration. There should be no unseemly hurry in those who feel themselves called to preach. The Lord has done without them a long time, and if they had never been born it would have made but little difference. Be as sure as possible of the divine call, that it is "not of blood, nor of the will of the flesh, nor of the will of man, but of God;" and then honestly accept every probationary step, until established and confirmed in the glorious but fearfully responsible work. And at whatever stage in the process of trial, if convinced that a mistake has been made, have the courage to retrace your steps.

About the literary and theological preparations for the ministry we have little to say beyond this, that a call to preach does not make them unnecessary. If possible they should be secured. A few years at college will save time and double the fruit of most ministers. The preacher loses much and gains nothing by starting before he is ready. Wesley's eight years spent in the university were a saving of time. Education is important, but with a fair English education much can be attained in our itinerant school. Good preachers have been and still can be made without the college or the theological seminary. The call to preach is also a call to study; but it is more than this—a call to a life of labor, of self-denial, and ordinarily of poverty. It is not a divine call to serve rich and flourishing stations, and to occupy the green and well-watered fields, but to go to domestic and foreign missions, and to build up the waste places. There is in the Christian life no self-renunciation equal to that involved in the call to preach. Let our young men count the cost, and be sure that their call is genuine.

THE MINISTERIAL WOE.

In Paul's case this woe was of the most serious import. Necessity was laid upon him of so grave a character that his salvation was involved. Of all the fearful things which a refusal to preach the gospel might have inflicted upon him, the loss of his own soul was that which he had chiefly in his mind. Taking all the circumstances of his conversion and call to the apostleship into the account, but one path was open to him. He was so unmistakably put into the ministry that it would have been the height of contumacy to have even doubted the fact. Disobedience to "the heavenly vision" would have placed him in an attitude of rebellion which must have ended in his eternal ruin. We might hesitate to apply Paul's convictions concerning himself to all who in the ordinary way are moved to preach. There are pains and penalties attached to every departure from duty in the religious life, and this self-evident proposition applies with peculiar force to the obligations of the ministry. To resist or to evade the impression that a dispensation of the gospel is committed to us may not in every case lead to the absolute forfeiture of eternal life, but there will be spiritual depression, loss of comfort, and often well-marked providential afflictions. The sin may not be "unto death," but the manifestations of the divine disapprobation will be neither few nor light. There are many good men in the Church, called in their youth to preach, whose lives have been embittered by conflict and disappointment, and whose temporal and spiritual welfare has been engloomed by this mistake of their earlier religious history. Their release from a distasteful duty has been attended by trouble and disaster, by the loss of peace and satisfaction, and by heart-felt sorrow and regret that they did not heed the voice of God. The young man who is called to this work will be happier in it than in any other condition, and if he does not lose his soul by declining to enter it, he will have cause to mourn over the most serious error of his life.

Disobedience to this conviction may entail eternal ruin upon the soul. The grieved Spirit departs from him who willfully resists his operations, and he is left alone to his idols. The refusal to obey this call is the beginning of a course of backsliding, which ultimately reaches apostasy. Thousands who have taken the responsibility of deciding against the clearest intimations of God's will concerning them have sealed their doom by this act. They have sought relief from their convictions by keeping aloof from all religious influences, and by plunging more deeply into the pursuits and pleasures of the world. They have fled from the presence of the Lord rather than accept the burden of calling sinners to repentance. The young man whom Christ called to follow him, although he went away sorrowing, still went away to keep his possessions and to lose his soul. Necessity is doubtless laid upon all who are called to preach. In some it may be a higher and more inexorable necessity than in others, but still there is a woe which follows disobedience. In some it is a more prominent element of conviction than in others, and in many it is nearly lost and overshadowed by a superabounding love for the work of saving souls. So glorious and delightful is this employment that they engage in it with the enthusiasm of volunteers, and are thankful for the privilege of proclaiming the riches of the grace of God in Christ. The point of perplexity is not whether they *must*, but whether they *may* preach the gospel. The blessing and not the woe stimulates and attracts, and they are drawn and allured by the constraining love of Christ. The sense of privilege may be greater than that of necessity, and so much greater that all consciousness of compulsion is lost in the freeness and gladness with which the divine commission is accepted. That view of the ministry which regards it as a species of servitude to which some believers are condemned is far from the true conception. It is rather the freest and noblest sphere of Christian duty, in which every peculiar sacrifice is offset by the grandest compensations. It is an invitation to the highest seat at the gospel-feast, and a distinction which angels might covet. Incidentally, and to serve the argument in hand, Paul exclaims, "Woe is unto me, if I preach not the gospel!" but generally he alludes to his ministerial vocation in terms of thankfulness and satisfaction. He magnifies his office, and glories in its tribulations and sufferings: "And I thank Christ Jesus our Lord, who hath enabled me, for that he counted me faithful, putting me into the ministry." The necessity was there, and in all his ministry, but it was outstripped by the nobler principles of faith and love, and overgrown by the fragrant bloom of a cheerful and joyous service. However it might have been on the service in the beginning of his career, it gave place and became subordinate to the impulse of a consecrated and holy heart.

We can scarcely think of John as uttering the Pauline woe at all. A nature like his needed not the lash to drive him into the field of duty, but it yielded readily to the divine drawings and the sweet entrancements of the spiritual life. His call was doubtless backed by as great a woe as that of Paul, but it may never have risen clearly into his consciousness, because its office was not needed. To him the ministry was altogether a call of privilege, a glory and a joy, and a service of perfect freedom. Prudential fear enters largely into ordinary Christian experience, but it loses prominence under the growing strength of the spiritual life, and almost fades from thought in the glowing and grateful affection of the believing heart. It is so in ministerial experience, in which the "Woe is unto me," however true in fact, is sunk in the all-pervading love of Christ and his work. Doubtless there are some preachers who have scarcely, even at the beginning of their career, felt any thing of it. The seraphim have touched their lips with fire from the altar, and when God has asked the question, "Whom shall I send, and who will go for us?" the response has been, "Here am I; send me."

There is an inward moral necessity which the minister of the gospel feels without any distinct reference to the consequences as they may affect himself. The burden of the word of the Lord is upon him, and he must relieve his heart of the burning truths that stir within. He cannot hold his peace if he would, and utterance must be given to the message that he feels commissioned to proclaim. The prophet's words describe at least the occasional feelings of the man who is called of God to preach: "But his word was in mine heart as a burning fire shut up in my bones, and I was weary with forbearing, and I could not stay." This burning fire shut up in the bones is a necessity different from that which is laid upon the conscience by the danger to our own salvation, and differing also somewhat from that grateful love which gladly and freely accepts this form of Christian consecration. Many are moved by this sense of woe to preach, many are perhaps held in their course by this influence; but it does not stand alone, nor is it the highest principle of duty. It is an element in all Christian life and in the ministerial call, but it is not at all times present in the mind, and in some instances it may not have been recognized where other motives have been in the ascendant.

An undue emphasis of Paul's words may lead to the error that the ministry is a path in which the highest incentives are not adequate, in which the believer is driven by the whip of necessity, and in which the principles and rewards of a religious life are not found. The apostle's "Woe is unto me" may also be perverted and misapplied by some who are exercised upon the subject of the call to preach. Perhaps they do not feel this woe; but is it needful in every case that they should? May they not be drawn by the love of Christ and moved by the word of the Lord in the heart? The permission may be stronger than the sense of requirement, and the privilege greater than the feeling of necessity. Love may be stronger than fear, and the sense of blessedness in this service may overtop the conceivable consequences of disobedience.

THE PREACHER AT WORK.

GODLY CRAFT.

PAUL made a bold and instructive confession when he said: "Nevertheless, being crafty, I caught you with guile." Soul-saving is an art, as much higher than all other arts as its object is greater than all other kinds of human enterprise. "He that winneth souls is wise," and there is a fertility of invention and a studied application of means which are needful to insure success. These alone will accomplish nothing, but they tell amazingly when united and in harmony with the operations of the Holy Spirit. While God gives the increase, and while only the good seed of the gospel bears living fruit, the skill of the sower has much to do with the result. As workers together with God, we may work in such a bungling way as to do little or nothing in bringing souls to Christ. Paul artfully accommodated himself to the conditions around him. "I am made all things to all men, that I might by all means save some." The guile which he employed consisted in the wise and dexterous use of the lawful and the expedient to move and allure to virtue and piety. Prejudices were conciliated, habits, tastes, and opinions were treated with careful delicacy, and all the springs of human action were touched with such a deft and adroit manipulation as to lead the opposers unconsciously up to the acceptance of religious truth. In this there was no compromise of any thing essential; but where occasion called for it, there was the most unflinching assertion of the offensive doctrines of the cross.

This combination of art and of fidelity is the element in

soul-saving which demands our study and imitation. It is to have craft and guile, and to be at the same time without low cunning and clear of blamable duplicity. It is to be wise to win, without abating the claims of the gospel; and to be all things to all men, while we know nothing among them but "Christ and him crucified." It will not do to fall back upon the divine power of the gospel, and to rest complacently in the conviction that the Holy Spirit is the adequate and only saving agent. If God accepts of human instrumentalities, and has made the world's salvation dependent upon them, we are responsible for their most effective disposition and use. While every thing is in the inspired word, there is much in the manner of its exposition and application. Christ might have put the substance of his teachings into a few propositions as dry and bald as the Thirty-nine Articles and as terse and compact as the Nicene Creed. He chose, however, a style ornate and lavishly embellished, illustrating by the most finished parables, and by the richest imagery, and by the largest affluence of figurative language. He taught with authority and with the utmost fidelity, and yet with consummate art. His life and intercourse with men show of whom Paul had learned his craft. To seek and to save the lost he also, in some sort, became all things to all men, adapting himself to the capacities and social customs of the times; but so that sin was always rebuked, sincerity, penitence, and faith were commended, and the afflicted were cheered and comforted. The apostles were to be "fishers of men," and to take with them into their higher calling the tact, judgment, and practical resources which had been developed by their toils and perils on the Sea of Galilee. Here was a stormier deep before them, and prizes of infinite value to be taken. And here was occasion for the exercise of all their mother-wit and all their daring and shrewdness. The line and the net were scarcely to be cast at random, but rather to be handled with ingenuity and skill. They were to catch men—not by casting their nets at a venture and by drawing it in a careless manner, but with elaborate art, with a view to results.

Our efforts to save men are too often perfunctory in their character, and we turn complacently from them with the doubtful satisfaction that we have done our part. If the sinner is not saved, it is his own fault. We have delivered our testimony, and here our responsibility ends. But have we used every possible art to awaken and attract him to the cross? Have we studied his character and adapted our means to reach his heart, and to interest him on the subject of personal salvation? The Christian, whether preacher or layman, cannot be clear unless he has brought all resources and all expedients to bear upon his work. "That I might by all means save some" was Paul's endeavor. The adequacy of the gospel, the necessity of the Spirit's operations, are all conceded; but still there was room for godly craft. Among the Greeks he reminded them of what their own poets had said, and illustrated the Christian warfare by allusions to their historic games and their military customs. He was at home in the literature of Athens and Crete, and knew when and how to quote their standard authors. Among the Jews he appealed to his own unblemished Hebrew lineage, and drew his weapons with wonderful tact from the armory of patriarchal and Levitical lore.

Of the eminent soul-savers among uninspired men it is enough to say that their business was an art in which means and expedients were studiously adapted to the great end in view. How to save souls, and how to save the most, is the thing aimed at. Whatever lawful expedients will reach this result are certainly legitimate. Luther and Wesley, scarcely less than Christ and Paul, had to break with the traditions and methods of their times. Whitefield wielded his mighty power at the expense of regularity and order in the Established Church, but with a single eye to saving results. A church is built to be filled; the gospel is proclaimed to be heard; Christian men and women are to leaven this great worldly mass, and to save the human race. Against the good is marshaled every form of cunning and the most multifarious devices and inventions of evil. Worldly sensations must be met with the religious, and the wisdom of the serpent, along with the harmlessness of the dove, must inform our religious life and enterprise. If Christians are solely intent upon saving souls, they will not stand upon dignity and order; they will not be content to move in the old ruts; they will not be satisfied with a stated round of duties which produce no fruit, but they will seek new and improved methods. The elaborate wiles which the devil throws around a single soul surpass description. The snares and allurements of the world are a most formidable and complex apparatus for the destruction of men. We must also be fruitful in the devices and allurements of love, study effect upon character to a sanctified end, and seek by the most varied appliances and by the highest art to compass the salvation of perishing souls.

COMFORTING GOD'S PEOPLE.

THE ministry is specially charged with this duty. Theirs is the office of consolation. "Comfort ye, comfort ye my people," was the message given to the prophet; and it is also a part of the great commission given to the preacher of the gospel.

God's people are an afflicted people. The ordinary calamities of life fall to their lot. Sorrows are sown thick along the path of many of them, and nearly all, soon or late, are made to drink of the bitter cup of misfortune. Religion does not exempt its possessor from pain and trouble. Among the most holy and devoted servants of God may be found instances of the most severe affliction. There is need of comfort, and it is alike the duty and privilege of the preacher to console those that are in distress.

The fact that Christians suffer is too manifest to call for proof. The reason for it is one chief element in the balm which the gospel offers. Trial is a part of our earthly probation, and its purpose is for discipline. God's paternal love is exhibited in the afflictions of his children. For spiritual ends, for the development of character, and to prepare us for the heavenly home, he has appointed these fiery trials. That they are of God and that they have a high and loving purpose are sufficient reasons for quiet and joyous endurance. With the assurance that all things work together for good to them that love God, there is no room for despondency. If God's particular and tender care is over his children, and if this conviction be strong in them, there is no occasion for misgiving. With the sure revelation of a future life, the resurrection of the dead, and eternal blessedness, the present pain is of small moment. There is comfort in this blessed hope that asserts itself in the most desperate straits of life, and that triumphs over temporal misfortunes.

The people of God are to be comforted—not only because they need it, but also because they are in a condition to receive consolation. The strong consolation is possible only to those who have fled for refuge to lay hold upon the hopes set before them. It is in fact impossible to comfort the impenitent and the unbelieving. Real comfort must flow from the divine promises, from Christ as our accepted Saviour, and from the hope that is born of the witness of the Spirit. For those who persist in sin and in opposition to

God there can be no particle of consolation. They deliberately place themselves beyond the reach of the great antidote to human sorrow. But the people of God have need to be reminded of the richness of their inheritance of grace, and to be directed to the abundant resources of comfort which their faith contains.

However we may explain it, there are Christians who do not seem to know how to summon the reserves of consolation in the time of trial. There is bewilderment under the first shock of sorrow, and sometimes a spirit of murmuring and distrust. With a cordial for every wound within reach, the hand that should be stretched forth is paralyzed. Just when the vision of the unseen world should be most clear and penetrating, the eyes of faith are holden. Until trouble came, the office of consolation in religion was subordinate and but little considered; and when the sudden blow fell, the refuge seemed to be shrouded in mist and wrapped in the obscurity of a far-off object. It is well to keep the elements of religious consolation in hand, so that when the emergency arises, and the fierce storm comes down upon us, we may be ready. For whatever reason the fact remains that tried and afflicted saints stand in need of this special ministry of comfort. The firm foundation, although built upon, must be measured and analyzed, and its deep and abiding character recalled to those who feel the shock of an unwonted conflict.

There are "sons of consolation"—those who have a special aptitude to help and strengthen weak and troubled souls. In temperament they are sympathetic, in discernment they detect the rooted sorrow, and because they have trodden the path of affliction themselves they are graciously qualified to succor those that are tempted. There are "sons of thunder," and also "sons of consolation;" but the complete ministry is that which combines the two. It may not be possible in all in an equal degree, and yet it is an excellence to be aimed at. To comfort is most Christ-like, and to be envied is he who is wise and strong in this ministry of consolation. In every congregation are troubled, tempted, discouraged disciples. They are waiting and hungering for a crumb of comfort, for a word of good cheer, and longing for the hand that shall lead them "beside the still waters."

The ministry of consolation is in accord with the office and work of the Holy Spirit as the Comforter. We may be sure that he is present to seal the message, to illumine the heart, and to apply the promises. It is a work in which we may suppose the Spirit especially delights. The methods and expedients of divine love are often severe, but their end in holiness is a supreme and everlasting consolation. It is the privilege of the man of God to be a co-worker with the triune God in this blessed work of bringing forth the wealth of consolation from the treasury of faith, and to comfort the people of God.

WHAT AND HOW TO PREACH.

A YOUNG preacher writes: "Could not some of you doctors of divinity give us an occasional hint about what to preach, or how to preach, or any thing of the kind? You know we are slow to learn, and need just as much precept as we can get." There are many excellent works on preaching, such as Vinet's "Pastoral Theology," Bautaine, Broadus, Bishop Simpson's "Yale Lectures," and "Ad Clerum," by Joseph Parker. Young preachers would do well to read works like these we have mentioned. A careful study of the Acts of the Apostles and Paul's Epistles, especially what are called the "Pastoral Epistles," will throw inspired light upon what and how to preach. It is plain, in general terms, that we are to preach the gospel. "Preach the word," is Paul's injunction. As embassadors for Christ the message is given, and it is the preacher's business to deliver it. Sinners are to be called to repentance, and believers are to be built up and instructed. The law of God must be explained and enforced; the plan of redemption in Christ, its means and conditions, must be made prominent; and all the duties and precepts of the Bible should be expounded and applied to the conscience and life.

In what relative proportion these subjects are to appear in our preaching depends much upon the character of our hearers and of the congregation before us. It is sometimes expedient to take such texts as are of an awakening character, such as are best adapted to produce conviction in the minds of the unconverted. Again, there are occasions when Christians are to be addressed upon matters of duty and experience. Ordinarily, however, we would aim to give every one his portion, whether saint or sinner, in every sermon. The object should be to touch the heart, conscience, and life of every person in the assembly, and so to declare the whole counsel of God that you can meet every hearer in the judgment without condemnation.

Our taste is in the expository preaching. The Bible is full of good texts, and instead of a sharply defined topic, with a mere scriptural motto appended, we greatly prefer a rich and juicy text that admits of unity of thought, and at the same time comprehends many aspects of doctrine and experience. There is life in the word, there is food in it, and there is the Holy Ghost in it. To get at the mind of the Spirit in any given text should be the main care. It may mean this or that, and many true and useful things may be said in connection with it, but the preacher should labor to bring out the precise shade of thought as accurately as possible, the precise thing intended by the inspired author.

Loose and careless exposition, or the quoting of texts without using them, or the perversion of Scripture to illustrate something foreign to their purpose, are all open to the charge of "handling the word of God deceitfully." A knowledge of the original languages in which the Scriptures were written is of great service to the expositor; but in these days good commentaries are abundant, and by their use any studious man may attain to excellence in exposition. Expository preaching has in it greater variety than the topical. Topics run out after awhile, but the word of God is deep, inexhaustible, and always abounding in fresh and varied materials. A good critical commentary, written by a man of true spiritual insight, in which the exact sense of the scripture is brought out, is, after the Bible, the most necessary book for the young preacher to study and consult. The habit of thorough analysis should be formed, and the method and arrangement should be such as to give the greatest clearness and force to the passage in hand. Attention to arrangement is important, because the maximum of power in the preacher cannot be reached by a rambling and disconnected discourse, and because the hearer needs method to assist attention and memory, and in order to any definite and powerful impression

The young preacher has the opportunity of forming right habits of study and also of delivery. After middle life not much change can be expected; but early in the ministerial life the power of extemporaneous speaking can usually be acquired. And if it can be, it is the better way. Every sermon should be thought out, and ordinarily the outlines put on paper; but it will be all the better if never so much as a *catch-word* be taken into the pulpit. Generally the use of notes and of manuscript is a habit gradually formed, and that might have been avoided. We mention what we regard as generally best. There are exceptions to the rule, but they are few. With a previously thorough study of the subject, memory and self-possession will seldom fail those who trust them.

Much has been written about the length of sermons. Young preachers do well to study brevity, and old ones too. From thirty to forty minutes is ordinarily long enough, though this depends on how often the people hear preaching, on the occasion, and on the preacher himself. As we advance in years the mental resources become more ample, the mind works more slowly, and the tendency is to grow prolix. Old men will not mend, but by considering in time young men may form the habit of preaching comparatively short sermons. Our bishops and great preachers preach long sermons, and they have a right to do so. People come a long distance to hear them, and would not be satisfied with a short sermon. But the measure of Marvin, Munsey, Kavanaugh, Doggett, and others like them, is not for us. Let us call to mind the fable of the frogs and the ox, and not attempt greatness in the direction of long sermons. There is much in the manner of preaching—the management of the voice, the gestures. Young preachers can improve themselves here. They can avoid and correct what is repulsive, and bring the physical powers into perfect harmony with the workings of mind and the emotions of the heart. It falls to the lot of few to become popular orators; but the most can speak so as not to offend good taste, and so as to command the attention and respect of sensible people.

It is scarcely needful to say that spirituality is the capital qualification. This, fully possessed, will shape our preaching wholesomely, both as to the matter and manner. There is a good deal of unspiritual preaching, dabbling in science, and a rage for sensational illustration. The preacher must walk with God and live a life of prayer and communion with Christ. There is a lack of spirituality even in preachers. They often have a certain type of zeal, they are clear thinkers, brilliant declaimers, and religious, but they need a deeper work of the Spirit in their own hearts. "The spirit of love, of power, and of a sound mind," is almost sure to be found in connection with a close and humble walk with God. The preacher cannot be too careful of his own spiritual condition. It is the essential element of a Christian ministry, and that which makes a personal ministry the appointed means of saving the world.

CUMULATIVE PREACHING.

As we were listening to a preacher the other Sunday we felt the force of the man's whole life poured upon us in a discourse of forty-five minutes. All that the man knew could not be told in that length of time, but the best that he knew on that particular subject could; and so we realized that we were getting the choicest results of a ministry of twenty-five years. The matter was evidently culled and chosen from a large stock, and did not, by any means, embrace all. A younger man could not have done so well, because the results of his thinking and gathering would have come from a scantier store. When Dr. Lyman Beecher declared that he was forty years in preparing a certain sermon he meant it in this sense, that it was the outcome of that many years of general study and of mental and spiritual training, although the actual writing of the sermon may not have occupied him more than a few hours.

We also thought that the cogent reasoning, the happy arrangement, the lucid statement, were the results of a quarter of a century of mental discipline and training added to the college course. It took time to develop these mental powers and to bring them to their present state of effectiveness and strength. These trained powers of mind were more completely exhibited in this single sermon than the stores of mere knowledge could be. So far as they were concerned, we were being served by the accumulated results of all the preacher's past years of study and mental effort. This treasure, of a mind brought to its ripest strength and polish through so long a course of training, was ministering, in its wholeness, to us in this one sermon. Just as all the weight of the costly and beautiful machinery bears upon the die in coining every precious piece, so the whole mind, with all that it had become, stamped itself upon this single piece of gospel gold.

There was also the spiritual element. Paul knew whom he had believed, because he had long been acquainted with Christ. It was the knowledge of long acquaintance, of walking with Christ for many years, and of trusting him under many and varied circumstances. In the case we were considering, besides the early conversion, the Scripture study, there were years of religious experience. In all this time there had been growth in grace and growth in the knowledge of Christ. The deep things of God had been sounded as they could not have been in the first years of the most devoted ministry. Here was a mature piety, with its wealth of increase, and with its strong and deep insight, and spiritual enlargement and freedom, coming full-handed to anoint us with the gathered unction of years of prayer and of spiritual struggles and victories.

We reflected further that nothing grows like character, and that the sum and might of it all are put into every word the preacher utters, into every blow he strikes. Up to the last hour before the sermon is preached something is added, and the entire power of a spotless and holy life goes into every sermon.

What, we asked ourselves, is the value of a sermon that

is the product of such manifold and rich materials gathered through many years of mental toil, heart-searchings, and consecrated living? And do we generally take into account what preaching is made of, and how much it costs those who are doing it? And it also occurred to us that one secret of good preaching and of a successful ministry lies in hoarding up, saving parsimoniously every thing in the way of thorough study, of religious experience, and of Christian character. Where this cumulative process goes on, time is an important factor of excellence. But this process, unfortunately, is not the universal rule. Perhaps there are not many who can put a whole life of thought and experience and character into every sermon. There have been miscarriages, negligences, mistakes. But for these they would be greater preachers than they are.

THE PREACHER IN METHODISM.

THE ITINERANT SCHOOL.

SOME years ago, after hearing one of our bishops, a brother said to us, "Is there any other system than ours that can develop such preaching as that?" The question came up in our own mind while meditating on the character and powers of our beloved and lamented Bishop Marvin. Those to whom we have referred, though exceptionally eminent, may be regarded as representatives of a class of preachers who have come up through the itinerant school, and who have been made what they were in a large measure by its peculiar advantages and discipline. It is doubtful whether many of them would ever have been heard of as preachers if such a system as ours had not been open for their reception. They were without the means to enter institutions of learning, and if the only path to the ministry had been through the college and seminary they must of necessity have turned to other pursuits. No matter how clear and strong the conviction that they were called to preach, but for this open door their way would have been closed, and many of its greatest and most useful preachers would have been lost to the Church. It is to be set down to the credit of the system that such men as McKendree, Bascom, Marvin, Winans, Pitts, Munsey, Green, and many others, came to be eminent messengers of the gospel. It afforded the opportunity, and gave them the chance without which they could never have entered upon that career in which they became so distinguished. The itinerant school gave them the needed opportunity for study and work, and by its provisions afforded the facilities for improvement in knowledge and for the exercise and development of their gifts in preaching.

That it would have been better if these men had been regularly educated may be true; but as this was impossible, it was the itinerant school that took them up and trained them for the work to which God had called them. With rarely more than the imperfect rudiments of an English education, but with minds fresh and thirsting for knowledge, with hearts glowing with love to Christ, and with bodies hardened by toil, they began their course as ministers of the gospel. What they read was of the most solid character, and in such measure as enabled them to digest it well. What they gathered from books was immediately incorporated into their own thinking and wrought into their daily preaching. There was a symmetrical development of the physical, mental, and spiritual man, and effective, soul-saving preaching was the object of all. They were called self-made men—self-educated—but perhaps it would be more correct to say that they were educated in the itinerant school. This was the only school they well could enter, and for them it was probably the best. It was a hard and rugged school, but where the root of the matter was in the men no system could bring it out so well. It was eminently practical, not hampered with too much art, and in it the individual gifts and characteristics were not so repressed as to bring all into one mold and to conform all to a single arbitrary pattern. Instead of unmaking and perverting the work of God, it simply guided, pruned, and stimulated the natural powers, and turned the gifts of grace into the most effective channels.

What the itinerant school alone has done and can do is seen in the history of many noted preachers who never went to any other school. Had this system taken them up at the end of a full college and seminary course they might have been more effective in some directions, but not as preachers. As preachers, to reach the masses and to persuade men to come to Christ, we doubt whether regular scholastic training would have contributed any thing to their popularity and power. On the contrary, they might have been considerably shorn of their strength by the more exact and scientific methods of the academies and universities. The training of the college and of the itinerant school are not necessarily incompatible, and it is generally desirable that our young men should have the advantages of both. The great men to whom we have alluded, however, stand as illustrations of what our itinerant system is capable of doing, and prove how wise, beneficent, and effective it has been in giving to the Church many of her noblest and most eloquent and devoted preachers. We know of no other system of ministerial training that has equaled it in turning out so many truly great and powerful preachers. In no other school do preachers come in such close contact with all classes of the people and have such opportunities of studying human nature. And as a school of eloquence what other can be compared with it? It may be truly said that not many, in comparison with the whole who have been educated in the itinerant school alone, have reached the eminence of a Marvin or a Munsey. But the same is true of every system, only we would claim that the average power and effectiveness is greater in ours. It does not better qualify for authorship, for teaching, or for scholarly pursuits, but it is the best school in the world for the training of preachers.

Henceforth our candidates for the ministry will be better educated than formerly. The times seem to demand it, and the opportunities are greater than they were forty years ago. A higher literary standard is required at the beginning of the preacher's course, but the discretion of the Conferences should be exercised with care. Some of the brightest names in Methodism have been saved to her ministry by recognizing the capabilities of the itinerant school in its functions of disciplining and informing the mind as well as in forming ministerial character. It may be that there are more educated young men applying than are needed to fill the ranks; but in drawing the line too strictly we may be throwing away some of our choicest material. In the itinerant school it does not take long to find out whether the novice is disposed to study and whether he has capacity. If he have these, and the natural and gracious gifts, he is in a school where he is sure to grow into a useful preacher. The old preachers, who came up from the start through the itinerant school, were usually most thorough in doctrine. If their information was not wide and varied, they knew theology well and they knew men well; and if not great in science and literature, they were mighty in the Scriptures.

What our peculiar school did for them is coming to be regarded as the very best preparation for effective preaching. It can make great preachers without the aid of other schools, although it does not depreciate their advantages; but with all that other schools can do, we cannot dispense with this. A system that can point to so many trophies of its wisdom is not to be despised as an educational institution. There must be something in its curriculum and methods to be admired and cherished when we remember the many great and devoted preachers who have been trained and developed under its influences. It has given to the Church some of the grandest characters that adorn the pages of its history. The mission of such a system cannot end until the world is saved.

ONE ADVANTAGE OF ITINERANCY.

The itinerancy comes nearer furnishing the Church with the ideal and perfect ministry than any other system. It is hardly possible that one man should possess all the excellences in their completest development and exercise. By a regular and comparatively frequent change of pastors each congregation shares the benefits of many and varied gifts. Some men are better pastors than others, some better church-builders and financiers, some have preëminently the wisdom and grace of good disciplinarians; and every church has need of these qualities in its pastor from time to time. As they are not usually found in one man, the advantage of them all is secured through the ministry of several. The strong and the brilliant, the solid and the entertaining, the instructive and the popular, are secured only through change and variety in the preachers. One in a thousand may unite all in his single ministry, and some are possessed of more varied resources than others; but generally it takes a great many preachers to make up a full and effective ministry. Paul planted and Apollos watered. It took them both to meet the demand and to do the husbandry of the house of God.

The doctrinal preacher builds up on the most holy faith. Under his teaching the church is instructed in the Articles of Religion, in the ordinances, and in the meaning of the atonement, the divinity of Christ, justification, sanctification. In the course of three or four years he has a well-instructed church, well grounded in doctrine, and everybody convinced and settled in religious opinions. Much good has been done, but some classes have not been reached, and among the elect there is desire for a change of spiritual food.

The more eloquent and hortatory man—one who moves on the wings of tropes and figures, and whose sermons swim in illustrations and anecdotes—has done a faithful work in his way, enlisting interest, drawing congregations, attracting the young people, and adding many to the Church; but in all his term he has perhaps never clearly and fully stated any one of the leading doctrines of redemption. His hearers cannot give the meaning of justification nor tell the difference between it and sanctification. General ideas they have of goodness, grace, and salvation, but there is lack of clear conceptions and of the gospel as a system of truths. Some will feel the need of something more solid, and others who do not feel the need are the ones who, for their own good, most require a change.

Let the doctrinal man take the place of the more sprightly, and let the eloquent and hortatory man take the place of the doctrinal. Each is the complement of the other—supplementing, perfecting, and completing what the other did not and perhaps could not do.

Every forcible preacher will, in an average pastoral term, impress himself upon the spiritual and intellectual condition of his people. Their type and degree of spirituality, and their grade of mind and thought, will answer more or less to his. They will reflect what is excellent, but at the same time they will bear the impress of his defects and infirmities. There are few preachers that reach equally well all classes. Some have gifts for the perfecting of the saints, the edification of the Church, and others reach with most power the unawakened and unconverted. There are those whose ministry is specially attractive to the poor and illiterate, but they fail in reaching the better. educated and those who move in the middle and higher walks of society. These "gifts differing" indicate the value and necessity of interchange of pastors.

Looking at the matter from this point of view only, the length of pastoral terms should vary greatly. Some men do all they can do profitably in a year, others in four years, others in ten. If the itinerancy requires for its harmony and maintenance a maximum limit, our four-years' term is probably about the best that can be fixed. It very nearly strikes the average capacity of highest usefulness. Some preachers might be more effective in a much longer pastorate, and some churches lose something by the change which comes by the limitation, but the majority are benefited. The rich and diverse gifts of many are so distributed as to work together for the building up of the whole Church. The benefits secured to the churches are sufficient to reconcile the itinerant to the discomforts of the system; but he should also consider that while it utilizes him to the greatest advantage to the Church it also secures to him better average appointments than a voluntary system of settled pastorates.

THE PREACHER, YOUNG AND OLD.

THE YOUNG PREACHER.

IN Methodism preachers generally start at an early age. The privileges of a collegiate education, and the growing opinion that a theological course, post-collegiate, is desirable, tend to give us in these days a more mature material for admission on trial; but still the classes received are usually made up of very young men—some of them not yet having reached their majority. Thousands of our middle-aged preachers were in the saddle and riding circuits before they were old enough to vote; and of the fathers and the old men fast passing away, the most of them began before they needed a razor, which the fashion of the times required beard-growing men to use. Our system of circuits and frequent changes is exceedingly favorable to the safe and advantageous employment of a youthful ministry. There are safeguards thrown around it in the presiding eldership and the senior preacher, and in the wise ordering of the appointing power against faults and errors in administration; and an undue strain upon the mind and its resources is obviated by the brief term of an annual pastorate, usually over a work of several appointments.

Not many sermons are needed at the beginning, and comparatively few are demanded to serve through the first Conference year. The horseback travel gives due exercise, promotes the flow of healthful spirits, and is a preventive of dyspepsia. It is killing work for a young man of limited education and without experience to maintain himself in a station during the first years of his ministry. The circuit is the best gymnasium in the world, and the most healthful school for the development of the ministerial character. It has given soundness of body and mind to our preachers, improved their common sense, and secured that practical qualification for the work which neither books nor lectures can afford. As a rule the circuit should be the young preacher's first work, whether he comes from college, the theological seminary, or the plow. Collegians can never be well-educated Methodist preachers until they have gone to this most important finishing school, and the willingness to matriculate in Brush College is a tolerable test of prospective fitness for their calling. The youth who begins with a high estimate of his claims to appointments, and is offended by the roughness and obscurity of the work to which he is sent, will hardly turn out well. He will probably be a dissatisfied man all his life, and will finally quit the ministry or seek a place in some other Church. As an itinerant the element of failure is in him, and it will sooner or later develop into disaster to his standing and character.

In no other ministry does real merit sooner obtain fitting recognition, and in no other does the man more surely reach the place to which he is best adapted. The bishops, as wise master-builders, are likely to put the living stones where they will most strengthen and adorn the temple, and the people will not be slow to see and appreciate the gifts and graces of those who minister to them in holy things. It is barely possible that some "gems of purest ray serene" may never come to the surface, and that some exquisite flowers may be left to "blush unseen," but, for the most part, with the fields and the laborers given, the man will reach the position for which he is best fitted by character and attainments. In no other ministry does a young man get on faster than in ours. His advancement is more rapid and the ground of his elevation broader than in other Churches. Our Connectional system puts its preachers into a field not limited by Conference boundaries, but as wide as the entire denomination, and his transfer to more important appointments is effected with facility, without detriment to the Church, and without damage to himself.

Woe to the man, however, who in the beginning seeks great things for himself, or who, in the maturity of his powers and experience, disparages his brethren and overestimates himself! The worm is in the bud, and blight will follow. To aim at greatness and usefulness for Christ is right, but there must be care, lest a wicked and selfish ambition come to be the overmastering passion. It requires a great deal of grace to begin, and still more of grace to continue in the work of the ministry. The simple and glowing piety of the first year, instead of being allowed to cool, must be fed and increased as the years roll on. There is no need for a man to think much about his position and appointments. Let him make himself the greatest and best of men, an effective preacher, a good pastor, and show himself "a workman that needeth not to be ashamed," and the rest will take care of itself. The finest-looking apple in the dish often has a blemish—there is a speck which tells of something wrong at the core. Many men feel that they are not appreciated, and wonder why they are kept in the background while others are advanced. Not always is the apple specked or decayed, but sometimes it is; and if not, it may not be as large as some others. Where a man's estimate of himself differs from that of his brethren, he should at least moderate his views or keep them to himself.

The young preacher filled with zeal and love is hopeful, and the freshness of the dawn is on his heart. If he has a modest opinion of himself, has made up his mind to endure hardness, and feels called to save souls, he will be thankful and satisfied with any appointment, and the first years will be the happiest of all in many respects. After thirty or forty years of faithful and possibly of eminent and honored labor, he will think of that first circuit as the toiler at evening remembers the blush and dew of the morning, and he will probably conclude that he has all along been appreciated and blessed far beyond his deservings.

The ministry of young men has its special value. We do not see how the Church could well do without it. This element of youth, this young blood, this almost beardless presence, in spite of its crudeness and incompleteness, puts color into the picture, and gives healthier tone to the canvas. Gray hairs we must have and the wisdom of years, but we also need the ruddy cheek and the locks that are not frosted. The gardener, the florist, the fruit-grower, understand that there must be a succession in their planting and culture. There is utility as well as beauty in it. Some crops yield their best results before they reach maturity. They are ripe for use long before they go to seed, and have a worth because they are immature. For some purposes there is virtue in the tender shoot and the fresh-blown flower even more than in the stalk and ear. The ministry of young men carries with it influences and sympathies of its own, and its sphere is productive of results of the greatest value to the Church. It has a temperament, a faith, and an elasticity which bring success and effect results peculiar to itself. The field of usefulness is not alone before the young man, and for which he is preparing, but it is around him, and he is gathering his best sheaves while he feels, perhaps, that he is only getting ready to sow. While he sharpens his sickle he is amidst the waving corn and thrusting it in. The first-fruits of our ministerial life are often the choicest, as they should be the earnest and promise of abundant usefulness in the future.

The young preacher must make himself. The kingdom is within him. Prayer, study, and work will develop and bring it out. After all the advantages of education, and after all the advice sought, the preacher must be self-made. Let him make the most of what he is and of what God has given him, and he will reach the highest round to which he is capable of mounting. He must grow like a tree rather than be built up like a wall. Let him take care about the too close imitation of admired models, and avoid dependence upon published skeletons. Above all, do not preach other men's sermons. The mind and heart will suffer from such a course, and the preaching will be barren and unfruitful. Some young men have fallen into this evil, this dishonest practice of supplying themselves with custom-made sermons, such as the English market supplies for a shilling apiece, and others use the stenographic reports of the popular preachers of the day. No matter whether the theft is found out or not, the man who forms this habit curses himself, and when detected he forfeits the respect of his hearers.

God bless the young preacher who sets out this year, in whatever Conference, and under whatever conditions of weakness or strength. It is the beginning of a path that has many rugged passages, many dark defiles of temptation and sorrow, and many conflicts with the powers of darkness. But it is also a course which has large and gracious compensations, and one that, if faithfully pursued, brings him to an incorruptible crown.

THE OLD PREACHER.

THE old as distinguished from the young—the man of age and experience rather than the novice. In our system the age of the man generally corresponds with his ministerial life. The man of forty has probably been preaching at least twenty years, and the man of sixty has usually seen his forty years of effective service. These years have been devoted to study and labor, and the education and character have been acquired while riding circuits and doing pastoral work. After so long a term, the fittest only are likely to survive. In some sort the office of natural selection has retained in the effective ranks the best physical constitutions, the most devoted piety, and the sturdiest qualities of soul. The diseased and feeble have fallen at their posts, the weak and vacillating have turned aside to other pursuits, the wicked have gone back to the world. Many, still faithful and true, by affliction have been compelled to retire from the more active sphere of toil. The residue of effective men is, as a class, made of choice material, and from forty to sixty-five should be at their best. The rich stores, so long in the gathering, should appear in the sermon, and a ripe experience and a mellow piety should make their visits to the homes of the people most comforting and edifying.

And so it is with the man of one work, who has gone steadily forward, developing his spiritual and intellectual powers in a strong and healthy way. He has become apt to teach. He is familiar with the processes of the Spirit in the awakening and conversion of souls, and as a fisher of men he has learned to handle the gospel-net with sound judgment and adroitness. With ordinarily good health, there should be no abatement in these middle years of fervidness of spirit, of sprightly thought, or of powerful and moving utterance. The breadth, depth, and strength should still be attended by the brightness and flexibility of youth. The old and the young tree are alike in the freshness of their foliage and in the sweetness and beauty of their blossoms. In order to continued and increased effectiveness, men must keep growing. They must grow both in grace and in knowledge. All the powers must be kept up to their full strength by assiduous culture, and the whole man kept in tone by unabated diligence. Alexander Hamilton, amidst the busiest cares of his profession and the engrossing occupations of statesmanship, went through his Euclid frequently. To keep the mind up to its highest working capacity there must be hard study for merely disciplinary purposes.

It is not unusual for middle-aged men, and for those who have passed the period when soldiers are drafted, to be painfully conscious of an inaptitude for severe mental labor. Growth has ceased, and regression, after a brief stand-still, is sure to set in. The very excellences of mature life are apt to degenerate into defects. In youth much pruning was to be done, and as intelligence increased and the taste became more severe and cultivated, extravagances in manner and style have been lopped off and repressed. Perhaps in this process the other extreme has been reached, and not only the wildness and over-exuberance have been checked, but baldness and comparative sterility have ensued. With improved taste and wider culture, the preacher should cultivate the imagination, and not be parsimonious in the descriptive colors which he throws into his well-studied themes. Let him not go too far in pruning, and let him aim to enrich and beautify while he strives after the solid and enduring. Many an old preacher would be the better for it if he should go back twenty years and pick up and put on what he then cast aside as blemishes and vanities.

The good-ground hearers are mostly young people, and to reach its greatest effectiveness there must be an element of youth in the sermon. A little of the sophomoric is wisdom sure enough in dealing with the average congregation. Young, fresh, and simple in style and thought, and with spiritual unction attending, there will always be a hearty response from those who are likely to be reached by any means whatever. It is the youthfulness of Mr. Spurgeon's preaching more than any thing else that accounts for his wonderful success in the pulpit. He is doctrinal, expository, descriptive, practical, sympathetic, and always young. He was a mere boy when he began, and he preaches very much like a boy now that he is in the forties. It is not difficult, in looking into some matronly faces, to recall the beauty and delicacy of girlhood. In spiritual faces, however changed by age and care, these qualities come out and glow with the distinctness of a transfiguration. The cloud of years, instead of obscuring, only gives greater softness and sweetness to the light that dwelt upon the brow of youth. It is most unfortunate for the brain to be allowed to grow stiff and inflexible in its action and for the heart to become dull and indifferent in its emotions. It is scarcely less unfortuate to lose the freshness and simplicity of early years and to fall into tastes and habits of thought which quench the fires of a more enthusiastic period. As youth reaches forward to grasp the wisdom of age, so age should strive to bring back and retain the freshness of youth.

Age, however, has invaluable qualities of its own, and resources of usefulness that only age can give. Our old preachers are a perpetual benediction to the Church, and their presence and labors are necessary to the completeness of the whole. Their preaching, while it may retain much of the characteristics of earlier days, has in it an authority, weight, and power which come of time well improved. Every congregation needs a due portion of such ministries, and should, if possible, have the privilege of profiting by them. Their knowledge of Scripture, their large acquaintance with men, and their profound experience in the deep things of God qualify them for usefulness to which younger men cannot attain. The fruit of old age is the most indispensable of all to the feeding of the flock of God. The hoary head is not only a crown of glory to him who wears it, but it is a diadem of beauty and power to the Christian ministry.

The abuse of this general principle lies chiefly in the special claims which old men sometimes base upon their years. Much is due them, no doubt, on the score of long service and ripe experience, but in their self-consciousness and utterances this ground of consideration may be made offensively prominent. It is better to let the fact assert itself, and to let character and influence stand upon their own merit. To be over-sensitive and exacting, and to seem jealous of the respect due to age, are infirmities to be guarded against. The psalmist enforces an important lesson by allusion to his years when he says: "I have been young, and now am old; yet have I not seen the righteous forsaken, nor his seed begging bread." The great apostle in his appeal to Philemon, for the only time in all his writings speaks of himself as "Paul the aged." We recall no other instances in which inspired men have sought to strengthen their declarations and teachings by reference to their years. Jacob, when in the presence of Pharaoh, makes but a modest reply to the monarch's question, "How old art thou?" when he says: "The days of the years of my pilgrimage are a hundred and thirty years; few and evil have the days of the years of my life been, and have not attained unto the days of the years of the life of my fathers in the days of their pilgrimage." That elderly men are not as much sought after and are not as acceptable as the younger may be partly their own fault. The clamor for young men may be largely unreasonable, but in the ministry, as in other pursuits, there must be effectiveness.

The most difficult thing of all is to recognize the advance of age in ourselves, and to yield gracefully to the inexorable lot. One of the trials of middle life is the thought of a destitute old age. On one occasion the preachers asked Mr.

Asbury what they were to do when they became old. The old Bishop comforted them with the sage reflection that not many of them would probably live to be old. Prudence and economy will help, but in most cases preachers can barely support their families and live. They must walk by faith, and not by sight. They will do rather better than the average of men in secular affairs at the worst. But the devoted preacher has a right to trust the Master whom he serves. God will take care of wife and children and old age, if he is faithful to his high calling. Some, in sheer affright and desperation, turn to other pursuits; but owing to lack of experience and business habits, and to an unfitness which their previous life has superinduced, they fail. Generally, it would be better and wiser to stick to the gospel-plow, though driven through the most barren soil. To quit in mid-career is to lose to the Church and themselves the results of years of study and experience. The sun sets with a peculiar splendor upon a full day's work faithfully done.

THE CHURCH IN THE WORLD.

ADDED TO THE CHURCH.

THIS, at any rate, is the scriptural way of stating the fact. A divine agency is recognized. The Lord added. The three thousand voluntarily joined the Christian company, but they were led to this by the moving of the Holy Spirit, and the apostles by divine authority received them. Besides their baptism and their formal reception, there was a work of grace in their hearts. It is Christ's prerogative to add people to the Church. Where the union is vital, and something more than a mere form, it is the work of Christ. Numbers may have been "joined in," as some express it, but whether they have been truly added depends on the part which Christ has performed.

The persons whom the Lord added are described as the saved—not such as should be saved, but the saved; so the best critics, Calvinistic and Arminian, agree. It is a fact in the narrative concerning the day of Pentecost. Those added to the Church on that day were of this sort. Our usage and discipline require that those received "desire to flee from the wrath to come, and to be saved from their sins;" and they are further required solemnly, in the presence of God and of the congregation, "to ratify and confirm the promise and vow of repentance, faith, and obedience contained in the baptismal covenant." If these conditions exist, they are as much as the Church can demand, and are a sufficient ground for admission to Church-membership. But surely, in view of the example in the Acts, less than these conditions should not be regarded as meeting the requirement.

The conduct of those added exhibits the reality of their union with the Church—steadfastness in doctrine. "They continued steadfastly in the apostle's doctrine." There was a doctrinal basis for their faith. They were well rooted in the truth, and were firm in their adherence to the gospel. "Fellowship" was with them distinctly realized. The communion of saints was a living and felt experience. Nothing more clearly distinguishes vital from formal Christianity than this. Fellowship is something spiritual, and none but the spiritually-minded know what it is. It is the living tie that binds the hearts of God's children in one; it is the antidote to bigotry, sectarian acrimony, and all uncharitableness. Thousands of Christians in name are strangers to the fellowship of the apostles. In this respect they have not been added to the Church; they are in it, but not of it.

The ordinances were observed by these first Church-members. Breaking of bread may stand for all—the Lord's Supper and the rest. They continued in them steadfastly. If fit to be in the Church, we are fit to partake of the Lord's Supper. In what good sense is any one added to the Church who neglects this plain duty and important means of grace? It is something very sacred, but it should not repel the truly penitent and those who intend to lead a new life. It was designed to help the weak, and to strengthen and comfort all. The sincere, the contrite, the soul that is striving to walk in the narrow path, should be steadfast "in breaking of bread." If baptism is the ordinance of admission, the Lord's Supper is the ordinance of continuance in the Church.

Those whom the Lord added to the Church are represented as continuing in prayers. They were converted in a prayer-meeting; in a meeting of great power and abundant supplication they were brought into the company of the disciples. As they began in prayer, so they kept on. "Prayer" is the word. Social prayer, family and private —this is the threefold cord that is not easily broken. How can a prayerless man be said to be a member of the Church? And if he does not pray in all these ways, is he of those whom the Lord has added? A man may have no family, he may be tongue-tied, or have other infirmities that shut him out from other than secret prayer; but his excuse must be a good one, or he is inevitably condemned. If the new member does not begin to pray and keep it up—in the prayer-meeting, in the family, and in the closet, he backslides rapidly, or he was never enough of a Christian to make backsliding possible.

We might notice other characteristics of those whom the Lord added to the Church, such as their liberality with their goods, their gladness and singleness of heart, and that they continued praising God, "having favor with all the people." Some of these thousands may have fallen out by the way, but they started off well, and continued for some time in a manner that proved that Christ himself had brought them into the Church, and augured favorably for their faithfulness to the end. Such additions are something added to the Church. Each one counts in making up the strength and power of the whole. The measure of resources is enlarged, there is an accession of workers, and the spiritual momentum is increased. Where there is a large increase of numbers without any corresponding increase of strength morally, spiritually, or financially, the Lord's hand is not as manifest as we could wish. If the Lord adds to the Church there will be results, the work will be lasting, and the fruits of the Spirit will appear in manifold ways.

Our dependence upon Christ is absolute. The means must be recognized and plied with earnestness; but let us be sure that the Lord does the work. In the main the hay, wood, and stubble are our work. Christ's hand is with ours in the gold, silver, and precious stones. Awakened people doubtless need instruction on the subject of joining the Church, and often need to be pressed to take the step, but the hard work is to lead them to repentance and prepare them for admission. When men are broken up under the hammer of the word, and deeply wrought upon by the Spirit, and when converted, it requires little effort to bring them into the Church; they cannot easily be kept out of it. Those that are saved, or are being saved, are pretty certain to seek the fellowship of God's people. The Lord adds such to the Church. They come as persons graciously drawn by the Saviour himself, and prepared to make a good profession.

CHURCH PILLARS.

THERE were a dozen apostles, but of these Paul tells us that James, Cephas, and John "seemed to be pillars" in the Church at Jerusalem. Very different kinds of men were they, but each one was strong and useful in his way. The living architecture of the house of God embraces this conception of the superior strength and value of some of its parts. In almost every organization, even of a denominational breadth, there are of necessity those who have this eminence of character and responsibility. On them largely rests the structure to which they belong; and the stability and safety of the whole depend upon their capacity and wisdom. In every society there are usually those who seem to be pillars—sometimes more in the seeming than in the reality. It is a fortunate thing for a Church to have in it enough of this sort of material—of men whose broad views, love for Christ, and weight of position and influence, can give tone and power to the whole body.

Both for strength and beauty are pillars needed. That

is an incomplete edifice, weak and impotent, that is without them. Many a Church enterprise has failed, and many an organization has come to naught, because it had none of these strong and capable shafts to support it. The house has not been built; or if built, it has tumbled down for the want of pillars. The character of a Church is usually shaped and determined by a few. Around them cluster the details of the structure, and the general effect is decided by the order and material of their composition. The piety, the intelligence, the method and quality of the benevolence, and the respect which a Church commands, depend upon the foremost spirits in it. Not all after the same pattern perhaps, but all should be sound and equal to the responsibility. Whether Doric or Corinthian, Roman, Byzantine, or Saracenic, they are to help in sustaining the precious burden that is laid upon them, and in maintaining the symmetry, harmony, and unity of the edifice. They are plain, ornate, solid, graceful, but all useful in their places, and all contributing to the stability and glory of the temple.

Church pillars may represent not alone the eminent in gifts and influence, but also the stable elements of the society or congregation. There is always a volatile and restless material, composed of those who float like the sea-weed. They are never well rooted, but move about from church to church, or simply hover on the outskirts, with no very vital tie to the main body. They have no earnest purpose, no serious idea of personal effort and work for Christ. Work for the Church, and in it, is not in their comprehension of duty and obligation. Their relation to the Church is that of incidental beneficiaries, who feel themselves entitled to what they may see and hear and enjoy, without contributing any thing beyond their fitful presence to the life and expansion of the divine kingdom in the world. They are pillars who constitute the nucleus of power and effectiveness, always in their places, and faithful to the post of duty under all circumstances. They are as much a part of the religious body as a pillar is a part of the house, and as permanent and steadfast in their relations to it as the columns which bore upon their capitals the arches and cornices of Carnac or the Parthenon.

The progress and prosperity of a Church depend greatly upon this strong, healthful heart, whose throbs keep up the circulation and vitality of the organization. This is to the whole as the citadel to the wide-spread and more vulnerable town. It is the stronghold and the hope of the cause of Christ in every Church and community. This old guard, well disciplined, always in battle array, and knowing nothing but fidelity and obedience, is the only dependence. In this respect every Christian may and ought to be a pillar. All should be planted in the house of the Lord, even built into it as an ornament and a support, and contributing in due measure to the firmness and comeliness of the building. In fact, however, the pillars—as compared with the lighter and more chaffy material—are few. The Church, as "the pillar and ground of the truth," is made up of the faithful ones, and by them the truth is exhibited and spread abroad. Between the real Church and the world there is this boundary between light and shade—a penumbra which partakes almost equally of the good and the bad.

Another aspect of Church pillars is given in the promise to the church in Philadelphia: " Him that overcometh will I make a pillar in the temple of my God, and he shall go no more out." The reference is probably to monumental pillars, as the promise continues: "And I will write upon him the name of my God, and the name of the city of my God, which is new Jerusalem, which cometh down out of heaven from my God; and I will write upon him my new name." A faithful Christian here is always a monument of grace. He bears inscriptions which God has written, but his office is service chiefly, rather than reward. To be made a pillar in heaven is the promise to him that overcometh. Whatever of this honor and glory comes within the experience here, the most is beyond earth, and in the world of light. Not every believer, by reason of extraordinary office or endowments, can be counted as a pillar in the house of God on earth, but the humblest who has overcome will be a pillar in heaven. And those who have been pillars in the militant church by their firmness and fidelity in the work of Christ, shall have the peculiar distinction of exhibiting through all eternity the love of Him who has redeemed them from sin and death.

From the earthly temple the pillars are removed; the strongest and most graceful are broken by age and death. The Jachin and Boaz of Solomon's temple, and the great temple itself, are no more. The pillars of Trajan, Pompey, and the Column Vendome must perish; the sculpture, the entablatures, the reliefs and hieroglyphics of ancient art, and all the devices and records of earthly heraldry, are doomed to pass and fade away. Him that overcometh shall alone bear the imperishable name and forever wear the memorials of triumph. "He shall go no more out." A monument of mercy and grace, shining resplendent with the glory of holiness and in the light of God, he is to shine on and forever. These are the pillar-saints of the Bible; not ascetics who have stood on pillars, but faithful workers in the Church below, crowned and emblazoned as pillars in heaven.

COUNTING THE COST.

THE Saviour introduces the cases of building a tower and of the king going to war to illustrate the importance of acquainting ourselves with the conditions of discipleship beforehand, and in vindication of his method of declaring to those who waited on his ministry what this discipleship implied. The illustrations are flanked by these strong declarations: "And whosoever doth not bear his cross and come after me cannot be my disciple." "So, likewise, whosoever he be of you that forsaketh not all that he hath, he cannot be my disciple." This was a severe method, apparently discouraging to awakened souls, and more calculated to repel than attract. But it was the Great Teacher's way, and, as he explains, the only true way. It was best that those who were concerned for their souls should fully comprehend the nature of his discipleship and the obligations which it imposed. Before laying the foundations of the tower, the cost of finishing it should be counted; before making war, the means of carrying it on should be estimated.

The illustration applies only to this one point: the absolute self-surrender and consecration which Christian discipleship demands. The help needed, the grace demanded to assure of perseverance are matters of promise and of faith. The question to be considered and settled at the outset is: Are we prepared to bear our cross and to forsake all that we have? The principle involved in those conditions runs through the entire Christian life. It describes a consecration of heart that is complete, and a life that is marked by self-sacrificing devotion. Christ's yoke is easy, but only so to those who take it; and his burden is light, but only so to those who bear it. After the surrender is made, and the service is heartily accepted, happiness flows in and satisfies the soul. In forsaking all, we gain all; and in bearing our cross, we attain to the fellowship of the Saviour's joy. Nevertheless, there is a yoke and there is a burden. If these are not consciously and willingly accepted—if all they involve is not apprehended—there is a fatal defect in our discipleship, and the probability is that the tower of Christian character will be left unfinished, and that the war upon which we have entered will end in humiliation and defeat.

Is it not better to lead inquirers on by some easier method, and to keep back these sterner features of discipleship until there has been some growth and maturity in experience? Can we not attract and lure people to Christ while these conditions are masked and wreathed with fragrant and encouraging promises? It is true that he who repents and believes shall be saved. He that is athirst may come, and whosoever will. Christ has said: "And him that cometh unto me I will in no wise cast out." He promises rest to the weary and heavy-laden if they will come unto him. And yet all these promises and invitations must be interpreted in the light of the declaration, "Whosoever he be of you that forsaketh not all that he hath, he cannot be my disciple." The Saviour puts this in the front of all his invitations, and insists that his discipleship is an impossibility until the surrender is made. What then? He would guard against self-deception, against a discipleship that was partial and wanting in reality and stability. The man who counted the cost and accepted Christ with all that the act implied, would hold out and be a disciple indeed; while he who followed impulses destitute of strong convictions would delude himself and fail in the end. The plain meaning of Christ's cautionary words is that a profession of religion, of faith in Christ, is a very serious and important step, and that people should know well what they are doing when they assume the vows of discipleship.

By whatever impulse moved, and under whatever influences, if there have been no self-surrender, no covenant of cross-bearing, no purpose of the absolute following of Christ, there is in the endeavor an element of weakness and failure. This kind of discipleship becomes a chronic seeking without finding, a periodical awakening which must be annually renewed—a religion that is utterly shallow, and devoid of living and abiding power. The cost of being a Christian must be counted at the start. The gate is strait herein. Christ puts the counting at the door of entrance. All sin must be given up, all unspiritual pleasures. Property and life must be laid upon the altar. Talents, learning, character, influence, time, must be devoted supremely to Christ; the affections, with the lusts, must be crucified. Here is a glance at the cost to be counted. Are we willing to have discipleship at this cost? Have we got our own full and unreserved consent to the surrender? If so, the way is open through faith into the holy of holies. The gleamings of the shekinah over the blood of the mercy-seat begin already to irradiate the soul. When the cost has been counted and accepted one great barrier to faith is broken down, and the way of the penitent to the cross is comparatively easy. He could never get there otherwise.

But we must not mislead. There are some who seem to halt between this self-surrender and faith. They have given up all, and yet the light does not dawn. Remember only a moral obstacle to faith has been removed, and faith does not look back even upon that, but forward and to the precious blood alone. Without giving up all we cannot believe unto salvation; but the giving up does not touch the ground of pardon. Christ is the whole and only ground. Faith leans not one particle upon our self-surrender, but rests entirely, confidently, peacefully on Christ.

Practically the great hinderance to discipleship and to salvation lies at this point of counting and accepting the cost. It costs too much in the way of self-denial, and men are unwilling to have discipleship on such terms. They are not persuaded in their own minds to give all for Christ. It is also the element of failure in thousands of professions that the conditions of a true discipleship have been overlooked. With no intelligent understanding of the duties and obligations assumed, religion has been a mere form, or the career has been of short duration. The tower that should have risen heavenward, strong and beautiful, is unfinished; the war that should have been crowned with victory ends in ignoble defeat.

GARMENTS NOT DEFILED.

WALKING in white in a dirty world requires no little care. There is uncleanness in every pathway, and the liability to jostle and contact is imminent. The clean and fine linen is easily soiled by the vile rubbish through which the saints have to pick their way to the better land. A capital part of every man's religion is this: "To keep himself unspotted from the world."

Even in our efforts to save people there is a timely admonition—"And others, save with fear, pulling them out of the fire, hating even the garment spotted by the flesh." It would seem that in pulling the fallen out of the ditch there is perilous risk of getting daubed with the slime. There is the possibility that in the effort at rescue we may get burned. Loving and pitying the sinner, we must keep up a most hearty hatred of the sin. "All things to all men" has this to qualify it: that we hate the spotted garment, and keep clear of any contagion there may be in it. Christians must not soil themselves in their ways and means of reaching and saving the world. The garments of the Church—the consciences and character of its members—are sometimes contaminated by dubious expedients. It is the filth of worldliness that is to be avoided—its spirit, frivolity, love of style and gain, its low motives, inordinate selfishness and love of pleasure. Catering to these may seemingly help the finances, and build brick walls and lofty spires, but it defaces and impoverishes the spiritual temple.

It is worldliness in its decent and respectable ways that is capable of defiling unawares. The pollen of flowers leaves a stain on the robe that brushes through the garden-walks. The very atmosphere of society is laden with the soot of unbelief and wickedness, and its polluting showers fall as silently and as unnoticed as the impalpable dust.

Sardis was a bad place, we have reason to believe, and only a few had escaped damage. It is noted rather as a wonder that any faithful ones should be found there. "Thou hast a few names even in Sardis which have not defiled their garments." There was one family worth saving from the flood, and one man with a portion of his family escaped from Sodom. There are more good people in proportion to the bad now, but the world is very much the same. It defiles the garments of the saints unless the followers of Christ look well to their ways and take heed to their steps. The Christian garb, smirched and mottled with avarice, fraud, and leesing, is an uncomely thing. Nothing is so repulsively untidy as robes pure and lustrous draggled in the mire, limp and begrimed with the foulness of the gutter. The defiled garment of Christian character and profession is a thing that may well excite the aversion as well as the pity and loathing of God and angels. Such objects are in every community. The plumage of more than angel-born, the crests of sons are seen drooping and besmeared with sensuality and diabolism. In the ways of business, of pleasure, of society, these spotted garments are trailed. The livery of what should be a holy and heavenly citizenship is flecked with the touches and pressures of evil associations and practices, and reeks with the odors and fumes of intemperance and lust.

And yet the blessed marvel is with us, in our world and in our day. It is something more than a perpetual miracle, and more extraordinary than if we were to see troops of angels in our fields, highways, and business marts—this fact that there are people who have not defiled their garments. This is the standing demonstration of our religion: the pure hearts and immaculate lives of at least a few who move about in the world and are not debauched and overwhelmed by its influence. If there is not much goodness, there is some. If not many, there are at least a few who have withstood the strong currents of worldliness and vice, and have kept themselves clean. The power of the gospel to save has its witnesses in every age, in every country, and in every community. There are names here and there bright and untarnished, shining like stars in the firmament, and attesting the greatness of redeeming grace and wisdom. Such exemplary piety may be comparatively rare, and yet there is altogether much of it. If in the worst of places there were a few names, we may believe that the aggregate of true devotion and faith is something to rejoice over. Proportionately there are doubtless far more holy souls and unblemished lives in the world than ever before, and we believe that the average type of our religion is higher and more complete than it was in those times when the few names were left in Sardis.

One of the worst forms of skepticism is that which doubts of all goodness, and cynically scouts at the reality of Christian purity. We are better for believing that there are clean hands and pure hearts, made so by the blood of Jesus and by the work of the Holy Spirit. The fact not only honors God and proves the gospel divine, but it lifts up to us all the possibility and the privilege of a like experience. How beautiful those lives must have been in their singular perfection, surrounded, as they were, by apostate professors and by the voluptuous vices of such a city as Sardis! How surpassingly beautiful are the holy lives we know of, made even more radiant by contrast with the wickedness of the age and by the general ungodliness of the world! It is the most delightful thought we can have in relation to the world—that there are good people in it, that there are souls sweet and pure in our midst, faithful ones whose garments show no stain.

It is not strange that the Master's prayer looked to this as the most vital of all interests. "I pray not that thou shouldest take them out of the world, but that thou shouldest keep them from the evil." The Saviour's concern was for the purity of his followers, the holiness of his Church —"not having spot or wrinkle or any such thing." The danger was from the evil of the world, that the garments might be defiled and the moral power lost. The disciples were needed in the world as its light, its salt, its salvation; but to be these they must be kept from the evil. They must keep themselves unspotted from the world, free from its covetousness, inordinate affection, and unbridled lust.

It would seem to stand for the highest eulogy upon the Christian that he has not defiled his garments. It means the consistent life, blameless conversation, the upright heart. And it must embrace much that is positive and active in the courageous confession and devoted service of Christ. It is not the life of the cloister, of the habitual recluse, but the stirring work of religious sacrifice, effort, and contact with the world in the great battle of Christian duty.

THE WORLD IN THE CHURCH

FORBIDDEN DIVERSIONS.

A PASTOR informs us that in the bounds of his circuit the people are almost universally given to social dancing-parties, and that it would be impossible to obtain a sound committee for the purpose of trying the offenders. We have reason to believe that this is not a solitary case. Such extreme instances may be exceptional, but everywhere there are these manifestations of the worldly spirit. In some places the worldly element has become so strong in the Church that the enforcement of discipline is exceedingly difficult, if not impracticable. This is an alarming state of things, and calls for serious consideration. How does it happen that the Church is largely composed, in places, of those who have no scruples on the subject of worldly amusement?

We fear that the General Rules are not read and explained from the pulpit as the Discipline requires. Once or twice a year the pastor should take a morning hour, in the presence of the largest congregations, for the purpose of enlarging upon the General Rules and of explaining the duties and obligations of membership in the Church. The pastoral address of the Bishops was ordered by the General Conference to be read to our congregations. Has this been done? In that address we have this: "An explicit utterance was given, by order of the last General Conference, in our pastoral address on the subject of worldly amusements. We now repeat that utterance. We abate none of its teachings with respect either to the manifest inconsistency of such indulgences with the spirit and profession of the gospel or the peril which they bring to the souls of men. Their multiplied and insidious forms are a source of perpetual temptation and damage, and are denounced by the word of God and by that part of our General Rules which forbids 'the taking of such diversions as cannot be used in the name of the Lord Jesus.' This denunciation is explicit and comprehensive. 'The name of the Lord Jesus' in this connection is a decisive test, and we are content to leave the issue to its sovereign arbitrament. Among those indulgences which cannot stand this solemn test is the modern dance, both in its private and public exhibition, as utterly opposed to the genius of Christianity as taught by us. When persisted in, it is a justifiable ground of judicial action by the Church authorities."

It will be seen from this extract that dancing is declared by the authoritative expounders of our Church law to be a justifiable ground of judicial action, and, by consequence, of expulsion from the Church; and yet there are thousands of members in the Church—not all of them young people —who pretend to believe that there is nothing in our rules which prohibits dancing and theater-going. Their ignorance may be owing to the fact that they do not read, and that their pastors have not taught them better.

There may be much backsliding after people get into the Church, but one reason for so much worldliness in the Church is owing to the way in which members are received. The door is not sufficiently guarded, and people are admitted before they have been instructed in reference to their duties and obligations. The Discipline says: "When persons offer themselves for Church-membership let the preacher in charge inquire into their spiritual condition, and receive them into the Church when they have given satisfactory assurance of their desire to flee from the wrath to come and to be saved from their sins; and also of the genuineness of their faith and of their willingness to keep the rules of the Church. When satisfied on these points, let the minister bring the candidates before the congregation whenever practicable, and receive them according to the prescribed form."

Are these points carefully inquired into by our preachers before the members are received? or do they not often receive them without having had any private conference with the applicants, and when it is almost certain that they have never read the Discipline, and that they know nothing about the General Rules? If there is any one point in a pastor's administration that should be more searchingly reviewed than another, it is whether he has fully complied with the law in the reception of members. The count of additions to the Church should go for little until we know how they have been received. It is far from clear that application for membership should be made publicly. Their reception is to be before the Church and by prescribed form; but as the applicant, if examined, may fail to give satisfaction, it would perhaps be better for the application to be made privately to the pastor. If after a thorough understanding of the rules and discipline of the Church—including the prohibition of dancing, drinking, theater-going, and the like—they are willing to assume the vows, their spiritual condition being satisfactory, they could then be received in accordance with the spirit and letter of the law.

Such carefulness in the reception of members would probably reduce the reported accessions, but we believe it would conduce to the soundness and spirituality of the Church. Under the old method of six months' probation, the worldly element was largely dropped without much trouble, but where no prescribed probation obtains we must insist that application for membership and reception into the Church be kept apart as separate and widely different transactions.

If people are invited to make application publicly, let it be well understood that it is an application, and is in no sense a reception into the Church. A prime cause of worldliness in the Church is in the careless way in which members are received. They are sometimes received while ignorant of our rules, unconverted, and not even thoroughly awakened. The world comes in at the door of admission, and until this is guarded against we shall continue to be troubled with dancing and theater-going people in the Church. We do not believe that guarding the door will effect a complete cure, but it will save the Church from being taken and governed by the world. We shall be able, at least, to maintain sufficient spirituality to administer discipline.

The business of the Church is, of course, to save as many souls as possible, but to this end she must keep herself pure and separate from the world, and maintain sound doctrine and strict moral discipline. The disposition in churches to bid for members as secular enterprises bid for patronage secures only an apparent and transient success. In the long run the "roomiest churches" will be empty or cease to be churches at all. Compromises with the worldly spirit may gain some members and keep them, but they are not saved thereby, and the spiritual power of the Church is weakened if not destroyed. Strictness in receiving members and in discipline after they are received will keep out some who will seek other and less scrupulous communions, but our gain in other directions will more than compensate. If the year's work foots up fewer members on the roll, the net result may be better. The count of the saved will be more, and the work will be more likely to stand the test of the fire in the revelations of that day.

LOOSE NOTIONS.

WE refer to the views which seem to obtain, to a considerable extent, among members of the Church in regard to sundry matters.

The observance of the Sabbath is one of them. It is not uncommon to take advantage of the cheap Sunday excursion-trains. A contemplated trip to the country, or return, may be made at one-fourth of the ordinary fare. If the cheap trains were run on week-days they would take them, but as they do not, our Christian friends pack up and go on Sunday. There is saving of some money. A country trip that otherwise might not be afforded is gained, but the law of God is violated. Can Christians afford to be economical in this way? Again, it happens that provisions for the Sabbath have not been made on Saturday. It may be the custom, or the housewife has "forgotten to take bread," and so the first thing on Sunday morning is a trip to the market. With some the day is largely devoted to visiting and dining, much more than to home reading and public worship. Some men of business, and others not particularly busy, cannot forego a visit to the post-office, and there are odds and ends of the week that demand a few moments at the store or a ride in the field

The relations of Christians to the whisky business ought to be above suspicion. As to its use, the Discipline takes the ground of total abstinence. Besides originating tract societies and Sunday-schools, Mr. Wesley put total abstinence into the organization of his societies. If a man who drinks liquor except in cases of necessity may be a good Christian, it is certain that he cannot be a good Methodist. In taking the vows of membership in the Church he has pledged himself to total abstinence. We doubt whether the habitual drinker of liquor can be a good Christian, but we are sure that the man cannot be who has solemnly vowed to abstain and yet continues to drink. The wrong of drinking carries with it the wrong of selling or buying liquor as a beverage. No reputable Christian will retail the poison; but do not some regarded as in good standing deal in the article in a wholesale way, or in connection with the more general business of groceries and supplies? The liquor business, if it must be tolerated by society, ought to be a specialty, and left altogether to worldlings and sinners. No Christian can touch it, even by wholesale, without defilement. It hurts his influence and damages his soul. The liquor trade yields large profits, no doubt, but these profits would be much less if all who profess to be Christians were to cease to use or buy or sell the miserable stuff. At any rate, the gain of sin is not for them.

Gambling—as, indulgence in games of chance—has a common principle in all its ramifications. The lottery, the card-table, the horse-race, the dice-box, and many other forms, come to the same thing. Betting on elections is in the same line, and attended with the most corrupting results in the politics of the country. The chance of getting much for little—or, practically, of something for nothing—is a severe test of principle. Gambling is bad as an amusement, because it becomes a passion. It is bad for the people, because it is unfriendly to industry, honesty, and labor, and because it impoverishes thousands where it makes one rich. Business gambling is as pernicious as any. It destroys confidence, unsettles values, and leads to the shipwreck of the most of those who indulge in it. The best business minds regard the inroad of the gambling spirit and methods into commercial affairs as a great evil. The dealing in futures certainly has about it something of the elements of a game of chance, and its influence in the business world is unwholesome in the extreme. By lottery-tickets, by futures, by other chance ventures, now and then somebody makes a fortune, and the fact is published, and multitudes are drawn into the vortex of ruin. Can a Christian consistently gamble, or touch that which has in it the gambling element?

There is a broad line between the kingdom of Christ and the world. Very loose notions prevail in regard to this distinction. What, in general, is the difference between a respectable worldling and a rather below average Church-member? Both may be found making the Sabbath a convenience for business or pleasure; both may be side by side selling whisky; both risking money on the same wild speculations or in schemes of chance; both filled with the love of the world; and both found together in the ball-room and the theater. With some sorts of religious people there seems to be no recognition of the principle and fact of a real separation from the world, and that in these days self-denial sacrifice, and even suffering, may be required in order to Christian fidelity. They accept things as they are, and do as the world does, oblivious of the broad distinction between Christian holiness and worldly-mindedness.

These loose notions concern the vital principles of practical righteousness, and their prevalence indicates a need of reform. The idea that people can gamble, dance, drink, sell whisky, and junket on Sunday with the world and as the world does, and yet save their souls, is a delusion that, with all its extravagance, needs to be exposed. Conformity to the world has always been a stumbling-block to the Church; and the most difficult thing in religious practice, as well as one of the clearest tests of religion pure and undefiled, is for the professed believer to keep himself unspotted from the world

RECREATION IN RELIGION.

THE Church is no more bound to furnish diversions for its people than it is to furnish them with employment. Religious principles apply to both, and the practical precepts of the Bible and rules of Church order and discipline indicate the line of Christian duty concerning them. If it be true that Christians must have amusements, and that the young people especially must have them, it does not follow that the Church is to furnish them. Religion is the business of the Church. Its mission is to preach the gospel, administer the ordinances, supply the means of grace, do what it can for benevolent and religious objects, and endeavor to bring the people to Christ.

Social reunions, however, under the guidance of pastors and Church-members, and conducted in accordance with the spirit of the gospel, may be productive of much good. Conversation, music, and literary entertainment might fill up the evening, and there would be a decided benefit socially to all concerned. In this direction our churches could do much more than they are doing to supply harmless and even beneficial diversions to the young people.

There is, apart from any expedients of this kind, an element of recreation in religion itself. As a relief from the weariness and cares of business and domestic affairs, there is nothing comparable to the duties of religion. The fatigued business man, the worried housewife, find refreshment in the weekly prayer-meeting. Nothing is more restful to the tired body and the exhausted nerves than an hour spent in social worship.

The craving for social intercourse is abundantly met and satisfied in the company of worshipers. The communion of saints is society in its religious aspects, and it is designed to be to the Christian what worldly society is to the worldly. Because of the higher purposes and benefits of religious association and worship, we are apt to underrate their value as a means of recreation. Thousands of people have scarcely any other society than that connected with their duties and relations to the Church, and the public and social services of the house of God are the only relief they have from the monotonous routine of secular affairs and daily toil. They find their recreation in their religion. Its duties are pleasant, and their spare time is occupied with them. The bow of care and labor is unbent, the strain upon mind and body is relaxed, and the isolation of home-life is expanded into a circle of the most congenial and helpful character.

Sunday with many religious people is a busy day. What with the Sunday-school, and the public services, and other meetings, the time is all occupied. And yet it is a change from the work of the week, and the effect is even more invigorating and refreshing than if the day had been spent in idleness and lounging at home. The Sabbath is indeed a day of true recreation to those who spend it in religious occupations. To those that labor, and to those that spend the day in pleasure-seeking, it is destructive of vitality.

The spiritually-minded Christian will find that his leisure is fully taken up with his religious duties, and the recreation there is in them will satisfy him. And this is about equal to saying that people who are zealously religious will have no desire to seek for mere diversions outside the path of religious duty. If the taste be formed for religious associations, and there be delight in religious services and exercises, and the mind and heart be filled and occupied with the truth and joy of divine wisdom, there will be no desire and no clamor for worldly amusements.

The recreation of spiritual men and women is in their religion, and not outside of it. Her ways are ways of pleasantness. There is cheerfulness, joy unspeakable, and the most delightful and satisfying entertainment in them. The services of religion are not a gloomy dirge nor a perpetual penance. They are not a yoke of bondage, a cruel task, nor a repulsive burden. Neither is religion in opposition to the healthy yearnings of our nature for that which shall entertain and invigorate. It is in itself the sum of all that is wholesome to the mind and body. It is the tree of life planted in the world to restore the wasting energies and to supply all the needs of the soul. It is every way and powerfully recreative. There is recreation in religion.

PERIL TO METHODIST EXPERIENCE.

THE Christian experience of the day is becoming confused and lamentably one-sided. The testimonies that we hear even in our Methodist love-feast in many cases lacks in the element of inward spiritual cleansing. One, and a very considerable current, seems to flow in the direction of a justification that is not attended by a conscious regeneration. Christ has paid the debt, and was delivered for our offenses. Resting in this, heaven is well assured. There may be no sense of victory over the easily-besetting sin, no realization of a pure heart, and yet there is confidence of being accepted, and of final salvation through the merits of Christ.

None hold to the atonement as the ground of pardon and final salvation more stringently than do our doctrinal standards; but we do not divorce this doctrine from that of sanctification. While Christ has paid it all, still without holiness no man shall see the Lord. There is a meetness of character, a personal righteousness, a purity of heart, that coincides with pardon, and goes along with it. It is this aspect of experience that has fallen out of our testimony to an alarming extent. The mere seeker and the backslider are now advanced to the front, often witnessing to an assurance of justification, based upon a mental operation rather than upon the felt power of a new life. Salvation is a matter of premises and conclusion, and not an actual sense of deliverance from the pollution and power of sin. Justification by faith is a wholesome doctrine, but it is a delusion to suppose that we are justified when sin still reigns in us and the fruits of the Spirit are unknown. The kingdom "is righteousness, peace, and joy in the Holy Ghost." The true believer receives the Spirit of adoption, crying, "Abba, Father!"

It has come to be a fashion to disclaim the very attainments in holiness which the Scriptures enjoin, and to seek to encourage the weak and troubled by relaxing the gospel demand of a perfect love. In some cases this may be the rebound from defective views of Christian perfection. It matters not how erroneously the doctrine has been advocated, we must insist upon a regenerated and sanctified nature, the attainment of personal holiness, and the witness of the Holy Spirit. The baneful breath of Antinomianism and of imputed righteousness is already to be detected in our love-feasts and in the common religious talk of many of our people. The heterogeneous muddle of doctrines in the so-called unsectarian evangelists of the past few years has helped to corrupt and mislead. The miscellaneous and popular religious songs put forth by irresponsible individuals, and eagerly caught up and used without discrimination in our social meetings, have contributed largely to the result. Our pulpits have in some degree given way to a shallow sensationalism, and our doctrines are not preached as fully and habitually as in other years. Do one-half of our people know the distinctive meaning of justification and sanctification? Are they made to realize that they may and must be saved from sin, and that the adoption of sons, with the corresponding Spirit of adoption, is a present inheritance and a blessing for the present hour?

Errors in doctrine are connected with false conceptions of experience. The true pulse of the Church may be better felt in the experience-meeting than anywhere else. And it is here that we think may be detected the beginnings of a serious disorder. There are false notes and discordant strains in the tone of our experiences. It is perhaps to be expected that the time of conversion and the attendant demonstration should be less marked now than fifty years ago. But conversion, as embracing faith in Christ and a new creature, must be the same. Inward holiness must not be dissevered from the clearest and strongest conceptions of Christ's merit as the ground of salvation. Our testimony needs to be strengthened in regard to the work and witness of the Spirit in the heart, and in regard to the cleansing power of the blood of Christ. We are glad to hear people declare that their purposes are right, and that they are trusting in the atoning blood; but we should be gratified to hear more about victory over sin and the blessedness of clean hearts.

The love-feast and the class-meeting are full of revelations and suggestions to the diligent and watchful pastor. He need not draw his bow at a venture if he be attentive to their voice.'

FAMILY RELIGION.

CHILDREN AT HOME.

IT is scarcely a home at all without children. A house in which there is none is desolate, whatever may be its spacious halls and rich upholstery. Grown people may move there in mirth and revelry, or live in quiet and orderly state; every thing may be kept prim and neat, with no traces of the disorder and abandon of young life; but there is a painful void. People who do not want children, and shun the care and worry of them, should by all means betake themselves to cloisters, or live, as troglodytes, away from the society of civilized men.

Not to sustain the parental relation is to be deprived of one of the most important conditions of our education. For moral and spiritual ends it is of invaluable service to have the parental affections awakened and developed, to be tried in our patience, and to feel the responsibility which the nurture and training of children demand. Where houses and people are childless through misfortune, Providence may have some compensating provisions; but the loss is one so serious that we can scarcely see how there can be any full reparation.

Parents can understand better than others those declarations and promises of Scripture that refer to this relation: "If ye, being evil, know how to give good gifts unto your children, how much more will your heavenly Father give the Holy Spirit to them that ask him?" Parents come nearer fathoming the fatherhood of God than even the angels do. They have a peculiar appreciation of the gift of the only-begotten Son. Do they not get deeper into this profound and affecting passage than the seraphim: "He that spared not his own Son, but delivered him up for us all, how shall he not with him freely give us all things?" There is a richness of tenderness and pathos in the parable of the prodigal son which none but fathers and mothers wholly comprehend. They have in them the image of the divine paternity, and are brought into completest sympathy with the highest manifestations of divine love and compassion. There are chords in the human heart which it would seem that God himself cannot make to vibrate except through the parental relation. It opens the understanding to some of the grandest disclosures of revelation, and presents a distinct field for the display of submission under sanctified sorrow. Children in the house, whether they are there to live or die, are a blessing. Their being and training call forth a class of affections and antagonize a selfishness which nothing else can reach. Their life is a discipline which has no substitute, and their death is a sorrow that has no kinship in the category of afflictions.

The home is the school of the children in it. Their characters are formed there, there they take their departure for a career of virtue and usefulness or for a course of vice, and to be the pests of society. Outside influences for evil are to be counteracted by the training in the family. Here —and effectually nowhere else—can they be fortified against the temptations which await them in the world. Neither secular nor Sunday schools can be intrusted with the work which must be done by the parents at home. Religion, morals, industry, neatness, practicalness, self-help, good manners, must all be taught in the house and in the childhood period. Herein parents should have no need of priests or dancing-masters. The home circle and the fireside should be the school-room for piety and politeness.

There is no adequate substitute for a good home, and to the young there is no privation more calamitous. In some families there is a tyranny that rebounds after awhile, and the children are the worse for it. Cunning, duplicity, and falsehood are fostered, and filial love and reverence are destroyed. In other households there is anarchy. The children run riot with excess of license, and are an annoyance to parents and guests. The broken chairs, the torn curtains, dirt, and general disorder, show the lack of all restraint. It is a positive trial to visit houses where the children govern the parents. The visitor feels embarrassment for the good, easy-going, slipshod, over-indulgent mother in her futile endeavors to quiet the chronic rumpus and to secure temporary peace. Surely there is a more excellent way. Government there must be; obedience must be exacted; and in well-ordered homes the children are olive-plants, green and beautiful and beautifying, and not nettles and stinging cactuses.

We think of the model household as having in it not a lone child kept as in a bandbox, but a group of merry, romping, loving boys and girls, from the elder ones blooming into their teens to the little bud that is the care and pet of all. They are not to be too neat in their every-day clothes, and there are looseness and comfort in their array rather than any affectation of expense and style. And this bunch of little folk is instinct with the spirit of obedience and deference to the parental will, with no trace of painful fear, but with every element of sunshine and gladness in it. Obedience, rightly implanted, brings in its train truth, honor, candor, and conscience.

About the rod and its use we cannot enter at large. The things we have indicated must be secured somehow, and generally they can be without much use of the classic birch. We have no quarrel with Solomon, but he turned out badly himself, and his children were not models. As a rule, the whipping should be done before the child is ten years old, and not much need be done after the sixth year. More children have been spoiled and ruined by harsh and injudicious use of the rod than have been saved by its wise application. Since we have been living in a large city, with close neighbors, we have rarely been free from the annoying screams and cries of whipped children. It is a nuisance, an evil, a barbarous cruelty throughout the world that needs to be abated. A parent irate, frenzied with anger, belaboring a helpless and ill-instructed child, ought to be indicted for felony. The rod may be good in some cases, but few parents have the wisdom, grace, and patience to use it aright. Firmness, love, prayerfulness, and self-control will be more effective than the harsher course with the average child.

THE BIBLE AT HOME.

GOD's Book was given us to be read. Some parts are more important and edifying than others, but every part is worth attention, and none should be neglected. It should be gone through in regular course from Genesis to Revelation. Portions adapted to our immediate condition and wants should be selected as occasion arises; but the habit of reading the Bible regularly through should be maintained.

The Bible should not be merely read; it should be studied, meditated on, and searched in a prayerful spirit. In general, we imagine Christians take too little pains in this matter, and that they devote too little time to it. Other books have usurped the place of *the* Book, and newspapers, magazines, and novels leave but a fragment of time for the word of God. It is a busy age, and many are occupied overmuch with the affairs of life. Remember, however, that the busiest must die, and that the treatment of God's

Book will be brought up in judgment. The Bible is entitled to our greatest care; it must be the first not only in our reverence, but in our actual use.

What we write now is for Christians in their private home-life. How are you treating the Bible? how do you read it? how much do you know of it and about it? We like to see Bibles about the house well worn, showing use, and with the signs of wear on the binding and gilding, and the pages opening with facility almost anywhere. Every one should have his own Bible, and be familiar with the location of its chapters and paragraphs. A neighbor's house may be just like ours, but we are more at home in our own. There are margins, fly-leaves, and marks that we appropriate, and the volume comes at length to have a history and many blessed associations. It is an old traveling companion; it has witnessed many trying ordeals in our lives; there are upon its pages the stain of storms and shipwrecks and the print of tears.

But the main thing is to read it understandingly. "Understandest thou what thou readest?" Do not pass over a verse without letting this question have its full force. Determine to find out the mind of the Spirit as far as possible, and bring all your thoughts to bear upon the words under your eye. A little self-examination will probably expose our ignorance and carelessness, and show how unworthily we have handled the word of life.

The reading will be a means of deepening piety, and the soul will be fed as it can be fed nowhere else. Without familiarity with the Bible the Christian cannot pray to much purpose, nor can he get the largest benefits from the preaching and ordinances of God's house. To be eminently useful, to have a uniform and stable experience, and to be truly happy in our religion, we must see to it that the word of Christ dwells richly in us. To stand and to be panoplied for the holy war, first of all the loins must be girt about with truth. To young Christians and to the old, to all who would keep themselves in the love of God, and persevere till the crown is gained, Bible-reading is of the first importance. There can be no permanent, vigorous, growing spiritual life without it.

PRAYER IN THE FAMILY.

THE first Church was a family Church, the first priesthood and ministry were over a household, and the first social prayer was doubtless in the home circle. It is not needful to be argued out, or set forth in the form of scriptural proof, that there should be prayer in the house. Our Methodist rules assume that it is one of several other duties which the "Spirit writes on truly awakened hearts." Such persons may neglect it, they may decline the performance from lack of courage, or from fancied incapacity, but they cannot be clear in their consciences.

It is good for the whole family—wife, children, guests, and servants—to worship God in this way. Even the cats and dogs and other domestic animals come to recognize the usage, and seem the better for it, though they may not understand the import as fully as their masters. Servants may avoid participation, but they feel the influence, and are conscious that God is under the roof as well as above it. Careless and ungodly neighbors come to know it, and in spite of themselves look upon that house as different from theirs, and better. It is a testimony to the world without, witnessing for the truth, and preaching in an humble way. Going to Church is in the line of respectability, and deep piety need not be supposed; but prayer and praise daily at home indicate more than conformity to the habits and fashion of a community. Can that be called a religious home in which there is no family worship? The world says nay, and so say we. There may be pious individuals in it, but there is no Church in the house. It does not stand in the aggregate as a religious household, and its testimony in this capacity is wanting.

The family is a good place in which to learn to pray. One can afford to pray indifferently here till practice gives greater facility and self-possession. It is a good school of training for the prayer-meeting and the public congregation and for the sick-room. People who do not pray in the family usually pray nowhere except in secret. Shrinking from the cross at home, it cannot be borne elsewhere.

After all endeavors to excuse themselves, we imagine that this omission rests as a cloud upon the consciences of many fathers and mothers. They cannot be quite satisfied, nor altogether easy, and there is a shade of God's displeasure upon them. They are living in the neglect of a means of grace and of an ordinance which is necessary for the welfare of their children. Without estimating the degree of guilt, or condemning too severely, we are persuaded that heads of families often lose ground and finally fall away altogether for the want of this most helpful assistant to godly living. The sons and daughters of a prayerless house cannot be expected to go out into the world braced for the inevitable conflict with sin and fortified against temptation. They have never heard the father pray, they have never heard him read the Bible, they have never felt the gracious dews which distill about the home altar. Their filial reverence and affection have never been raised and purified by the noblest exhibition of paternal dignity and love. The father who does not pray with his family never rises to the highest and best realization of his position as the head of his household.

Prayer operates as a restraint upon doubtful and hurtful pastimes. It gives a sanctity to the home which rebukes and excludes reveling and pernicious games. Dancing and cards are not likely to be allowed where the morning and evening sacrifices are regularly offered. The houses of professors of religion may sometimes be desecrated by these practices, but not the homes that are hallowed by family worship. They cannot well exist in the same atmosphere and be indulged in the same hour with prayer. Whatever is hurtful to the Christian life will be banished by the erection of the family altar.

Prayer in the family requires a deep and consistent piety. Wife, children, and servants know us better than we are known in the Church or in the community. Conscious inconsistency in temper, language, and manners is an embarrassment which reaches its closest quarters at home. It is hard to pray with those who know our faults too well. Careful living and much grace are the conditions of free and comfortable praying in the family.

As to the manner there should be time, each one should take part in reading the Scriptures, and all should join in the Lord's Prayer. If not always, yet occasionally let the Commandments and the Apostles' Creed, as given in connection with the vows of baptism and Church-membership, be repeated by all. Singing should not be omitted. At least sing the doxology to Old Hundred or Sessions. Let there be always this much of praise. The Scripture-lesson should usually be short, attended sometimes with brief exposition and questions, and let the prayer be short. Do not weary and disgust the children by prolixity in any thing, and let the whole service be lively and cheerful. It is family worship, the Church in the house; the children are all members, and let all have something to do. There are no aliens, no outsiders, no strangers here. The promise is to you and to your children: "Thou shalt be saved, and thy house." It is the place to gather the family under the wings of Jehovah, and to adore and praise him who hath "set the solitary in families."

THE SON OF THINE HANDMAID.

DAVID, in times of great distress, recalls the character of his mother, and pleads with God the fact that she was a handmaid, or servant of the Lord. "Give thy strength unto thy servant, and save the son of thine handmaid." Himself a servant, he was also the son of God's servant. He was not only devoted to God, and of his own choice the servant of the Most High, but his mother before him had been faithful in her allegiance to Israel's God. He thus recalls his mother, and dwells with peculiar satisfaction and comfort on her religious life. It strengthens his faith and it encourages his trust in God, and he seems to urge it as a reason for divine deliverance. As a servant, he brings himself within the range of many gracious promises; but as the son of God's handmaid, he seems to regard himself as entitled to the benefit of other promises—of such as are given to parental piety and faithfulness. As the sins of parents, their negligences and their evil example, fall upon the children in many ways, so parental piety leaves an inheritance of manifold blessings to them.

He doubtless felt that, having honored his godly mother by obeying her counsel and walking in her footsteps, this might be pleaded in connection with the promise to faithful and obedient children. He might also have many precious memories of the lessons received at his mother's knees, the prayers she habitually put up for him, and of some special act of declaration in which she had dedicated her child to God. We hear often in the history of the father Jesse, and the title "son of Jesse" is of frequent occurrence. In one of the grand Messianic Psalms it is impressively applied: "The prayers of David, the son of Jesse, are ended." But to the mother there is hardly an allusion, except the two which David makes, and in these she is simply described as "thine handmaid." Why should he not have pleaded the piety of his father as well, and have dwelt upon his uprightness and his character as God's servant? That he was a man of pure and righteous character we have no reason to doubt, and yet the son of Jesse is still more the son of his mother. He honors her with such mention as indicates his deepest love and reverence, and as if his own character, as the servant of the Lord, were the outgrowth of hers as the Lord's handmaid.

We gather from these references that the mother's memory was habitually cherished, and that the impress of her teachings and example was such as to leave a lasting influence, and also that her relation to God, as "thine handmaid," was to him a source of strength and hope. He had come to a throne, and had come to be possessor of great riches and power. Great and famous as he was, he refers to his mother, and counts it as his greatest honor that she was a servant of God, and that he had walked in the same path. It was something to be thankful for that he had such a mother; and the thought of her in his troubles was an inspiration to his faith and trust in God. Besides the broader field of promises which her relation to God opened to David's mind, there may have been also the remembrance of her prayers, and the feeling that the power of them still lingered at the throne, and might be as a shield to him in times of calamity. She may have been long dead, but he felt that her consecrated life and her fervent prayers were not forgotten before God. He prays as if God's strength and deliverance were somehow to reach him through her, and that, beyond his own relation to God as his servant, and beyond his own faith, hers were to be counted and were to contribute to his welfare. He seems to feel that his mother stood related to him and to God as the highest of any earthly priesthood. In his great trial, while he flies to God and hides himself in his pavilion, he also nestles in the bosom that pillowed his infant head. He comes to him who dwells between the cherubim for refuge and support, and yet in his coming he is emboldened by the memory of his mother's exemplary and holy life. He had not ceased to feel the power of it in his own heart, and he also felt that God had not forgotten it. Sure of being the servant of God, and claiming promises on that score, he strengthens his case and makes his position firmer by reference to his mother's holy and consecrated service. In this hour of conflict and of prayer the only earthly name and the only human memory are the name and memory of his mother. No other influence is like this in its depth and power; no other—except that of God himself—so penetrates the whole being and survives the changes and fortunes of life.

But for these brief allusions we should have known almost nothing of David's mother; but, brief as they are, they disclose the fact that the greatness, glory, and piety of her royal son were chiefly due to her as the Lord's handmaid. All this is the reiteration of a commonplace truth, and only an illustration of a mother's influence. And yet it is an illustration drawn from a somewhat peculiar aspect of that influence, as having its highest manifestation in the cry of the soul after God.

Happy is the son who can revere his mother as the handmaid of the Lord, and who, though dead, yet speaks by the faith which she exhibited. And happy is the mother who realizes the responsibility of her position, and who, as God's handmaid, consecrates her children to Christ, and stamps them indelibly with her own pure and heavenly character. Genuine piety in the mother cannot fail to tell upon the character of the children; but it must be of such depth and of such a type as to command the respect and the love of the children. There are thousands of devoted mothers, unselfish, careful, affectionate, blameless in general deportment, and attentive to the ordinary needs of their children; but the impression upon their children is not that they are first and chiefly the servants of God. Their religion is not the main thing, their nearness and consecration to God do not so dominate the character and life as to make these the most memorable things in the thoughts and memories of their children. The mother's religion is apt to be that of the child. The son who has not seen it so exemplified in her as to command his respect and his conviction of its truth and excellence may doubt of it ever afterward. A mother's piety is about the strongest bulwark against the attacks of skepticism and the inroads of vice that a young man can have. Her character as a Christian should be so decided, so unquestioned, and so clear in its exhibition of the Christian graces as to refute every device of the adversary of the soul. Fortunate are the children who in the hour of adversity can gain heart and hope from the recollection of a mother's piety, and who, even in their prayers, can make mention of her as "thine handmaid."

SOUL EDUCATION.

TRAINING FOR THE LIFE TO COME.

IT gives dignity and importance to the most insignificant things in our experience if we habitually look upon them as a part of our education for the future world. There are a thousand little things—important for the present welfare—that we do not regard as having any bearing upon the endless hereafter. The child is taught industry, economy, and thrift, because these elements of character are the conditions of success in this world. He is given a practical education, is taught such branches as have an immediate application in his daily work. He learns a trade that he may win his bread and provide for his temporal comfort. Thus a great part of the training of youth has reference mainly to the preparations for the life that now is.

The toil of men in the field of active pursuits is incited, first of all, by the great argument of necessity. Food and raiment and an enjoyable home can only be secured by the drudgery of daily labor. Much of it is spent in menial services or in attention to details which in themselves have no interest or significance whatever. The farmer plods wearily after the plow. It is the same dull round of sowing and reaping, and the effort to extort from the soil that which is yielded with reluctance to his persevering industry. The mechanic shoves the plane and drives nails; he lays brick and plasters walls; he builds houses and repairs them. The thrifty housewife is busy all the day with the affairs of kitchen, laundry, and the sweeping, dusting, and mending and making. Woman's work is never done, and much of it is made up of items both petty and irksome. Clerks, sewing-women, agents in all sorts of business, find nothing in their tasks beyond the money they command. It is very much the same with the merchant who is engrossed with the management of heavy operations, and with lawyers and doctors who spend their lives in ministering to their clients and patients.

What a world of care, anxiety, and weariness is represented by these manifold aspects of human activity and toil! And then we are to consider in this connection the failures, the poverty, the sore travail, the sharp pain of body, the heart-aches that are incidental to almost every condition. Surely all must have large reference to our eternal future. They must be for our learning not with sole nor with chief regard to this world. There must be something in these petty and groveling affairs which necessarily occupy the most of our time that tells upon a nobler future. The earthly ends are ennobled by the love and sacrifice and patience that are in them. But these ends are only shadows of something higher. The discipline of the boy which fits him for the work of this life is also fitting him for some grander arena, and that which prepares him for his work here only introduces him to the more thorough school which is to complete his character and open to him the boundless future.

The real discipline is in the practical and the arduous pursuits, in the duties which in themselves we loathe, and in the things that annoy, vex, and disgust us. For a time it would seem best that we should be bound down to the clods of earth, and that the powers and aspirations which have been divinely breathed into us should for awhile be chastened and repressed by this worldly turmoil and care. Out of this dark and trying condition pure and noble souls come up like the verdure and bloom that spring from the garden mold. It is the hardness of our lot in this ever-pressing round of trivial cares and labors that makes up the training element in it. The discipline that comes from what is seemingly mean and contemptible is what the soul needs for its future destiny. The temptation to fret and pine under this dispensation of forced and uncongenial toil must be met and cured by the abiding conviction that it is a stage in the process by which the blossoms and fruitage of the skies are to be reached.

We do not now refer to the discipline of affliction in its deepest manifestation. It is more difficult to see the good in our allotments of lowly toil and exacting and wearisome duties than it is to realize the mission of sorrow and bereavement. Our self-respect and our claims upon the respect of others are raised consciously by mighty and exceptional griefs. These griefs command the homage of men as they do the special notice of the divine promises. They lift the soul up so powerfully and so graciously that a sense of their exalting influence is felt and realized. But these daily and hourly servitudes, and this inexorable bondage to the tyranny of earthly needs, require a patience, submission, and a faith of a higher order.

Our blessed Lord, found in fashion as a man, " took upon him the form of a servant." The most of his earthly life was probably spent in Joseph's work-shop. Obscure toil was his. Those were long years—weary ones—that he spent in such work as the poorest peasant might have done. The healing hands, the miracle-working hands, the hands afterward lifted in blessings as he ascended, were used to the rough tools of the carpenter. This mind of minds, this grandest and purest of souls, was for a period subjected to the ordeal of the most lowly and the most trying of earthly conditions. It was a part and much the longest period of his human training. It is so with the most of his disciples. We are moving in the Master's footsteps, if the training be accepted by us with a contented and courageous spirit. There is a joy set before us as there was before him. Those who endure and labor with cheerful patience shall in due time go up from this training-school to the thrones and glories of the brighter world.

AT THE FEET OF JESUS.

THIS is the attitude of a true disciple. It is expressive of humility, docility, dependence. The disciple has every thing to learn. He is ignorant; he may be under the dominion of error, and he comprehends but partially and imperfectly the things which make for peace and righteousness. He is a learner, and is willing and anxious to be taught. He sits at Jesus' feet. His heart is open, his ear is attent, his eye is upon the gracious Teacher. He is more absorbed in him than in the outward affairs of life. These may occupy his hands and make his daily hours busy with the cares of the world, but he does not withdraw himself from Christ. He may intermeddle with all knowledge, and study what the great and good have written; but Christ alone is his Master, and directly from him he receives the word of life. The art of Christian discipleship, if such an art there be, is in this absolute deference and submission to Christ, and all real disciples are taught of God through Christ. Mary "sat at Jesus' feet, and heard his word." This is a picture of beauty as clearly cut as a cameo, and as spirited in its lines as the most exquisite engraving. It stands for all time as the best type of the humble, unworldly, reverent, studious disciple as a learner in the school of Christ. It illustrates the Master's words: "Take my yoke upon you, and learn of me; for I am meek and lowly in heart, and ye shall find rest unto your souls." All the riches of wisdom and knowledge are hid in Christ, and it is at his feet that these riches are discovered to us. The attitude of the soul toward Christ is every thing. The glory of the Lord will never be seen in his face until in humility, self-abasement, and faith we sit at his feet. The glory beams only upon those who look up, and the rays fall only upon the lowly and contrite ones. We may be sure that Jesus delights in such disciples; but how complete and satisfying is the joy of those who have come to realize that Christ is their Teacher and Lord!

There is in him the teaching of himself. The Teacher is himself "the power of God and the wisdom of God." If he had only lived and said nothing, the light flashing from his person would have been greater than that which shines in the words of prophets and scribes. If man never spake like this man, it is also true that never man lived like this man. In other cases the treasure is in earthen vessels, but in him it is in a golden. His teaching life and his teaching character are absolutely perfect. At the feet of such a person we can sit, and feel that we are honored by such intimacy. Whatever he may say, the background of his personality is steadily luminous. He is himself the great lesson, and the faultless illustration of a perfect and glorious manhood. It is not so of Moses, Paul, or John. In them the ideal is blurred, and the outlines, at some points, are indistinct. In Christ the Teacher himself is perfect.

When we pass to the word-teaching of Christ we have at least the seed-truths of all truth and the words which are spirit and life. Here we sit at his feet not only when we study his own words, but also when we pore over those of Christ-inspired men. It is the Spirit of Christ in them that gives authority to the words of evangelists and apostles. We sit at the feet of Paul only as he sits at the feet of Christ; and thus, whether our text be in the prophets, Gospels, or Epistles, we sit at the feet of Jesus and hear his word. The Spirit of Christ is the inspiration of all Scripture, and in some sense it is true that the devout in all ages have sat at the feet of Jesus. The disposition of the heart and the recognition of a personal Redeemer have been the same. In this inquiring, receptive state of mind, how powerfully and clearly Christ teaches! Under the spell of his words, how the heart burns, and how the whole Bible glows with promises and consolations! The good part, once chosen at the feet of Jesus, becomes a precious treasure that cannot be wrested from us. It is there that the heart surrenders, the final choice is made, and the imperishable blessing is received.

In some degree all true believers are taught by the Spirit. How much and how truly depends upon this attitude of discipleship! The "Spirit of truth" was given to those who sat at the feet of Jesus after he ascended. They were at the feet of their invisible and glorified Lord when the baptism of fire came upon them. It is while at his feet that the Spirit of the Son is sent forth into our hearts, "crying, Abba, Father!" "For God, who commanded the light to shine out of darkness, hath shined in our hearts, to give the light of the knowledge of the glory of God in the face of Jesus Christ." Christ teaches through the Spirit, even as he is glorified by the Spirit. This is the complement of his office as our Teacher, and the completion of the work. The need of the Holy Spirit is absolute. We have sat at the feet of Christ to little purpose if we have not realized this divine illumination and felt the presence of the Comforter. How and where is the gift of the Holy Spirit to be sought? It is at the feet of Jesus. This attitude of discipleship includes all the conditions. Divested of pride, purged of self, humble, contrite, believing with the whole heart open and waiting and expecting the promised blessing. The only difficulty is in coming to Jesus—sitting at his feet. It is only the upward look—the eye that gazes from the lowliest vale of humility—that gets so much as a glimpse of the spirit-giving Saviour.

What fullness of blessings are for us in Christ, in him who lived that we might learn of him, who spake that we might hear, and who ascended that he might flood the trusting and waiting soul with supernatural light! At Jesus' feet is the only place of rest and peace. Here only have the perplexed and the sorrowing, the guilty and the penitent, found rest unto their souls. At Jesus' feet, if we can only get there and there abide, we shall be so charmed with the sweetness and quietude of its bliss as to desire nothing more this side of heaven.

WAITING FOR THE LORD.

THIS attitude of waiting is insisted upon by Christ and by the apostolical writers. It is the condition of readiness and of preparation for the end. Whether of the end of the world, the end of existing order of society and of governments, or their own end, the substance of the admonition is to be ready. To be prepared for the second coming of Christ and for the final judgment is to be ready for whatever may happen. In such a state the Christian is ready for tribulation, for bereavement, for tumults and revolution, for sickness, and for death. If it be a definite looking for the personal coming—for the great *parousia*—this insures a spiritual readiness for whatever may come to pass. "Looking for that blessed hope, and the glorious appearing of the great God and our Saviour Jesus Christ," is connected with the operations of the grace of God in the heart. To "love his appearing" is a mark of the true believer.

This looking and loving is, however, consistent with the

conviction that the manifestation of Christ is yet very distant. Ages may roll between us and that event, and it may come long after we have entered the paradise of God. All this does not affect the blessedness of the hope nor the waiting for the Lord's coming. Whether here on earth battling with temptation and sin, or yonder in the home of those who have entered into rest, the looking, the waiting, the expectation are common to all the saints. We are waiting and they are waiting, "that they without us should not be made perfect." This polar star of hope never sets, but shines alike upon those who linger on earth and upon those who have crossed the flood. Every eye is turned toward this grandest and most momentous event. Every sanctified heart on earth and in glory is yearning for the appearing.

As to ourselves, this waiting is practical. It is not a state of inaction, of wonder-worship, of indifference to the duties of life. The loins are girded, and the lights are burning, and the servants are diligently improving the gifts intrusted to them. There is no fanatical excitement, no interruption of the work given us to do. Rather does this expectation quicken the spiritual life and incite to greater zeal in laboring for the spread of the gospel and for the salvation of the world. If saved at all, the world must be saved before "the appearing of the great God and of our Saviour Jesus Christ." The grace of God and the present instrumentalities must achieve the salvation of the human race. The coming of Christ is the end, the consummation of all things, the last judgment, and the final and complete reward and glorifying of the good.

With reference to such results, how necessarily the belief leads to vigilance, to the diligent use of the grace and opportunities given, and to ever-increasing effort to advance the cause of Christ. It is the hour of our opportunity and of our responsibility. We know not when the end may come; but our accountability will be gauged by its imminence—by the possibility of its coming at any time. How much time God will give the Church to execute the great commission cannot be known. He never intended that we should know, and he has left it in obscurity, that every generation should do its utmost to bring the world to Christ. The premillennial theory, based upon the idea that present gospel methods are a comparative failure and that the personal reign of Christ on earth is to bring in more powerful and effectual means of bringing men to repentance, is a theory that paralyzes effort and weakens faith. Consistently with such a theory, we might wait inactive and with folded hands, and our missionary zeal might sleep until the voice of the archangel and the trump of God call us to awake. It is, however, the delay of that trump and the silence of that voice that loudly call us to action. The world must be saved before the Lord descends from heaven with a shout; and our own souls must be arrayed in righteousness, and we must be perfected in love before that day.

Waiting is, therefore, working. It is laying broad and deep foundations, and building for the ages. It is an intense realization of the fact that the gospel is the only hope of the world, and that there is nothing more in the way of means and instrumentalities to come forth from God. The coming that saves and redeems is already consummated and at work; the coming that judges and glorifies is that for which we look. How would preachers preach, how would Christians live, how would they all run in the race of usefulness, if they were thus waiting for their Lord? Their greatest readiness would be in their complete consecration and in the absorbing endeavor to pluck from the fire as many brands as possible.

And yet there is a waiting that is full of self-deception and danger—a current talk about a millennium that is to usher in a new and different dispensation, and in which the old gospel methods are to be superseded. Perhaps the servant who buried his talent was one of these sincere but deluded souls. He was waiting for his Lord, but not wisely waiting. He was looking for him, but only to be met with rebuke and shame. The foolish virgins were also waiting for their Lord, and they slept the sleep of carnal security. They thought they were ready, but the doors of heaven were shut against them. The true waiting is thus distinguished from the false. It is a right apprehension of what the Lord's coming is—a coming to judge, to punish, and to reward, and a coming that closes the gospel offer to the world. It is such a life as takes its tone and impetus from a blessed hope that also rivets upon the conscience and heart the vast issues involved. This true waiting brings Christian men face to face with their great and fearful responsibilities, and arouses in them all the faith and zeal and watchfulness of a trumpet-blast from the throne of judgment. Waiting for their Lord, they are in the vestibule of eternity, in the ante-chamber of the august Presence, and in joyous readiness to lay their charges down at the Master's feet. Waiting here with fidelity, they move at length into brighter conditions of waiting until he comes.

CHRISTIAN DUTIES.

THE DUTY OF PLEASING.

THERE are cynical and half brutal natures that take an evident satisfaction in crossing the desires and thwarting the plans of others. They are rough, uncouth, and disobliging in their intercourse for no other apparent reason than that they like so to be. It is a way they have of asserting their individuality and independence, or of taking their revenge for the selfishness and wrong which they imagine the world has shown toward them. Those who have, through long and severe struggles, attained to wealth, and feel themselves masters of the situation, are often harsh and inconsiderate in their dealings with subordinates and with those who have been less successful in life. They sought to please when there was an object and when there were selfish ends to gain, but when secure in their wealth and position, they became domineering and repellant. Prosperity often mars the manners and destroys their amiability. The outward deportment becomes worse as the man's circumstances become improved.

There are also stern types of morality, and even of godliness—men and women, in their way both benevolent and devout, who regard it as a sin to make themselves perfectly agreeable. They act as if they feared some danger in the ordinary amenities of social intercourse, and as if remembering to be courteous would somehow compromise their high calling and stain the garments of their Christian profession. Their principles are good. They are stanch in asserting them and conscientious in making them as repulsive as possible to those of a different persuasion. As the carnal mind is enmity against God, and as the cross is foolishness to the natural man, they would, as they believe, be chargeable with wickedness to attempt to conciliate the world. There is offense in the cross, and it is a mark of fidelity in the Christian that he make himself other than agreeable to the worldly. So far from seeking to please, they would regard such a course as a betrayal of the grace of God. They are religious scolds and ascetics, who are really better than they seem. They are such saints as children are afraid of, and such as Christians of a sunnier mold respect rather than love.

The art of pleasing as it exists in society is for the most part selfish. True politeness is the expression of benevolence in little things. In social intercourse, and in all our relations with one another, it is a thing of great value. A right-minded and intelligent Christian must be polite. Charity "doth not behave itself unseemly." And yet the pages of Chesterfield exhibit the hypocrisy and the immoral designs which are often underneath the garment of outward elegance and decorum. The money-shaver is the blandest of men until he gets his victim in his power. It pays for the dealer to show his wares with a smile upon his face. The good salesman is the man with good manners. We are indebted to sharp competition for three-quarters of all the politeness that is shown us in business intercourse and on the thoroughfares of travel. To make headway in society, in business, or in politics, people must be affable. Popularity is cultivated as the means to the attainment of selfish ends, and as the path of success in securing wealth, influence, and honor.

It is not unlikely, however, that with the most of people it is pleasant to please. If no self-interest is sacrificed thereby, they would rather make themselves agreeable than repulsive. They rise above indifference, and would rather impart pleasure when it is in their power to do so. It may be akin to selfishness, and it may be something better. It may not spring from any high principle, but if a wild flower it has a certain beauty and fragrance. We meet with teasing, hectoring spirits now and then; but they are the exceptions, and with them humor is largely in the ascendant. It is their way of giving and receiving pleasure.

We come out of all these aspects of the subject to the high Christian assertion of the duty of pleasing. Paul was a gentleman indeed, and in his inspired moods he was careful to say, "Let every one of us please his neighbor for his good to edification;" and he points to the perfect Example when he declares: "For even Christ pleased not himself; but as it is written, The reproaches of them that reproached thee fell on me." This was a principle of action in all his intercourse with men. He was probably the most courteous and affable man of his age. There was nothing gruff or boorish about him. He writes to his brethren, and cites his own uniform course: "Give none offense, neither to the Jews, nor to the Gentiles, nor to the Church of God; even as I please all men in all things, not seeking mine own profit, but the profit of many, that they may be saved." We know not how the Christian duty of pleasing could be set forth more completely. The end is purely a benevolent one, divested utterly of the hollowness and selfishness which often taint the elegances and courtesies of worldly intercourse.

Christians do well to study this masterly exhibition of a duty which, in its highest import, is too much neglected. No principle is to be compromised, no truth is to be surrendered; and yet we are to seek to please, to make ourselves as attractive and agreeable as possible, and with the single purpose of benefiting our neighbor—"Not seeking mine own profit, but the profit of many, that they may be saved."

The art of pleasing is not to be surrendered to human vanity, selfishness, and venality, but it is to be appropriated and sanctified as a means of bringing souls to Christ, and of winning them from the service and bondage of sin.

However the principle may apply to the minister of the gospel, as influencing his intercourse with the people and the manner of his pulpit ministrations, it is also very suggestive in its adaptation to our every-day Christian life. That the children of the house sometimes become averse to instruction and worship, and regard the Bible as the most dismal of books, may not be their fault altogether. There has been stern parental discipline and peremptory insistence upon obedience, but the element of pleasing has been overlooked. Religion, and especially religion at home, is a thing of beauty; but it has not been made so. Our neighbors have no good opinion of our faith, because we have taken little or no pains to add something to their happiness by such considerate attentions as would secure their friendship. Our course may have been such as needlessly to awaken opposition and excite prejudice. We have been dogmatic rather than kind. We have been harsh in tone and censorious in spirit, forgetting that "the sweetness of the lips increaseth learning."

The Christ-like man will study how to please his neighbor for his good to edification. He will please that he may lure him to the cross and bring him to Christ. He will endeavor to catch men with this godly guile, and to lead them to the sanctuary by the strong but silken cords of love. The school of Christ is a school in which the duty of pleasing stands out prominently. The law cannot be silenced, sin must be exposed and rebuked, and the world's enmity must be encountered; but the unselfish and earnest purpose to make men better and happier is a mighty force in the Christian's work.

HELPING ONE ANOTHER.

AMONGST other ways in which Methodists are to evidence their desire of salvation is the following, as found in the General Rules: "By doing good, especially to them that are of the household of faith, or groaning so to be; employing them preferably to others; buying one of another; helping each other in business; and so much the more because the world will love its own, and them only."

The duty of doing good to all men is clearly recognized —"of every possible sort, and, as far as possible, to all men." The preference which the rule declares for the household of faith is taken from Paul's words: "As we have therefore opportunity, let us do good unto all men, especially unto them who are of the household of faith." The apostle doubtless had reference to works of charity and gifts to the destitute and suffering, but Mr. Wesley has not gone beyond the spirit of the passage in applying it to business affairs. To help each other in business is the natural and spontaneous tendency of fraternal feeling and brotherly-kindness. The preference which the relation of brethren demands in the bestowal of alms is certainly not less obligatory in the industrial pursuits of life. Believers are described as "the household of faith"—intimately united in fellowship to Christ and to each other. Christ takes his disciples under his special care, denouncing the heaviest judgments upon those who shall cause them to stumble, and assuring him of a special reward who shall give "unto one of these little ones a cup of cold water only in the name of a disciple." Christ recognizes and rewards the good done unto his disciples as done unto himself: "Inasmuch as ye have done it unto one of the least of these my brethren, ye have done it unto me."

The help which Christians can afford each other in the way of business is often considerable, and it is the most prudent and rational mode of bestowing benefits. Where the poor can be placed in positions to earn their bread and to become independent of charity, they are more effectively aided than if gratuitously maintained. Many a worthy mechanic, tradesman, or merchant, vainly struggling for a start in business, might have been saved from poverty and failure by a little encouragement and patronage from his brethren in Christ. Young men seeking employment are perhaps neglected by members of the same Church, who might with little trouble secure them positions. Where there is already abundant prosperity, the relation to the household of faith should still decide our choice in business transactions. We may hope that the wealth to which our patronage has contributed will be more expended to the glory of God in the hands of a Christian than in the hands of an unbeliever. Better enrich the man who consecrates his money to the support of the gospel than build up the fortune of another who lives only to hoard his gains or to expend them upon his lusts.

This duty of employing Christians preferably to others, and buying one of another, is of easy and wide application. Every day there are opportunities in some direction to practice it, and yet it is often most grievously neglected. We do not mean that we are to buy of each other without respect to price, nor that we are to employ Christians without regard to qualifications. Other things being equal, the preference is to be given them in trade and in employment. If the Methodist does not do as well by me as another, then I must go where I can do the best; but, with the rule thus qualified, we ought to be at some pains and inconvenience to make our connections in business with those who are known to be exemplary and good people. While we would reprobate an offensively clannish and bigoted spirit, we believe that the rule of "helping each other in business" is of scriptural obligation, and not to be neglected without censure and condemnation. However much we may affect a broad and liberal spirit, we cannot set aside the inspired declaration, "Especially unto those who are of the household of faith." The rule is often broken through want of consideration and from the idea that business has nothing to do with the Church and religion. The claims of Christ's disciples are not thought of in such a connection. They have never thought of their merchant, their grocer, their employés as having any religion at all, but only as serving them to the best possible advantage. The duty, as Christians, of helping each other in business has never amounted to a practical and serious conviction. It is not our purpose to give this subject a sectarian application, though in this respect Methodists need to be reminded of their delinquency. While we do not abate our catholicity of spirit, there is need that the ties of our brotherhood be drawn closer in the temporal affairs of life.

SERVING THE WILL OF GOD.

DAVID was a notable man—a king and a personage who left an impress upon his own age and upon all ages such as few can expect to do; and yet in that single stroke of Paul's concerning the great monarch of Israel we have a revelation of what all lives should be. The true order of the words is given in the margin: "After he had, in his own age, served the will of God." The way to benefit others, and to contribute to the general welfare, is to be governed by this principle of obedience to God. The highest ends of benevolence and usefulness are reached through this supreme regard for the counsel of him who appoints to every man his work. The divine plan covers all the ages and moves toward a beneficent consummation. It has for its object the salvation of the world. Each consecrated person is a factor in this great achievement. To be consciously in our place, and to do our part, would seem to be what is meant by serving the will or counsel of God in our generation.

It is much to serve our generation, to help those who are immediately about us, to lessen the miseries of our day, and to add something to the stock of its happiness. This, in itself, is a worthy purpose—infinitely better than a sordid selfishness. It is the limit of ordinary philanthropy and of pious zeal. But to serve the will of God in our generation is broader, because it looks beyond our own times and considers each individual life and each generation of lives as contributing to the completion of a divine purpose embracing the welfare of all ages. Recognizing what the will of God is in its grand sweep of mercy and in its far-reaching plan for a redeemed world, the man of faith puts himself in harmony with the divine counsel, enters into it with absolute devotion and self-renunciation, and feels himself to be vitally connected with the kingdom of God in its progress and development. His work is delivered in his own generation, but it is related to what others have done before him and to that which shall come after. While David served the will of God in his own generation, he served that which is the light and hope of this and of all generations. What he did and what he was have come on down to us. The service to our generation is greater than that which he rendered to his own.

In some sort we are like the madrepores, that build up the coral-reefs and raise up islands and continents. Each tiny creature serves the counsel of the Creator in its brief generation, and helps in carrying out a plan that stretches through centuries of the earth's history. The Christian man, however, is a conscious and intelligent worker, and comprehends the system of which he is a part. There is this breadth and grandeur in serving the will of God: It touches most practically and beneficently the people and the times nearest to us, while it tells upon future generations and will be felt in the consummation of all things. Local and temporary as to its field, the results of serving the will of God are universal and immortal. The life and character are divested of all narrowness, and are made sublime by the conviction that our works of love are tributary to a stream as vast as the needs of the world. For all time the world is blessed and made better by those who see the will of God and serve it.

Serve it. His will of mercy and goodness, his plan for the world's salvation, his counsel of goodness toward us, may be delayed, and even thwarted. We can serve his will, or we can stand in the way, and by perverseness, opposition, or indifference, hinder the fulfillment of his purpose of love. God would have all men to be saved. His counsel in redemption embraces all in the provisions of salvation. We may help or hinder in this work; and we do. Our time is short, and our life-mission is to serve the will of God, eminently as that will goes out after the lost and as it has its expression in Christ as the Saviour of all men. The world was not saved in David's time, but he did what he could. It may not be wholly reached by the gospel in our day, but it is for us to lay something upon this rising monument of truth and grace, and to help swell the advancing tide till it covers the earth with the glory of the Lord. We might say—and many do say practically—that the counsel of God will take care of itself, and that his purpose for the salvation of the world will ripen in good time. But David served the will of God, placed himself in harmony with it, and wrought mightily and earnestly to bring it about; and this is enough to say of all who have wrought righteousness and have lived to much purpose in the world.

In its highest and best sense, no man serves his generation unless that service has had reference to the kingdom of heaven advancing in the world and gilding all the ages with its promises and realizations of grace and the hope of immortality. In serving themselves men build railroads and factories, and fill the world with their cunning and useful inventions. Trade, commerce, and all the industries are advanced thereby, and material comforts and luxuries are multiplied. They have served their generation incidentally; but there has been no thought of the will of God, no concern about the kingdom which contains in itself the real essentials of human progress and happiness. Compare the great railroad magnate recently dead with Paul or with Sir Francis Lycett. Tom Scott served his generation; Jay Gould is serving his. But as to serving the will of God in their generation, how does the matter stand? It is a practical age. Nobody is considered of much account unless he be an inventor or a builder or a bold projector of industrial enterprises. The danger is that, as a people, we shall come to the fearful pass of "having no hope, and without God in the world." The course of things must be reversed and the divine order must be restored. Men must serve the will of God, and by such serving reach the highest good for all generations.

CHRISTIAN GRACES.

CONTENTMENT.

CHRISTIAN contentment has reference to the dispositions of Providence. When clearly in the path of duty the Christian accepts the conditions of his lot. Contentment can hardly be called a grace. It is rather a state and habit of mind to which several graces contribute. Faith, patience, submission, are some of the elements of it.

It is not of course to be regarded as opposed to the spirit of progress. The inert character of the Orientals, the lack of all enterprise and improvement in some races, and the complacent thriftlessness of some individuals, are not illustrations of this scriptural duty. Inertness, laziness, idleness, are as far from it as light is from darkness. Neither is it that aspect of fatalism which neglects the means and opportunities of improvement, and then affects a pious resignation to the will of God. When we have done the best we can, have used our gifts and opportunities as we could, have followed the indications of Providence, and have sought in all things the glory of God, there is then occasion to be content. Men are to make their condition as good as possible—they are to be active, industrious, provident, energetic. It is right for them to desire prosperity and temporal blessings—to pray for them and to work for them. But if adversity come, they are to recognize the hand of God in their afflictions, and to acquiesce in the dispensation.

Paul has more to say about contentment than any other inspired writer; and the connection in which he enjoins it indicates that it is to be specially cultivated under circumstances of trial. He had learned, in whatsoever state he was, to be content. "Everywhere and in all things I am instructed both to be full and to be hungry, both to abound and to suffer need." He was sure of his divine calling, and if want overtook him in it he did not fret or repine, but patiently and even cheerfully endured. As MacKnight translates his words, "I have learned to be self-sufficient." A contented mind is indeed a kingdom in itself. He had in a measure made himself independent of outward conditions by a trustful and submissive spirit. This is the application for many: contentment in poverty, in affliction, in adversity. And this, we may be sure, does not exclude the desire of the soul for a brighter and happier world. It rather ministers to contentment, under trial and in tribulations, that there is a gracious purpose in them and a beneficent end. They are working out for us a weight of glory —they are working together for good. Why should we rebel and murmur against that which may be needful for our spiritual and eternal welfare?

In other places contentment is urged as opposed to covetousness, to the spirit of those "that will be rich." "Let your conversation be without covetousness; and be content with such things as ye have; for he hath said, I will never leave thee, nor forsake thee." "And having food and raiment, let us therewith be content." This is an illustration of contentment as opposed to inordinate desires. The determination to be rich, without regard to the means, or whether consistent with our Christian duties, is a form of discontent. If Providence has provided things necessary, but denied us the luxury and style of large fortune, we are to have thankful hearts, and not to sacrifice principle and conscience for wealth. The religious man is not grasping; he is not absorbed in the pursuits of gain. There is generally less contentment among people who are prosperous and well-to-do than among the impoverished and suffering. Their discontent takes the form of greed—is the unsatisfied craving of avarice. However large the accumulation, it is seldom that rich men have enough. Not satisfied with moderate profits and with the safe and slow increase of their possessions, they launch out into wild speculations and recklessly run in debt. In the mad pursuit of riches they become selfish, indifferent to their obligations, and utterly forgetful of God. Contentment antagonizes the love of money, and clears the soul of it as the root of all evil.

Does religion bring contentment? In other words, does it lead to patient, trustful submission to the providence of God? and does it so moderate the desires as to restrain from covetousness and all inordinate affection? Certainly the grace of God does not teach us to be idle, and to make no endeavor after earthly things. It does not instruct us to be sick if we can be healed, nor to abide in poverty if we can get out of it. Contentment there may be in connection with enterprise and prosperous undertakings. The most laborious and energetic and successful may be content. They may be clear of covetousness and actuated by consecrated motives.

Contentment shines in both adversity and prosperity. It is the habit of the believing heart. It is another word for moderation, for resignation, and for peace. It is tranquillity in danger, joy in tribulation, a faith unshaken by the storms of sorrow. It is a state of mind that equalizes all conditions, and makes God and his will the sum of our happiness. It is that state wherein the affections are set on things above, wherein the mind is stayed on God, and wherein there is perfect peace. True contentment can be found only in Christ as the soul's refuge and as the stronghold of the tempted and distracted spirit.

LOVE IN RELIGION.

LOVE is a positive grace. It is not merely the absence of ill-will or hate. There may be no conscious enmity toward God, but there is indifference. There is no sense of love as supremely centered in God as its object. Not to hate any one is far from loving all. It is sometimes a confession meant for a state of grace: "I have no ill-will toward anybody in the world." This is more than the devil can say, but it falls below what the Christian feels. Love is not a religion of negations. It is actual and positive. God and man are not objects of indifference, or merely tolerated without aversion. They are loved. The degree of love, to be loved at all, has this positive quality. The highest conception of it is in the Saviour's interpretation of the Commandments. God is to be loved with all the heart, mind, soul, and strength, "and thy neighbor as thyself."

Paul's description of charity comes up to that of Christ. He describes the temper, behavior, and conduct which mark the possession and the fruits of it. Here is given the picture of a complete inward life and the corresponding outward conduct. If we come short of this standard of excellence, by that much there is defect in our Christian character. Love is the essential in religion. Evidently men may die for their religion, they may give largely, they may work industriously, but there may be no particle of love in them. The force of Paul's delineation lies in the contrast between a religion of love and a religion without love. Witness such words as these: "Charity suffereth long, and is kind; charity envieth not; charity vaunteth not itself, is not puffed up, doth not behave itself unseemly, seeketh not her own, is not easily provoked, thinketh no evil; rejoiceth not in iniquity, but rejoiceth in the truth; beareth all things, believeth all things, hopeth all things, endureth all things."

The true Christian character is not here drawn in contrast with that which is avowedly worldly and sinful, but rather as opposed to a type of religion in which there is pride, envy, and a puffed-up and carnal spirit. It is a test of the genuine as opposed to the false, as a detecter of the counterfeit and debased coin that somehow gets into circulation in the religious world. It gives the ring of the pure gold, and the image and superscription which attest the genuine money. Spurious forms of religion had already manifested themselves in the Church. Miracles and other extraordinary gifts had been perverted. Selfishness, ambition, vanity, and sordidness had crept in. Vaunting on account of superior gifts and attainments had become common. Unseemly behavior had followed. Men had become intent upon the desire and pursuit of the wonderful and the sensational. Paul's picture of charity is drawn to offset this miserable travesty of religion, and to correct it.

We do not expect to find love in the world. We may find the very opposite of it among people who claim to be Christians. And yet love draws the line at the point of what is absolutely essential in Christian character. Without love, whatever his profession and whatever his attainments and possessions, he is nothing. It would seem to be a description of that which we must have in order to salvation. Not an impracticable ideal, but a character to be realized in the experience of all who expect to be saved. It is manifestly something above ordinary morality, something in advance of all forms of religion. It is the heart and essence of Christianity, greater than faith or hope, because it is their object and end realized—the heaven of character and also of happiness.

Love is a point of perfectibility. It is said to be made perfect, and that perfect love casteth out fear. The inference is doubtless sustained by a large experience, that there may be love in us, and yet, in degree, imperfect. Certainly perfection in it is set before us. At this point, if any, are Christians to go on to perfection, and to perfect holiness in the fear of God. We may take Christ's declaration of the law of love—to love God with all the heart, soul, mind, and strength, and thy neighbor as thyself—or we may look at Paul's description of the more excellent way, or we may come to the ripe and mellow strains of John as he emphasizes the nature and necessity of it. The perfect love may not be ours, and yet, in part, we dwell in love. It is of advantage to bring our self-examination to this one point, since love embraces all. To take in the whole life in detail may not be possible, but we may test ourselves by this one principle. In connection with this test the defects of heart and life are sure to be brought out.

Love is something so positive, so pure, so unselfish, so energetic for good withal, that the least deviation is readily detected. Perfect love, besides correcting what is uncomely and harmful in word and conduct, casts out the fear of death and the judgment. There is no fear in love. The second death can have no power over him that dwelleth in love.

Love perfected must prove itself. It must keep a sweet temper under great provocation; it must maintain humility in the midst of "visions and revelations;" it must assert its dominion in the presence of gainsayers and under the contradiction of sinners. If cleansed from all sin, the work will be displayed in the perfect love that reigns within. "When that which is perfect is come, then that which is in part shall be done away." If sin is anywhere left intrenched in the soul, it will be revealed as a flaw in our love, and the swell and glow and power of a full salvation will be in the consciousness of love being perfected.

THE DENIAL OF SELF.

This is the first element of discipleship, and one of the profoundest of religious principles. Self has been to the unconverted the center of all. A powerful centripetal force draws every thing in this direction. An all-ingulfing selfishness governs the natural man. The first, the last, the only thought is self. If somewhat modified and thrown out from his own person by natural affection, it is selfishness still moving in an orbit which knows no other center. There is no higher law than his own will; he turns "to his own way," and self is his only law. It is self in its rebellion against God that must be denied. Where it exalts and opposes itself against the divine authority, where it seeks to follow the bent and purposes of the carnal mind, where it presumes to dictate to infinite wisdom, it must be denied. A man must disown himself in order that he may come under the Saviour's yoke; he must break off all connections with every other master that Christ may be received and confessed as his Lord. In putting off the old man with his deeds, he puts on the Lord Jesus Christ. Instead of obeying self, living to himself, and being full of himself, he is now full of Christ; imaginations and every high thing are cast down, "bringing into captivity every thought to the obedience of Christ."

The soul, divested of self-will and the spirit of revolt against the divine authority, revolves in a new sphere, and is drawn to Christ as the supreme and all-controlling good. This act and state of self-denial leads, of course, to the renunciation of sin and the disregard of all personal considerations in the path of duty. Ease, honor, liberty, and life itself will be counted but loss for the excellency of the knowledge of Christ. The fountain of all, however, is in the comprehensible principle by virtue of which a man denies himself, disowns himself, and realizes that he is the absolute property of God. Here is the beginning of humility, which forbids him "to think of himself more highly than he ought to think," and which divests him of the intolerable egotism and conceit which sprout so rankly in the soil of the unregenerate heart. A life of unexceptionable temperance and morality may be wholly selfish. The anchorite and the extremest ascetic in religion may live to self as completely as the veriest voluptuary in the world. Saint Simeon Stylites, on his pillow, with his fastings and exposure to the rigors of the seasons, was as full of himself as any of the pleasure-loving throng who wondered at his almost supernatural endurance.

To realize the self-denial of the gospel, it is not needful to seek the occasion nor to make it. It is *himself* that the believer denies, and in this renunciation every possible thing is embraced. It is not a fragment of appetite or of ambition that is sacrificed here and there, nor is it the mere fringes and periphery of the life's garment which are trimmed and shorn now and then. Christ strikes more profoundly and more comprehensively. He does not begin by lopping off the branches, but the ax is laid at the *root* of the tree. "If any man will come after me, let him deny *himself*." The poor body may be starved and lacerated and the soul remain supremely selfish. Men may stand on pillars, live in caves, wear sackcloth, shut themselves up in cells, fare abstemiously, and yet know nothing of self-renunciation. A true Christian life will touch the point of sacrifice in every direction, simply because the denial of self underlies all. It is not so much in isolated instances and in partial phases of duty, but in the whole of life's purposes and achievements. It will appear in the government of appetites, in the abandonment of ease and pleasure, in giving, in working for God. The stream will rise to the altitude of its source, and the disowning of self and the renunciation of self will enter into every performance. While a man may submit to flagellation till the flesh drops from his bones, and even give his body to be burned, and yet know nothing of true self-denial, it is not possible for him to possess it and fail to exhibit it in every breath and pulsation of his being.

The trouble should not be to find wherein we deny ourselves, but rather wherein we do not. And yet there are probably multitudes of professed Christians to whom this matter of self-denial is but little more than a gospel fiction. They are following their ease and pleasure. Their giving is measured by their convenience; their work in the Church never goes beyond what is perfectly agreeable. They lay up treasure on earth; they indulge in the fashionable pleasures of the world. To give something, to do little, and to keep within the ordinary bounds of continence and sobriety, is the measure of their devotion. There are those whose highest conception of this principle is exhibited in refraining from sinful appetites and in observing the outward duties of the religious profession. To be crucified with Christ, to endure hardness as good soldiers, and to bring their entire practice up to the measure of this denial of self, is beyond their thought.

Thousands are selfish, sensuous, even voluptuous, in their religion. A comfortable place in the Church, where the little work that is done is done by others, and where entertaining sermons, inspiring music, and good society contribute to the agreeableness of worship, is the chief and crowning object. Self-indulgence comes not only in worldly but also in religious forms, and spreads its enervating spell over the Church. The softness, shameful effeminacy, and cowardice of thus living to self is rebuked by the Master's call to self-denial. If Christians are to save themselves, they must have this salt of the religious life in themselves; and if the Church is to save the world, her members must gird themselves for the great work by denying themselves and by becoming imbued with the constraining love of Christ, "that they which live should not henceforth live unto themselves, but unto him which died for them, and rose again."

THE GRACE OF GENTLENESS.

To be gentle is to be godlike. In nature the rough and violent processes are exceptional. The storms that sweep the ocean and the tornadoes that devastate the land are fitful and unfrequent as compared with the general tranquillity and more quiet movements of the elements. The shocks of the earthquake are alarming because seldom repeated. For the most part, the mighty forces of the material universe work quietly and even slowly. The continents and islands are rising and sinking without perceptible and startling convulsions. The wonderful contrivance for watering the earth, the falling showers, the refreshing dew, the growth of vegetation, the movement of the stars, the revolution of the earth, are all illustrations of gentleness in the work of God. The world was made, and is preserved, with but little violent demonstration. Every thing goes on with wonderful stillness and smoothness, as if all the ministers of nature were shod with wool. The worlds roll on with no clatter of wheels, the seasons continue their noiseless procession, the birth and decay of the oak, and the blossoming and withering of the rose proceed in silence. The omnipotent hand, guided by wisdom and love, touches the vast and the minute, and forms and wields all with an infinite delicacy. It is a gentleness without feebleness and a quietude united with the most untiring activity.

This is largely true in the dealings of God with his accountable creatures. Severity in the order of Providence, like that of nature, is exceptional. There is gentleness even with the unthankful and the impenitent. Long-suffering and forbearance usually attend their course. The ministries of love and persuasion are more than those of wrath. After the fire is "the still small voice," and before it also; and this is the constant and life-long appeal. David says once, if not twice, "Thy gentleness hath made me great." What would he have been without this gentleness of mercy in his hour of guilt and crime? And what would any of us have been—and such greater and better, as Abraham and Moses— without this same tenderness to the weak and erring? The operations of the Spirit are often mighty in their gentleness —like the dew upon Hermon and as the early and the latter rain. In all the wide ministrations of the Spirit—moving on millions of hearts, hovering and warming dead consciences into life, inspiring faith and love, and peace and joy—there is much of this quiet march of power. All the visible instrumentalities, all the thousands of vocal tongues, all the stir and uproar of earnest declamation, are as nothing compared with the unseen and often unconscious work of the Holy Ghost. This great power of life and light is abroad, ever acting in the world, awakening, converting, comforting, and sanctifying. It lies at the bottom of the events in the moral and spiritual movements of every age, molding, preparing, and consummating the great revolutions in character and history. In the sweep of centuries the effects are manifest, and in the individual experience the results are known and felt; but the Divine Agent himself is moving with an awful stillness, and in methods which defy analysis.

When we come to him "who is in the bosom of the Father," the prophetical portraiture is fully realized in his character and ministry. " He shall not strive nor cry, neither shall any man hear his voice in the streets." On occasion he could launch the withering anathema and hurl the bolts of wrath, but Christ was preëminently tender. He was considerate of the bruised reed and the smoking flax. He gives his own highest and most attractive qualification as a teacher: "Learn of me, for I am meek and lowly in heart." His was a great spirit—always calm, and marked by the gentleness of a temper ever under the sweetest spell of love and compassion. Paul, when he appeals to the Corinthians, beseeches them " by the meekness and gentleness of Christ." Of his own conduct to the Thessalonians he declares that "we were gentle among you, even as a nurse cherisheth her children." This grace he especially enjoins upon the ministry: "The servant of the Lord must not strive; but be gentle unto all men, apt to teach, patient; in meekness instructing those that oppose themselves." Christians are exhorted "to be no brawlers, but gentle, showing all meekness unto all men." Gentleness is enumerated among the fruits of the Spirit in such company as this: "Love, joy, peace, long-suffering, *gentleness*, goodness, faith, meekness, temperance." James, in describing the attributes of the wisdom that is from above, places this in the resplendent train: "But the wisdom that is from above is first pure, then peaceable, *gentle*, and easy to be entreated, full of mercy and good fruits, without partiality and without hypocrisy." Paul's celebrated monograph on charity sets gentleness as a conspicuous gem in the crown of the queen of the graces. Unseemly behavior, self-vaunting, all roughness and harshness of demeanor are opposed to the love which towers above faith and hope.

Conventional usage has borrowed the word and given it an indiscriminate application. Gentleman and gentlewoman is a character of the most exalted religious excellence. How often it is a misnomer in worldly society it is needless to indicate. But among religious people gentleness has not always the prominence to which it is entitled. There is flurry and bluster where quietness would be more seemly and far more effective. A hard, overbearing, and intolerant spirit mars and deforms the character which abounds in strength and energy. Firmness and uprightness are destitute, perhaps, of tenderness and compassion, and the most invincible and admirable courage is utterly without delicacy or refinement of feeling. There is a supposed incompatibility between strength and gentleness, and that it is rather in the way of vigorous action. The push and snap of vigorous enterprise and aggression would be rendered impotent by the quiet temper and the patient spirit. Gentleness is thought to neutralize power and to stand for all that is merely negative in character. But it is not so in God. The meekness and gentleness of Christ did not weaken his ministry, and Moses and Paul were the gentlest of men. It is the work of the Holy Spirit, and no subordinate part of it, to make men gentle. It is one of the brightest features of charity that it polishes the inward and outward man and softens the harsh and dictatorial disposition. It is often the one blemish of the otherwise good and great that they are not gentle. Christians though they be, they are neither *gentle*men nor *gentle*women. Whatever other graces they have, they have not this. Other and admirable qualities shine with a somewhat compensating light, but gentleness is something foreign to their composition.

THE EDIFYING GRACE.

IN one of his characteristic parentheses, Paul, if he does not add something to his wonderful delineation of love, epitomizes the marks by which it is to be recognized. "Knowledge puffeth up, but charity edifieth." The controversy in the Church was concerning "the eating of those things that are offered in sacrifice unto idols." On the part of some there was assumption of superior wisdom, and they were so puffed up as to disregard the views and scruples of others. The temper was dogmatic rather than charitable. There was a disposition to despise and override the opinions and feelings of those who could not agree with them. Their course was calculated to breed dissension and to pull down and destroy. Certain opinions and convictions are knowledge in the apostle's meaning; and these, when held without love, are the fruitful source of trouble. Knowledge thus held puffs up the professors of it, leads them to think more highly of themselves than they ought to think, and to brand those who differ from them as perversely ignorant and opposed to the truth.

Practically, this knowledge without love is a false knowledge, a conceit and a delusion, and one of the worst aspects of self-deception. "And if any man think that he knoweth any thing, he knoweth nothing yet as he ought to know." As a matter of experience, the test lies in the spirit manifested. The same experience may be differently apprehended, and, if formulated as a doctrine, the terms of the statement may vary; but if called to judge those who claim the experience, we must be governed by the apostle's declaration that "knowledge puffeth up, but charity edifieth." Charity, we are sure, is not puffed up, but there is a phase of knowledge or opinion that is. Genuine love is always humble, considerate, and of seemly behavior. It takes the wind of pride and the stubbornness of dogmatism out of the heart, and those who have it will esteem their fellow-Christians more highly than themselves.

If the matter in dispute happens to be love itself, then the test is all the more conclusive. The puffed-up spirit, that assumes superior sanctity and that sows the seeds of caste and divisions among Christians of the same communion, is a wrong spirit. It may be mysticism and fanaticism, but it is not the spirit of the gospel. That which engenders strife is not charity. An experience that cannot be professed and held so as to promote harmony and peace among converted people, and so as to elevate without disintegrating the body of Christ, must be wanting in the great essential. Charity edifieth. It builds up the Church. Its sweetness and beauty are diffused in the society, and it is as a precious aroma in the house of God. It is at the point where good men differ that this edifying grace is most conspicuously manifest. Here love comes in, if anywhere; and it is here that its power to heal and build up is exhibited. If at this point there is a puffed-up spirit, a temper of intolerance toward those who apprehend the matter as we do not, and a disposition to disparage their spiritual attainments, the presumption is that in disputing about love we have lost it. The measures of opinion may be intolerant and tend to schism, but those of love will always make for peace. The methods of the one are likely to be exclusive and separating; those of the other will be to unify and to promote the fellowship of all who have faith in Christ and are led by the Spirit of God.

The differences among Methodists on the subject of Christian perfection have led to a good deal of trouble and to much uncharitable controversy, especially among our brethren in the North. The variance seems to be largely in the way this experience is apprehended and in the manner of its attainment. It is agreed that the substance of perfection is love. In a letter to one of his correspondents, Mr. Wesley says: "I want you to be all love. This is the perfection I believe and teach; and this perfection is consistent with a thousand nervous disorders which that high-strained perfection is not. Indeed, my judgment is that, in this case particularly, to overdo is to undo, and that to set perfection too high is the most effectual way of driving it out of the world." As thus explained to Bishop Gibson, the prelate replied: "Why, Mr. Wesley, if this is what you mean by perfection, who can be against it?" And we believe that among Methodists at this time there is agreement on the point that love is the bond of perfectness, and that love so perfect as to cast out fear is the rightful experience and privilege of the children of God. There are differences as to whether it be a growth, a second blessing, and as to whether a residue of sin is left in the heart after regeneration which must be removed by a specific act of faith.

Good and holy people entertain these different views; and, for aught we know, they always will. This should, however, lead to no divisions and to no parties in the Church. If love pervades all who differ, there will be no trouble, there will be no invidious distinctions and judgments; and while love is preached and sought and professed, special phases of opinion will cease to rend and divide the followers of Christ. Love is the fulfilling of the law, and love builds up. We have enlarged somewhat upon Paul's parenthesis wherein he gives us the contrast between the knowledge that puffeth up and the charity that edifieth. We may take this, in connection with his larger description of charity, as our guide in reference to what perfection is, and as the grounds of self-examination. Every lineament in the picture unfolds this feature and expression of love. It is the edifying grace. It strengthens and encourages the weak and struggling. It is not provoked by the supposed ignorance and misconception of those who may be regarded as weaker brethren. It does not separate itself from those who may be on the lower rungs of the ladder of grace, but draws and cheers and comforts "till we all come in the unity of the faith, and of the knowledge of the Son of God, unto a perfect man, unto the measure of the stature of the fullness of Christ."

Charity edifies the whole body of Christ by uniting it in the bonds of love. It counter-works the tendency to fanaticism, because it leavens the entire spirit and tempers the harshness of strong convictions with the consciousness that all are liable to err. The true and the false in religion are often much alike in certain stages of development, but the tares and the wheat are manifest in what they produce. The principle of discrimination is given in reference to the most vital question of religious life. That which puffs up, whatever be the profession, is a delusion at the least, if it be not an error bordering on sin. That which edifies is the true and genuine doctrine and the experience which answers to the word of God. The edifying power of charity is in the life, tempers, and words of those who possess it. Thus exhibited, it is sharper than the blade of the polemic and clearer and stronger than the statement of the best-constructed creeds.

THE SURPRISES OF GRACE.

The Scriptures furnish some instances of remarkable goodness and piety existing under circumstances where we would least expect to find them. The case of the Syrophenician woman is in point. Living in a heathen coast, herself a Gentile, and probably without the advantages of the religious training of the Jews, she astonishes the Saviour by the greatness of her faith. The centurion whose servant was sick affords another illustration of wonderful faith where none would be likely to look for it. A pagan by birth and education, but by the chances of his profession thrown in contact with the Jews and their religion, he rises above all in the grasp and simplicity of his trust in Christ.

The apostles, and others who enjoyed the most intimate personal converse with Jesus, and who had been thoroughly instructed in the doctrines and worship of the Old Testament, were inferior to this soldier in their faith. Up to that time—howsoever it might have been later—Christ had "not found so great faith; no, not in Israel." Extraordinary eminence is given to this Roman soldier by the Saviour's words.

A kindred truth is brought out in the healing of the ten lepers, where the only one who returned to thank their benefactor was a Samaritan. He was the last one of whom such a return could have been expected. If any were delinquent, this was the likeliest to be wanting in gratitude, as men usually judge. The evangelist's brief touch is a master-stroke, bringing out the striking feature of the scene with almost startling effect—"And he was a Samaritan." In that inimitable parable, given in answer to the question, Who is my neighbor? the priest and the Levite, of whom we have a right to expect the most enlarged benevolence, are altogether wanting in compassion, while the Samaritan alone fulfills the commandment of love to our neighbor. In the parables of the prodigal son and of the Pharisee and publican there is the same exhibition of good in contrast with those whose circumstances were more favorable but whose conduct was not in keeping with their privileges or profession.

Instances of contrition and repentance—such as that of the woman who washed the Saviour's feet with her tears and wiped them with the hairs of her head, and such as that of Zaccheus the publican, who came down and received his Lord joyfully—are in the same line of illustration. The thief on the cross has been the subject of meditation and study throughout the gospel ages, and his repentance and faith are more wonderful and instructive because exhibited in such close connection with crime and its punishment. Of all the hardened and deriding spectators of the Saviour's crucifixion, only this malefactor was moved to repentance; and only the centurion who commanded and those who were watching with him were constrained to confess, " Truly this was the Son of God."

The conversion of Cornelius was every way remarkable, but the chief surprise in his case is that a man in his calling—an eminent military character, whose life had been spent in camps and courts—should be found so devout and spiritual before the gospel was preached to him. In form and profession he was neither a Jew nor a Christian; but still he was a man of prayer, and doubtless accepted with God. Of all the people in Philippi we should scarcely have picked out the jailer as the most hopeful subject of conversion. His business was calculated to harden his nature, and his associations, except during that one memorable night, must have been unfavorable in the extreme. His contemplated suicide in the moments of greatest consternation shows that at that time he was in the depth of pagan darkness and ignorance. He passes, however, from this condition of sheer heathenism to that of Christian assurance and faith in the space of a few hours. The conversion of St. Paul might be enlarged upon in this connection. It was a surprise to Jews and Christians alike. He was the last man of that generation that either would have thought of as likely to be changed in his course. There were miraculous causes in his awakening; but, with these fully considered, the conversion of Paul stands as a marvel that human calculations would never have anticipated.

History and observation supply us with illustrations in accord with those which we find in the Bible. Such deep piety and pure faith as were exhibited in the Dairyman's Daughter, and conversions like those of Thomas Oliver, Colonel Gardner, and John Newton, are of like import. Sincere and humble piety like that of Cornelius has doubtless illustrations in the heathen lands of to-day. There is exalted virtue, remarkable faith, and a deep insight and experience of divine things far removed from the ordinary track of privileges and opportunities. Here and there they are brought to light as revelations of what God is doing apart from the more favorable conditions of salvation, and as exhibitions of his abounding mercy and his power to save to the uttermost. The hopefulness of Christian charity should be stimulated healthfully by these instances, which are only astonishing because they seem to set at naught the circumstances and methods which have come to be regarded as essential to the attainment of salvation. There is danger of limiting the ample breadth of infinite goodness and of bounding our faith in the power of the gospel by lines altogether too narrow. Every now and then we are rebuked by the discovery of gems where no intimation of their existence was seen. A mine of riches opens where no one had thought of looking for the precious metal. There are springs of water gushing up in the desert, and the wilderness is gladdened and beautified by a bloom and fragrance altogether in contrast with the gloomy solitudes which they adorn.

It may often happen that those whom we have regarded as nearest the kingdom of God are most distant, and that those whom we have marked as most hopeless are already about to yield to the drawings of the Spirit. The final day will doubtless reveal many surprises of grace. What we have found in the sacred page, and in the imperfect field of observation and experience, will prove to have been only the tokens and predictions of that which awaits us in the world of light. The wonders of grace will then be uncovered, and we shall witness the fruits of redemption as they have been gathered from the entire scope of human history and from all the varied conditions and circumstances of human experience. The surprises of grace here are as the shells on the shore, while those of glory will be as the unmeasured wealth in the ocean's depths.

THE BELIEVER'S POSSESSIONS.

"ALL THINGS ARE YOURS."

GOD himself is the supreme proprietor. "For whom are all things." And Christ is the supreme possessor, since all things were made by him and for him. Coming into the relation of sons through faith in Christ, Christians are heirs of God and joint heirs with Christ. In Christ and with him they are the heirs and virtual possessors of all things. In this relation to Christ, and in union with him, all things are for their sakes. The end of the creation of the world is in them, and they are the vindication of the divine wisdom and goodness. The present world is theirs for probationary uses. "All things are yours." They may own not a rood of ground, and be without a place to lay their heads, and yet all things are theirs, and made to contribute to their good.

The meek shall inherit the earth as well as heaven, because the earth is the scene of their redemption and of their adoption, and the theater of their triumph over sin. They have put it to its highest and only true use in the pursuit of spiritual objects. While others have seemingly possessed and enjoyed it, the righteous alone have gathered from it the imperishable treasures. Those who gain the whole world and lose their own souls are in no true sense the possessors of the world. Nothing is theirs. Even in this present time they have, in losing themselves, lost all. They have failed to get any good out of the world, and have, in effect, forfeited every thing. Christians are heirs of all things, and they are also the real possessors of "things present." Through Christ they possess the present world even as they are heirs of the world to come. All things in it work together for their good. Every thing is made tributary to their welfare, whether the world or life or death, or things present or things to come. The title is in their sonship, and the soul that cries "Abba, Father!" can claim the universe as its own.

Neither this world nor any other can be really enjoyed out of Christ. Beyond mere animal gratifications, what is there possible to atheism? What room is there for the appreciation of the beautiful and the sublime where there is no intelligence in creation? The irreligious possess the earth in much the same sense in which the herds possess the fields in which they graze. They see no God in the blooming herbage beneath their feet, and the blue vault above them has for them no suggestion of a far-off and cloudless heaven. The earth yields them food, raiment, and sensual pleasure, but nothing more.

It is only through Christ that the natural world can be seen as a thing of beauty, because it is through him that we discern the hand that formed and preserves all. Sin excludes from the enjoyment of heaven, but does it not also shut us out from the highest and most satisfying enjoyment of the world? The Christian has all things, because through Christ he is capable of grasping and enjoying them. A feeling of devotion and a sense of God are essential elements in the beautiful and the sublime. Without these, flowers and landscapes and mountains are beyond the touch and reach of the soul. The imperial quality in all things is the spiritual, and this can be detected and enjoyed only by the spiritual.

The domain of science, to a large extent, seems to have fallen into the hands of unbelievers. But what have they in it? They gather facts and pursue their labors to sustain a godless theory. There is, as they profess, no design, no omnipotent personal will, no trace of God in the rocks or the stars, or in the history of living things. Who are the true possessors of science, the devout Faradays or the sneering and skeptical Huxleys? And who will, in the end, be the owners of this great wealth of discovery and scientific toil? Doubtless Christianity will gather and appropriate all, and all will ultimately contribute to the overthrow of infidelity. To the blind workers there is nothing but chance or the evolutions of a stupid and material force; but to the devout spirit the Infinite God, in all his wisdom, power, and goodness, shines. Atheists may push forward the explorations of science, but the men of faith are the possessors of it.

Modern inventions seem to be mainly in the interest of commerce and the accumulation of wealth. The railroad, the steam-ship, and the telegraph are recognized incidentally as aiding in the spread of the gospel. But, in the order of Providence, this is their chief purpose. The builders and the owners of them, the great railway kings of the day, and the merchant princes, have not thought of Christ. But God is in these enterprises, and they are doing his work in bringing about the universal brotherhood of humanity and in spreading the glad tidings of salvation to the uttermost parts. Is there any thing in the line of science, exploration, travel, or invention that Christianity does not fall heir to? They are carried on mostly for mere temporal purposes; they are often under a godless control; they belong to capitalists, who care nothing for God. And yet in their best and highest uses they belong to God's people; they are the instruments of a world's salvation.

It is also true that the money of the world is largely in the hands of the ungodly. But the believer alone owns money; with sinners the money owns them. Those that consecrate their wealth to Christ are the only ones who get the worth of their money out of it even in this life. The blessedness of giving it and using it for God makes it truly the possession of the believer. The Christian would at once turn all the streams of gold into the channels of religious and benevolent enterprise; but, indirectly, do they not tend that way? and at length will they not flow into the Lord's treasury?

The wealth of the world, and its science, and its wonderful inventions, await the converting power of the gospel, and believers will possess them all some day. The heavenly inheritance is among the "all things," and this earth, purified by fire, may be the scene of future glory, but here and now "all things are yours." In this world believers are "as having nothing, and yet possessing all things."

THE SECRET OF THE LORD.

THE knowledge of God is spiritual, and only reached through the spiritual nature. He remains "the unknown God" until manifested to the faith. We could not know him without a material universe to exhibit his power, and without a special revelation through his word. And yet with these volumes open before us we may fail to know him. He is a hidden God until the soul is supernaturally opened to behold him. The secret of the Lord is this something which neither nature nor the word of God discloses until the fear of God is planted in the heart. All is mystery and uncertainty, perplexity and doubt, until the disposition to know and obey God is formed within. It was true in David's time, and also in ours, that the secret of the Lord is with them that fear him. They have a profound insight of the divine nature and a clear and satisfactory conception of the divine character. The glory of God is given to them in the face of Jesus Christ. God shines into their hearts, because their hearts are opened to the heavenly rays.

It is a secret of grace, the hidden mystery, that baffles all science, and pours contempt upon human wisdom. The wonderful things of God are unfolded to the devout spirit. To him the very heart of the Infinite Father is revealed. He feels God in the assurance of sins forgiven, in love enthroned, in the spirit of adoption. The plan of redemption is practically clear to the soul that has come to Christ in penitence and in humble trust. The secret of the Lord has been unfolded to him as it never can be to him who seeks to find out God by scientific research or by merely intellectual methods. It is with them that fear him, because this is the condition of the manifestation. "God is a Spirit, and they that worship him must worship him in spirit and in truth." In no other way than through the spiritual in us can we attain to a true and spiritual worship. God knows the proud afar off. He moves farther and farther away from those who would be independent of his help. Their searchings, without prayer and without humility, will carry them farther away from the object they are seeking.

The world by wisdom knew not God. It never has made any advances in this direction by philosophy or by science. Nature yields up some of her secrets to the investigator. The laws of matter are to some extent defined, and the processes of life and growth are grasped. But the secret of the Lord, his personality, holiness, and love, the essential nature of him who is in all, and lies back of all phenomena, is undiscovered. This is disclosed to him who fears God. The God-fearing, praying man, in conversation and in the revelations of the Spirit, is the only one who possesses this wonderful secret. It cannot be extorted by reason, it cannot be attained by metaphysical studies, it cannot be reached through geological or astronomical exploration. The name of God is secret, the sublime and awful secret of Jehovah, but it is known to them that fear him. What the wise and learned have never been able to wrest from the domain of nature is discovered in joy and peace, and assurance to devout and prayerful souls.

There is to most men a great mystery connected with the Divine Providence; so much so that they are disposed to question the presence and reign of God in the world. The hand of God is to them not manifest. We doubt if it ever is, except to them that fear God. To them it is almost as an open vision. The principles of providential government are explained in connection with human probation, the existence of sin, and the deed of discipline. To them it is not difficult to believe that God cares for the sparrows, and that he cares still more for his children. The pure in heart see God in providence, in the pages of history, in the rise and fall of empires, and in the individual experience. In God's dealings with us as individuals there is an aspect of mystery. To the superficial view his ways are inscrutable, and under the first shock of some great sorrow we are often in great darkness.

What God's purposes are as to ourselves we may not wholly know. They are good as interpreted by the loving heart. In a general way the great secret of Providence is clear. "For we know that all things work together for good to them that love God." But, besides this, the devout believer will often see in himself the reason of the chastisements sent upon him. It is as a personal secret between him and his God. Paul understood the meaning of the thorn in the flesh. In this thing the secret of the Lord was with him. It was a preventive discipline to keep him humble, and that the power of Christ might be manifested in his infirmities. The meaning of affliction is one of the secrets of the Lord which is revealed to them that fear him. The general gracious purpose is clear, and often also the particular reason of the stroke. To the irreligious, in times of trouble, all is confusion and darkness. They do not see God in their personal affairs, and in their troubles they do not understand him. They doubt of God, or they rebel against him. They do not penetrate the secret—the wise and merciful end, and the rebuke of their sin and worldliness.

The nearness and intimacy of the believing soul with God, the spiritual communion and close friendship enjoyed, are connected with the unfolding of God to the spiritually-minded. God does not keep himself aloof from them, he does not hide himself. Rather he takes them into a sacred intimacy and nearness to himself. He tells them his name, clears up the mysteries of grace, and breaks the seal from the book of Providence. He causes his face to shine upon them, opens to them the deepest secrets of his nature, and shielding them in the cleft of the rock, and, passing by them in fearful grandeur, proclaims himself, and makes all his goodness to pass before them. The secret of the Lord is the desire and the experience of them that fear God. Jacob, Moses, David, Paul, and John had the strong desire, and rejoiced in the inward revelation. To them, and to all spiritual souls, God is not an object of conjecture or of speculative thought, but as dwelling in them and guiding them. The mystery of all mysteries, the hidden source of all things, shines as a Father's love and presence in their hearts.

CHRIST'S SYMPATHY.

Goodness may not always be sympathetic. We can well believe in the love of God when we have so many evidences of it in the provisions of salvation. There is tenderness, pity, compassion in the Infinite Father toward his erring creatures. God alone perfectly comprehends the consequences of guilt and sin in its future and eternal developments. Neither men nor angels can completely fathom the depths of that wretchedness which the lost soul is doomed to experience. God alone knows the sufferings endured in this world. No human capacity can go over the terrible array in detail, much less can it gather up and grasp the whole at a single glance; and yet, with his knowledge of sin and suffering, and with his love for the fallen and wretched passing all human love, we can scarcely conceive of God as "touched with the feeling of our infirmities."

In angelic natures the impossibility of this fellowship in suffering is apparent. They are moved by a benevolence only less boundless than that of God himself. They can truly rejoice over the repentance of one sinner and minister tenderly to the heirs of salvation, but they can have no proper feeling of such weakness as springs from the flesh in its companionship with a corrupt and fallen nature. Their pinions of light know nothing of weariness, and their spirits of flame have never been darkened and saddened by the shadow of sin. In the wilderness and in Gethsemane they could do scarcely more than gather upon the outskirts of those terrible passages in the Redeemer's conflict with the powers of darkness. However near they may come to us in their vigilance and solicitude, there is still a vast distance between them and our human nature. The general import is clear enough. The unseen and spiritual enemies are more manifest to them than to us, and the tremendous interests involved are measured as no human intelligence can take them in. But there are elements in the struggle which baffle their efforts to fully conceive. So far as they are like ourselves, they are capable of sympathy; but beyond this, and as we enter the conditions of our depraved and bodily natures, they can be little more than anxious spectators of a scene which there is nothing in themselves to explain.

The capacity of man to feel for his fellows is limited by his very imperfections. Without goodness and benevolence, indifference prevails. Where the moral condition is right, there is wanting complete perception of the suffering in any given case, and of those variations and modifying circumstances which may exist. It is a difficulty with the best of benevolent natures to adequately feel for others. There are points in which experiences touch, but there are also many in which they are far removed. It is hard for the strong to enter into the trials of the weak, for the well to appreciate the temper of the sick, for the learned to have perfect patience with the ignorant and illiterate, and for great and highly endowed minds to deal kindly and considerately with those of low and medium gifts. Both selfishness and incapacity are in the way of complete sympathy. To feel all and to feel perfectly would crush. Only a superhuman organization could bear a weight and strain like this. And yet human sympathy, in its best manifestations, is the most beautiful, helpful, and healing of virtues. "One touch of nature" thus refined and purified "makes the whole world kin." However helpful our sympathy may be, it is often helpless. What it inspires us to undertake is altogether beyond our performance. In the physical pain of others, in their mental anguish, and in their spiritual perplexities, we may be profoundly moved, and wrought up to the highest tension of desire to assume the burden or in any way to relieve the sufferer; but we are absolutely helpless.

The sympathy of Christ stands out in relief as something different from the love and compassion of God, to be distinguished from the benevolence of angels, and as every way more perfect and effective than our purest and deepest fellowship in human suffering. He knows, as he only can know, the anatomy of the body and the soul, and how every fiber and faculty of this wondrous compound is swayed and tortured under the force of pain and anguish. Without sin, he approached so nearly its conditions as to meet the most powerful assaults of temptation. He was tempted "like as we are." The diabolical, the fleshly, the worldly were encountered in their fullest strength, and his soul passed through every strait of anguish known to us in the conflict with sin. All the lines of a perfect sympathy meet in him as in no other being in the universe. Knowledge, feeling, and helpfulness are all complete in him.

And it is a comforting assurance which we have that in his heavenly exaltation the Saviour retains his sympathetic character. He is at the right-hand of the Majesty on high in his humanity; and it is there, and now, and ever that he is "touched with the feeling of our infirmities." It is as the ascended and glorified Christ that it is written of him: "For in that he himself hath suffered being tempted, he is able to succor them that are tempted." He was qualified by the assumption of our nature, and by the temptations and sufferings of his life on earth, to be in heaven "a friend that sticketh closer than a brother." Enthroned as he is above all, and invested with the purple of everlasting and universal empire, and by the mightiness and splendors of his regal state almost lifted beyond the gaze of the seraphim, he is still touched with the feeling of our infirmities. The sorrows and trials of the humblest saint, the death-throes of the obscurest believer, penetrate through all these ranks and atmospheres of dazzling radiance, and touch the Redeemer's heart. If we cannot apprehend God, if we wearily ponder and speculate where we find no ground to tread on, we may rest in this blessed assurance. We may feel how inadequate, how utterly powerless, is earthly tenderness to sustain, and at the same time turn to the loving and ever-living Christ. No submissive sufferer, no earnest seeker, is without his sympathy. Especially in the great battle of believers for salvation does Christ claim his rightful relationship as brother and near of kin. From his throne he is not ashamed to call them brethren, and in all their warfare he cheers them by his presence and sustains them to the end.

MELODY IN THE HEART.

The heart may be out of tune even more than a cabinet organ, even more than the voice. There is in it the discord of conflicting passions. The life is not in accord with the conscience, and there is not harmony in our relations with others. The greatest of all discords is between the soul and God. The cares of the world fill us, and there is no spirit of praise. "How shall we sing the Lord's song in a strange land?" How, indeed, if we are far from God and in a state of estrangement from the comfort of the Holy Spirit? It is well to attend to the instrument, to cultivate the voice, and to master the science of music. Both in the Old Testament and in the New we are commanded to sing. Singing stands upon the same authority as praying. One may be more vitally important than the other, but by precept and by example both are enjoined. Everybody can pray, even vocally and in public, but some may not be able to sing. Some! With proper convictions in reference to it as a duty, the most can. Conscientious study and practice will enable nearly all to assist in congregational singing and also to hum a tune in private when the spirit of praise and rejoicing is in us. But we can, without exception, make melody in the heart unto the Lord. This depends largely on the spiritual state, and the condition is very much under our own control. A dumb person may sing, and this is one of the miracles, literal as well as metaphorical, which an ancient seer predicted.

Paul and Silas in prison, with their feet in the cruel stocks and at midnight, sung praises to God. The song may have been from the Psalms, or it may have been improvised from the fullness of hearts filled with the love of Jesus. We can hardly think of Paul as having much melody of voice. He probably carried the bass with a jar and a crack, while Silas with more sweetness and strength sung the air, sending the music through all the corridors and cells of the jail, so that the prisoners heard. What was in the heart could not be repressed, and the singing under such circumstances fell upon the ears of the criminals as something bordering upon the supernatural. It may have had as much to do with the awakening of the jailer as did the earthquake. Martyrs have sung on their way to execution and in the flames. Dying saints have breathed their life out in song. The melody of the heart rises superior to outward conditions, and reaches its sweetest and purest notes amidst the severest trials of faith and fortitude.

We do not from hence conclude that the inward melody always finds utterance—only that it often does in spite of the most untoward circumstances, and that it may and should exist in all Christian hearts. The heart as inevitably sings under the breathings of the Spirit as do the Æolian strings when swept by the evening breeze. The chords are tuned by the divine hand, and they respond to the touchings of the infinite love.

While we are enjoined to sing with grace in the heart and to sing with the spirit and the understanding, may we not comfort those who cannot utter themselves musically by supposing that some of the most perfect psalms and hymns and spiritual songs have vibrated in believing souls without ever having reached the grosser birth of vocal expression? Is not this the perfect melody, and the only perfect? Words are inadequate; voice and ear and science are necessarily defective, but the voiceless music of a pure heart may be without a flaw. Angels may catch some of its strains, but only the ear of God takes in every note. It is said that we must sing here if we expect to sing in heaven. This opens a poor prospect to those of us who never can turn a tune, and almost forces us to withdraw our approbation from those who are silent because they respect the feelings of their fellow-worshipers. But is not the probationary aspect of music chiefly that of the heart? However well we may sing, we shall not be the fitter for heaven on that account unless we have learned to sing with grace and to make melody in the heart. Better be in heaven without a tongue than to be there with no capacity for this higher music of the soul. As God regards the matter, there is more real melody in a silent Quaker meeting than in the professional quartet of a fashionable church. In the heavenly atmosphere our merely vocal attainments here would be the veriest discord. The medium of vibrations there may be such that the heart diffuses melody as flowers give out fragrance. What the bird, with frenzied effort, tries to sing, the flower is. The song of heaven is the music of holy hearts; and may it not be that the song that, for lack of suitable organs, has been shut up through all this mortal life will burst forth as a prisoner from his long and weary confinement? or, as the sweet odors spring forth from the broken vase, so may it not be with the soul when the earthly tabernacle is dissolved? At any rate, those who can sing must not be too severe on those who cannot. In this, as in other things, the first may be last and the last first.

As a matter of religion and of worship, singing must be with grace in the heart. It is a dead and offensive thing unless the spirit go along with the understanding. In our singing we must make melody in our hearts unto the Lord. The main thing is the state of the heart. We need better singing than we have, and nine-tenths of religious people are culpable because of their personal indifference on the subject; but probably the greater and almost universal guilt is that our hearts are not filled with praise. It is a part of worship both as sacred and as spiritual as prayer, and yet many have come to regard it as an artistic entertainment, belonging more to the region of æsthetics than to the domain of piety and devotion. The well-tuned heart is an important preparation for the service of song, giving it that unction which it needs quite as much as the prayer or the sermon; and we believe that where there is melody in the heart the worthiest expression will be studied, sought, and attained. Praise in itself is comely, and it will seek to array itself in comely utterance. The spiritual soul will love spiritual songs, and the pure heart will hate discordant notes as it hates unhallowed desire and unholy tempers. The heart and the voice, let them be cultivated together. They will act and react, and the harmonies of the outward expression and of the inner feeling will be blended in a worship that is adorned with the beauty of holiness.

DIVINE COMPANIONSHIP.

THERE is a personal intimacy with God which is consistent with the deepest reverence. Enoch, Abraham, and Moses in their career exhibit this habitual companionship. They adored, worshiped, and were filled with awe, and yet they walked with God. To them there were theophanies—

extraordinary manifestations to the senses—but apart from these was the habitual consciousness of God as ever about them. They communed with him in spirit and in thought. They endured as seeing him who is invisible. God was not only near to them, but they were near to God. There was companionship. They were the friends of God, and enjoyed the privileges of a personal intimacy with the Infinite Jehovah. This was the most considerable fact in their history, and the one thing most descriptive of their character and lives. These names point us to the higher altitudes of faith and godliness, but they also exhibit an experience common to all devout souls.

There is a type of religion which occupies itself exclusively with the worship of a far-off God. It is not wanting in reverence, in fear, in the sense of divine authority, and in sublime conceptions of the attributes of the living God; but God is distant, awful, and even appalling. To such worshipers the thought of walking with God as a child with his father, or as a friend with a friend, would be rejected as impertinent and irreverent.

Still further from the temper and ideas of natural men— the unbelieving world—is this association of the human with the infinite and ineffable Spirit. What a vast chasm yawns between Enoch and Abraham and Mr. Spencer's conception of the unknowable First Cause! To the ordinary worldly-minded, whether philosophical or thoughtless and sensual, God is the remotest and most unreal of all objects. To Moses he was the nearest and most real. To him the material world was a mere shadow, transitory and changeful. Personality, spirit, intelligence, were to him the substance and basis of all things.

We do not know that these ancient worthies speculated much, if at all, whether knowledge is possible with man, or whether God could be known. They simply sat upon the sun-crowned heights, ever dwelling near the sky, and were filled with the light of God. God came to them through the open avenues of their spiritual nature, and they came to God through that faith which is "the evidence of things not seen." Walking with God, they did not walk with a shadow; the friends of God, they were not the companions of a vapor; seeing him who is invisible, they saw God more clearly than the eye beholds the sun. God somehow took these spiritual souls up into himself, permitting them even to share his counsels, and manifesting himself by an inward glory which surpassed the splendors of the outward world.

In Christ this divine companionship is distinctly and vividly realized. Walking with God "as dear children" is one of Paul's declarations. Union with Christ brings us to the experience. In him God is brought inexpressibly near, and through him we reach that companionship with God which dispels the last shadow of doubt. The far-off "are made nigh by the blood of Christ," and God is declared to us by "the only-begotten Son which is in the bosom of the Father."

Always the privilege and the characteristic of God's people, this divine companionship in the gospel stands out in peculiar brightness. As Enoch, Abraham, and Moses exhibit it in the dispensation of types and shadows, John, the eagle-eyed and eagle-pinioned, is its most conspicuous representative in the latest manifestation of truth. "And truly our fellowship is with the Father, and with his Son Jesus Christ." It is a companionship of light. This light broke upon the path of the most spiritual of the patriarchs; its flashes gleamed along their toilsome pilgrimage. But under the gospel and in the heart of John it swells into the warmth and brightness of the vernal day. As his pen tells the story, walking with God is walking in the light, because

"God is light, and in him is no darkness at all." This is the substance of all: "But if we walk in the light, as he is in the light, we have fellowship one with another, and the blood of Jesus Christ, his Son, cleanseth us from all sin."

PRAYER.

LEARNING TO PRAY.

THE request of the disciples, "Lord, teach us to pray, as John also taught his disciples," was evidently suggested by the Saviour's prayer which they had just heard. It was as he was praying in a certain place, when he ceased, that they asked to be taught. His prayer on that occasion seems to have convinced them that they were ignorant of this most solemn and important duty. They were not ignorant of what John had enjoined; the forms prescribed by Jewish doctors and teachers were familiar to them. More than their acquaintance with these was their knowledge of the prayers recorded in the Old Testament Scriptures. We might suppose that the disciples had enough instruction on the subject, with the prophets and the Psalms before them, with some forms of prayer, public and private, which they had probably used from their childhood, and having already been with the Master for two or three years. Then if this was a second delivery of the Lord's Prayer, they had heard prayer explained and enforced, and the form given in the Sermon on the Mount, perhaps not more than twelve months before.

What was there in this particular prayer of Jesus that apparently for the first time awakened in them the conviction that as yet they knew not how to pray? When we have heard a truly great and admirable sermon we have gone away with the feeling that we could not preach at all; and we have had similar humiliating confessions to make about prayer when we have been led at the throne of grace by some one specially anointed and qualified for this most spiritual exercise. Something akin to this must have been the thoughts of those who were with Christ and heard that memorable prayer. There was nothing in David or Isaiah that excited in them the sense of their ignorance and destitution, or that aroused in them aspirations for the excellent gift. All their lives they had been praying, and praying well, as they supposed; but there was something in this prayer of Christ that revealed the feebleness and poverty of their souls, and their utter lack of that grasp of faith and communion with God which Christ exhibited.

There is no mention anywhere that the disciples asked their Master to teach them how to preach. This he did by example and precept, looking forward to the gift of the Holy Ghost as the most essential and complete endowment for his work. But we do not find that the feeling of insufficiency ever so came upon them during the ministry of Christ that they straightly and urgently asked to be taught to preach. With the Saviour's incomparable discourses fresh in their minds, they might have questioned whether they or any other could ever fittingly proclaim the gospel; but this duty was as yet at a distance, and until after the Saviour's resurrection they probably thought little about it. At any rate, the thing they asked for was how to pray. However poorly qualified to preach, they felt themselves still worse off in the duty of prayer; and they may have thought that if they only could pray aright the preaching would be assured in its own time, and when the occasion came.

Besides the sense of spiritual want and the need of a stronger faith, there was the conviction that this new dispensation demanded an order of prayer in accord with its superior light and privileges. The prayers of the Old Testament, to be used now, must be vivified and illuminated by the spirit of the New. Compare the prayers of Christ and Paul with those of Moses and David and the later prophets, and the difference is apparent. Praying under the gospel and in the dispensation of the Spirit is as superior as the conditions of grace and opportunity under which we live. On this occasion the Saviour gave the prayer previously enjoined, and with amplifications and illustrations. The friend and the three loaves, the son that asked for bread, the condition of asking, seeking, knocking, and then that promise of promises, "How much more shall your heavenly Father give the Holy Spirit to them that ask him?" are in the sequel. This is prayer in the new dispensation. God's fatherhood is prominent, the sonship of believers is embraced, the gift of the Holy Spirit emphasized. The disciples, from the teachings and still more from the prayer of Jesus, saw that their praying must be adjusted to the new and happier conditions of the perfect law of liberty, and that their love, faith, and spiritual life must find expression in forms adapted to the clearness and completeness of the gospel. John's twilight prayers would not answer, and the inspired supplications of the Old Testament must receive the interpretations of the new and more exalted Christian life. In substance the request was: Lord, teach us to pray as thy disciples—as Christians.

There is no literal repetition of the Lord's Prayer in the Gospel of John, nor in the Epistles, but we can see—in the writings of Paul especially—how the nature and spirit of Christian prayer had been learned. The letter of Christ's teaching was completed and vitalized by the Holy Spirit. The Epistles abound in examples of prayer, and are abundant in precept, and the Spirit's office is emphatically recognized. We are to pray in the Holy Ghost, and his aid is specially declared: "Likewise the Spirit also helpeth our infirmities; for we know not what we should pray for as we ought; but the Spirit itself maketh intercession for us with groanings which cannot be uttered."

Prayer is something to be learned. The request of the disciples should be that of all who are sincerely bent on serving their Lord. The formula of the Lord's Prayer, repeated from infancy, does not meet the requirement. The fluency and ease of extempore prayer may amount to a singular gift, and the petitions, framed in secret as a religious habit, may be continually offered, and we may not know how to pray. We can teach prayers to our children, but God must teach them to pray. It is to be learned of Christ; his word and Spirit must guide us. True Christian prayer that looks to a finished atonement—to a risen and interceding Saviour and to the Spirit poured out, that embraces the fatherhood of God and aspires to adoption, that sinks into perfect submission to the divine will and rejoices in the divine fellowship—must be taught us by God himself.

And when we think of the power of prayer—that it is, after all, the supreme instrument—how essential that it should be learned! Every other aspect of the art of doing good is subordinate to this, and yet it is of that of which we are most ignorant. And this ignorance is not always the first to be felt. We may not know how to preach, how to train our children, how to lead our friends to Christ, but do we suspect that our most lamentable defect is in not knowing how to pray? The simplest thing in the world, yet the most difficult. Something that seminaries cannot impart, an art that archangels cannot help us to attain, the very loftiest reach of wisdom and grace. Lord, teach us to pray.

CHRIST'S EXAMPLE IN PRAYER.

THE force and authority of the Saviour's example in prayer are deserving of special consideration. He is our pattern in holy living. A close imitation is necessary in reference to the tempers and conduct in general. The true following of Christ largely consists in building upon his perfect model, and in seeking the mind that was in him. We are to learn of him as the "meek and lowly in heart." The believer is to walk "even as he walked." In this, as in other respects, we are to put on the Lord Jesus Christ. His love is to be the ideal of ours, and his self-denial and submission are to be the aim of his disciples. Likeness to him in spirit and conduct is the great aim and achievement of the Christian life. The Saviour's actions were shaped designedly with this purpose. He is always the great Teacher, whether speaking or acting, living or dying, working miracles or discoursing in parables.

His precepts and commands in reference to prayer are explicit and full, and his illustrations of it are luminous and inimitable. He twice delivered that summary of all prayer known as "the Lord's Prayer" by way of eminence. He enjoins and reëstablishes secret prayer in its truth and purity. He declares the character of it as the condition of the highest blessings of the kingdom, affirming that "every one that asketh receiveth, and he that seeketh findeth, and to him that knocketh it shall be opened." The power of persevering and importunate supplication is illustrated in the case of the Syrophenician woman, and in the parable of the unjust judge. Prayer and fasting are connected and enjoined for special ends, as the casting out of certain kinds of evil spirits; and certain eminent subjects of prayer are proposed, as the sending out of laborers into the gospel field and as a safeguard against temptation.

But he who so emphatically commanded and illustrated this most vital duty prayed himself. We do not now refer to such occasions as the raising of Lazarus, the agony in Gethsemane, and the petition for his murderers on the cross, but to those incidental glimpses of a praying Saviour which occur in the ordinary progress of his ministry. We pause over a passage like this, which immediately precedes the calling of the twelve apostles: "And it came to pass in those days that he went out into a mountain to pray, and continued all night in prayer to God." The connection suggests that this season of prayer was in some measure related to the choice of the apostles; but beyond this it lets us into the devotional habit and life of Jesus. It was secret, it was prolonged, it was importunate. The soul of the Redeemer was there drawn out in earnest supplication and absorbed in divine communion. After the feeding of the five thousand and the dismissal of the disciples and the multitude, the narrative proceeds to say: "And when he had sent them away, he departed into a mountain to pray." As in the other instance the entire night was employed, in this the most of a day seems to have been consumed. The wonderful miracle was followed by a season of prayer. The Saviour withdraws from the world, sends away even his most intimate followers, and seeks a place of solitude where he may conclude the day in this blessed and delightful exercise. Here was much apparent painstaking and trouble to secure the conditions of secret and undisturbed communion with the Father. The transfiguration was ushered in by prayer, and opens out of it as the flower bursts from its bud. On this occasion the favored three were with or near him, witnesses rather than parties to the solemn exercise. "He took Peter, John, and James, and went up into a mountain to pray." We might infer that this had been the Saviour's custom, sometimes going alone, at other times permitting the presence of some or of all whom he had specially called to proclaim the gospel. The power of prayer was here displayed in its most wonderful and glorious effects, at the same time that the sublime and expressive transaction brings out in bold relief a habit that pervaded the Saviour's life.

We are scarcely permitted to conjecture what were the subjects of prayer which occupied the mind of Christ during these long and solitary hours. That sublimest of all inspired scriptures, the seventeenth chapter of John, may, however, impart some conception of the scope and grandeur, as well as the indescribable pathos and love of those prayers which were uttered upon the lonely mountain-top. Whether the apostle's language refers exclusively to Gethsemane we do not know, when he says: "Who in the days of his flesh, when he had offered up prayers and supplications with strong crying and tears unto him that was able to save him from death, and was heard in that he feared." These seasons of retirement were doubtless marked by sore temptation, by agony of soul, and by the greatest triumphs and sweetest consolations. The Redeemer could not achieve his work without prayer. He prayed because he needed to pray, and because he fully assumed our nature, and in all things was "made like unto his brethren."

We dwell, however, upon the fact as an example to us, and insist upon this particular application. It is for this, doubtless, in a large measure, that the circumstance has such explicit statement in the record. It is to enforce upon all the preëminent necessity of prayer; that it is the very life of the soul, and the most characteristic and distinctive of the Christian's duties. It is a sufficient warrant for it, and an adequate solution of all supposed difficulties connected with it, that Christ prayed. He gave a practical exhibition of his well-pronounced precepts upon the subject. If our lives are conformed to his, they must be lives of prayer, of habitual supplication, and patient waiting upon God. He was our example herein, and the close and devoted imitator will be careful to follow the Master's footprints in this regard. Let the praying Saviour rebuke us and condemn us, and send us with more frequency and with greater boldness "to the throne of grace." Let this single feature of the perfect life imbue us with the purpose and desire to be more Christ-like in prayer.

PRAYER AND THE HOLY SPIRIT.

THE Holy Spirit is one of the objects of prayer. "How much more shall your heavenly Father give the Holy Spirit to them that ask him?" Thus the Saviour puts the matter, making prayer the condition upon which the most comprehensive gift is bestowed. The Spirit is to be asked for directly, and all the promises of his bestowal, as the Sanctifier and Comforter, are doubtless subject to this qualification. David, in his penitential Psalm, deprecates the departure of the Spirit of God, and prays with alarming earnestness, "Take not thy Holy Spirit from me;" and again, in conscious guilt and weakness, "Uphold me with thy free Spirit." The very character of the Holy Ghost as a gift, as promised, and to be sent, implies this condition of prayer. There are certain operations of the Spirit in awakening and conviction which take place in the unconverted before prayer is possible; but for the penitent and the converted, for all sincere and humble seekers, the Spirit is certainly to be asked for. The guilty but penitent backslider by prayer may arrest his departure from the soul, and experience his restoring and healing power. The faithful Christian may obtain larger manifestations of the Spirit in his work in the heart by devoutly seeking for them.

So dependent are we upon the Spirit for every grace, and so manifold are his offices and operations in the work of salvation, it is not strange that he is set before us as an object of prayer. It is possible, however, that believers do not ask for him as directly and as importunately as they should. It may often happen that the Spirit is grieved by the careless and comparatively indifferent way in which he is mentioned or thought of in their praying. A thousand things are in the mind, and many of them asked for before him, while the gift of the Spirit should be the burden of desire and supplication. This is above all the richest heritage of a loving heart—the boon which Paul had in his mind when he declared the import of Isaiah's wonderful strain: "Eye hath not seen, nor ear heard, neither have entered into the heart of man, the things which God hath prepared for them that love him. But God hath revealed them unto us by his Spirit." To obtain a spiritual apprehension and experience of the deep things of God, the Holy Spirit must be made the habitual desire and burden of prayer. All sincere and honest souls have reason to ponder this subject. They cannot afford to ignore the promised gift and its condition. Such a test of prayer as this God has made himself. Let the seeker, troubled with doubts and pressed by the conflicts of inward temptation and conviction, try it. It is precisely what the dark and troubled soul needs, and God has promised as a Father to give the Holy Spirit to them that ask him.

The Holy Spirit is intimately connected with prayer in another sense as the qualification essential to its exercise. Hence, we have these suggestive scriptures: "Praying always with all prayer and supplication in spirit," and "praying in the Holy Ghost." Besides the letter of revelation and the objects for which we are warranted to pray, there is a gracious preparation which the Spirit supplies. When we consider the coldness and formality, and the dullness and inconstancy to which even secret prayer is liable, we can comprehend how much the Spirit is needed to quicken desire and to strengthen faith. Praying *in* the Holy Ghost is something different from praying *for* him, and implies that the heart is filled and guided by him. It is prayer united with communion, and with love shed abroad, and with such hungering and thirsting after righteousness as only the spiritual nature feels. It is not the prayer of a sinner seeking pardon, but rather of a saint of maturest experience struggling after higher and grander blessings. Prayer is often earthly and selfish—it is on a level with the sensual and sordid soul which utters it. There may be a willfulness in it, or a narrowness, a querulous and dictatorial spirit. Praying in the Holy Ghost is eminently spiritual, submissive, and humble. Especially in intercession this is the essential quality, because it secures holiness, charity, and faith. There is a nearness to God which moves the arm of Omnipotence, and it is in answer to such prayer that God is delighted to send down his richest blessings. Praying in the Spirit thus distinguishes the true prayer of the believers from all that is merely formal and from all that is actuated by low and unworthy motives.

Still another relation of the Holy Spirit to prayer is that of helpfulness in the Christian's trials and conflicts. "Likewise the Spirit also helpeth our infirmities; for we know not what we should pray for as we ought; but the Spirit itself maketh intercession for us with groanings which cannot be uttered." Here the office of the Spirit is to help our infirmities, our ignorance of what is best, our impatience and distrust in affliction, and to inspire submission and confidence. In the perplexing dispensation of Providence it is natural to fret under the yoke of trial, and to choose for ourselves the path of deliverance. The intercession which the Spirit makes is within the troubled soul, and its end is to bring about a right spirit—a submission which Job framed into such words as these: "Though he slay me, yet will I trust in him;" and which our great Father exhibited in the pathos of Gethsemane: "O my Father, if this cup may not pass away from me, except I drink it, thy will be done." The Spirit's help is to work in us this patience and subjection to the will of God, to raise and purify the affections, and so to inspire desires which accord with our highest good.

None but those who have passed through the severest ordeals of affliction, and have wrestled successfully with their own infirmities of ignorance and pride, can altogether comprehend these unutterable groanings. It is with an enlarged application, however, that we may dwell upon the assurance that the Spirit helps our infirmities in prayer. If given up to his guidance, and humbly seeking his aid, the Christian will be strengthened and directed. His heart will go out after right objects, he will rise above every thing groveling and sensual, and he will thirst for the living God. His understanding will be enlightened, his faith will be purified and strengthened, and he will walk with God. With these relations of the Holy Spirit to prayer, it is evident that there is no other duty or privilege which brings us into so intimate contact with the most awful and most mysterious workings of God. It is something so spiritual, so entirely interpenetrated and surrounded by the Holy Spirit, that its nature and efficacy belong alone to the domain of Christian consciousness. It is the profoundest proof and expression of the supernatural and spiritual in religion.

PRAYER ENDED.

IN the conclusion of that grand Messianic Psalm wherein Christ and his kingdom are portrayed with such wonderful beauty and power, the author almost startles us with the declaration that "the prayers of David, the son of Jesse, are ended." It may be that in his mind the sum of all had been said in this rich and devout composition, and that nothing was left to be asked for. Or possibly the aged king was consciously near the end of life, and that the time of prayer with him was over. In this last respect the end comes to all when, with all other privileges, labors, and opportunities, prayer is laid aside forever. Whatever may be the benefits to ourselves, and however availing in bringing down blessings upon others, death seals the lips of supplication. The Christian, whose days and nights through many years have been marked by "praying always with all prayer and supplication," and whose earnest wrestlings with God in behalf of sinners and the Church have known no abatement, is done with prayer as soon as he is done with earth. The last word uttered, the last sigh may be a prayer, but it is the last prayer of a prayful life and of the praying soul.

Prayer is a most important part of the believer's work on earth; it belongs to his probationary duties and responsibilities, and ceases with the hour of his release from the affairs and activities of time. Praise, heightened and glorified, will go on endlessly. Death cannot break it, nor will there be any pause when the great transition passes upon the redeemed spirit. What other employments there may be in the heavenly world, there is no warrant for the supposition that intercessions for those who remain on earth will enter the glorified state. Prayers may not be answered until long after the saint that breathed them has entered paradise. They are not forgotten before God, and his angelic ministers and the ordering of his providence are being disposed, and are moving toward the gracious result. Gathered and garnered there is a mighty store of power and benedictions which shall be manifest some time. Like good seed scattered up and down the Christian's earthly path, the prayers of the righteous sprout and blossom and bear fruit long after the grave closes upon those who have uttered them. No form of Christian work has so great a tenacity of life, and none continues so long to multiply and develop after the workman is dead. But whether as a seed-sowing or a reaping, the praying that we do terminates with the present life. This most wonderful gift and privilege, this most powerful means of good to the world, has an end. Every dying man can say with truth, My prayers are ended. Of this as of other things the admonition bears with emphasis: "Whatsoever thy hand findeth to do, do it with thy might; for there is no work, nor device, nor knowledge, nor wisdom in the grave whither thou goest." Devout people who realize their responsibility in reference to active labor in the cause of Christ, and who are stimulated to giving and doing by the shortness of life, do not always extend the application to prayer.

Prayer, as to certain objects, is ended by other circumstances than that of our own death. The time comes when those we have prayed for are taken away. The parents we have been long accustomed to remember before God are gone, and the life-time habit, begun at the mother's knee and cherished and strengthened by an intelligent and ripened piety, is abruptly and sadly broken by the tidings of sorrow. We know not which is more sad, the thought that they no longer live to pray for us or the conviction which flashes upon us that they have passed absolutely beyond the mention always heretofore given them in our secret devotions. Children have the central place in the parental prayer. They are called up by name and personal form when the believing parent is closeted with God. From earliest infancy through childhood, youth, and on through maturer years, they are kept at the mercy-seat. Natural affection, deepened and ennobled, and purified into something higher and better, and the solemn sense of accountability for the eternal welfare of those whom God hath given them, inspire a fervor and faith which reach their mightiest and sublimest expression in the intercessions of believing parents. The death of children, as it touches this habit and life of prayer, is most deeply felt. While living they may go beyond our sight, and they may outgrow the tender and sweet dependence of infancy and childhood, but only death separates them from our prayers.

Of all relations and friendships we might indulge the same reflections. Those for whose salvation we have been specially concerned, those in whose welfare we have become greatly enlisted—whether neighbors, associates, kindred, or friends—for them our prayer is ended as they are numbered with the dead. Their names must be left off henceforth from the catalogue of those for whom our prayers have gone up. Their memory may be precious, the form and features are clear and full, love still clings to them, and they live in our daily thoughts and appear in our nightly dreams, but they have no more place in our prayers. It ought to quicken our earnestness and diligence in prayer when we reflect that the objects of intercessions, even the most precious and best loved, are liable at any time to be removed from the reach of our supplications. Prayer may not only be ended by our own death, but it may be ended as to some of its most cherished objects by the stroke which bereaves. Those whom God has placed within the circle of our prayers are by his dispensation taken from us.

We doubt not these instances of prayer ended are among the most melancholy recollections and experiences of many. There is a shade of gloom—and perhaps an approach to remorse—growing out of the half-disguised conviction of their own unfaithfulness. If the dead could be called back to life, with what fervor and agonizing they would pray for them! There is healing balm for the wound in the consciousness that we were diligent and importunate, and especial comfort in the assurance that our prayers were answered— that when our prayer for them ended, it had been answered in placing them where prayer is not only impossible, but where it is no longer needed.

MISSIONS.

LOOSING FROM TROAS.

THERE are many devoted preachers who are annually exercised about the field which they should enter. The Bishops usually allow a man to choose his Conference, and hence the question, Shall I transfer, and where? The only trouble in the case should be to know the mind of the Spirit in the premises, and when that has been reached to go or stay. Before Paul and Silas came to Troas they "were forbidden of the Holy Ghost to preach the word in Asia." Afterward "they assayed to go into Bithynia; but the Spirit suffered them not." At Troas the vision appeared to Paul in the night. "There stood a man of Macedonia, and prayed him, saying, Come over into Macedonia, and help us." Gathering from this that the Lord had called them to preach the gospel in Macedonia, thither they went, to preach to Lydia and others, to cast out evil spirits, and to save the Philippian jailer and his house. The case is plain enough with these devoted men. The Lord had a will concerning their movements, forbidding them to preach in some places and commanding their departure to others. Asia was without the gospel for the most part. Mysia, Bithynia, and Troas were without Christ, but the mind of the Spirit was that they should go to Macedonia. God has a mind in the movement of his ministers now, and this is the point of solicitude.

Unquestioning submission is the first thing to be attained. To get clear of any willfulness in the matter, and to look only at the claims of duty, is perhaps the most difficult achievement. How it is to be ascertained, though sometimes perplexing, is not so difficult as unconditional obedience to the divine command. There are so many merely temporal considerations involved—grounds of personal preference growing out of local circumstances, family ties, and pecuniary support—that we are apt to look at these almost exclusively. The country where men hope to do best for themselves is too often the Macedonia to which they gravitate. Their call to preach is a general one, and so they preach. The place may be determined by other influences than those which moved them to assume the obligations of the sacred office. The vision which took Paul and Silas by "a straight course" to Samothracia and Philippi was a divine call to preach in that particular region rather than anywhere else. Neither salary, health, nor personal advancement had any thing to do with it; and when they had assuredly gathered that the Lord had called them there, they forthwith endeavored to go, and they went. They loosed from Troas with no misgivings, and doubtless with the persuasion that he who called them would give them a prosperous voyage, and stand by them in their times of trial. To be like-minded with them is the true attitude of the gospel minister. He is ready to obey the heavenly vision, and to subordinate all other considerations to the will of God concerning him. So he preaches, it is a matter of indifference where. Paul would have gone to Asia; he then thought Bithynia was a good field; it was desirable to tarry at Troas. But he was mistaken. Macedonia was the open door; and of all the places in the world this one, which he had never thought of, was that which God had chosen for him. Abraham preached the same lesson of obedience when he went out from his own country, shaping his course not by the stars of heaven nor by the green pastures of earth, but by the guiding hand of Jehovah.

When, however, we imagine we have attained to complete submission, and are ready to move at the divine command, there comes the perplexing question, How are we to know the will of the Lord concerning us? Does the Holy Ghost forbid, and does he move us? Is there any vision of the night, praying and saying, "Come over into Macedonia, and help us?" Doubtless there are indications nearly as plain as those which the apostle had. If the steps of the good man are ordered of the Lord, the path of the devoted preacher ought not to be less clear. There are many things to be taken into the account in reaching the right conclusion, because the will of God is in accord with our conditions and necessities, and may be intimated by the providential adjustments which surround us. The men in a full and overrunning Conference are not called away from it necessarily, and in some instances a man may be called from a destitute field to one that is already pretty well supplied. The generally accepted idea, however, is probably the true one—that the more destitute fields appeal to the preacher's conscience. To them he ought to go if he can; and if others hold back who might go, all the more reason for him to let go the fastenings and set sail. But this loosing from Troas is a hard thing with many upon whom the impression is strong that a distant Macedonia requires their labors. The breaking up of old associations, the sundering of social ties, pecuniary sacrifices, and domestic interests involved, are calculated to deter. There are probable hardships to be encountered, a scant and uncertain support, and the ordeal of a new climate is to be undergone. Once in Macedonia, it is a trial to stay. There are older communities and Conferences, and richer and more inviting lands. To have come was the uttermost of effort, and not to go back is more than many can endure.

Alas for us that the grace to endure hardness as good soldiers of Jesus Christ is so often lacking! In some Conferences there are more men than places—there are men in the local ranks because the itinerant cohorts are full, and there are strong and experienced preachers who could be spared without much detriment to the work where they are. It is more agreeable every way for them to stay; but meanwhile "the regions beyond" are without the gospel, and the people are perishing. We may speak for Louisiana, where nearly half of our parishes are almost without the gospel, and in which some large presiding elders' districts have not more than three or four effective preachers. In some sections our churches and parsonages are going to ruin, and our flocks are being scattered and devoured for want of pastoral oversight. This may be true of other destitute Conferences in the West, but we doubt whether any are worse off than Louisiana. Will not the night vision wake up a host of recruits for these needy and sorely suffering regions? Weird and solemn and beseeching was the appeal as it came to Paul. Across the seas and amidst the shadows of paganism there stood a man of Macedonia. Was it the embodiment of heathen ignorance and misery crying to Christ's ministers for deliverance? or was it Christ himself already there and waiting for his heralds to proclaim life to the dying?

In Louisiana, in Arkansas, in Montana, in California, there stands a man who identifies himself with all the waste places, who speaks the language of their perishing people, and calls upon his servants to come to the rescue. There he stands, the impersonation and representative of famishing and neglected souls thirsting for the waters of life and hungry for the bread of heaven. He who called to Paul out of the night and across the Ægean calls to hundreds among us to break away from the older Conferences, to surrender local for itinerant work, and to yield to the Spirit's call for a self-denying but glorious ministry. Loosing from Troas, with a Hellespont of some sort to cross—there is the rub! Struggling and dying souls implore; the Man of Calvary prays us to come. The needle is true to the pole when suspended upon a burnished point and freed from perturbing influences. So it is with preachers in the line of duty if they swing free and clear upon the perfectly polished pivot of obedience to the divine will, and divest themselves of the disturbing forces which tempt them to swerve from the path of duty. The eye of love will be clear to see, the ear of love will be quick to hear, unless blinded and deadened by mistaken views. Where there is a Pauline heroism and an apostolic zeal, the man of Macedonia will not pray in vain for help. Loosing from Troas will be an easy matter when the spirit of burning fully imbues the ministry, and when the Master's voice is heard sounding across the waters and from the dreary desolations, "Come over, and help us!"

JONAH AND FOREIGN MISSIONS.

JONAH's mission to Nineveh antedates the birth of Christ about eight hundred years. In that age there was on the part of the Jews little thought or concern about the salvation of the heathen. The selfishness and exclusiveness of the elect people were such that other nations were regarded with abhorrence and enmity rather than compassion. In itself considered, the idea of sending a missionary from the banks of the Jordan to the Tigris would seem to have been something anomalous. No prophet had hitherto been commissioned for such a purpose. It was hard for converted men after the day of Pentecost to comprehend the new departure of going abroad and preaching to the Gentiles. It is not strange that the son of Amittai had his misgivings when commanded to go to the great Assyrian metropolis. It came to him as a clap of thunder out of a clear sky. Jerusalem was full of wickedness, the people of the covenant were themselves fearfully given to idolatry, corruption abounded throughout the borders of Israel. There was work enough at home, and it looked like the veriest folly to send a missionary to a place so distant and to a nation who needed repentance scarcely more than that where the prophet lived. To the faithful and devout who constituted the true Church of the time it must have been a great surprise. God's care for them they believed. That he should raise up prophets for their warning and instruction was reasonable, but how preposterous that the God of Israel should show compassion to the uncircumcised, and so much compassion as to send a special messenger to call the Ninevites to repentance!

In this matter Jonah was not of the same mind with his Master. He partook of the religious exclusiveness and selfishness of the Church of the day, and was imbued with that benevolent utilitarianism which demands that all shall be done at home before we attempt any thing abroad. The sacrifice of his personal comfort, the hardships of so long a journey, and the personal peril to which he would be exposed may have wrought upon his fears, and there may have been in him something of national prejudice and enmity toward those who were, by prophetical announcement, one day to be a scourge to Israel. If the Gentiles were to be called to repentance through him, Jonah would have preferred some other field. But the one comprehensive key to his conduct is found in his almost invincible convictions against the character of his mission. He did not believe in foreign missions, and to the end he was anxious that the result should vindicate his reluctance to engage in the work. Under constraint he went to Nineveh and preached unto it the preaching that God bid him, but he would have been gratified if the wicked city had not repented; but, as the penitent city was spared, he recalls what he had pleaded before he left his own country: that God would repent him of the threatened evil, and that the peril of the city was not such as to require this extraordinary intervention. Contradictory and inconsistent as the prophet seems to be with himself in his expostulations and complaints, there is throughout this persistent and perverse opposition to carrying the message of warning to a distant Gentile people. He thought it better to stay at home, and confine his labors to Jerusalem and the coasts of Israel.

As in some sort anticipatory of the great commission, and the world-wide scope of the gospel provisions of grace, the history of Jonah stood as a monumental light until the new dispensation came in, and even now its lessons to the Church are impressively significant. These lessons bear upon the central and absorbing work of the Church as an organization to preach the preaching given to it by Christ to the nations. Jonah stands out in the ancient times as the type of hardshellism, as the representative of nearly every phase of opposition to foreign missions. He illustrates this opposition not so much as it comes from the world but as it exists in the Church. It is a prejudice and an antipathy which pleads the state of the people about us, that questions the peril of the heathen, and that doubts the power of the gospel to save them. Jonah exhibits this opposition as manifested in the face of the divine command to go. "Arise, go to Nineveh, that great city, and cry against it; for their wickedness is come up before me;" and this is not plainer than the marching orders to us as delivered by the Captain of our salvation: "Go ye into all the world, and preach the gospel to every creature."

The grand import of Jonah's mission justified the striking miracle by which his flight from the presence of the Lord was arrested. It remains as a sign, accommodated as the type of the burial and resurrection of Christ, but, in a figure, the type of judgment upon our disobedience to the divine command and the gracious effects of that judgment in the spiritual resurrection of the Church and its renewed life of obedience and power in proclaiming salvation to all nations. The Saviour's reference, besides warranting this application, connects his own resurrection with the cause of missions, as the sign, the convincing miraculous attestation of our duty and of our success. To Jonah and his times, and to Nineveh, the sign was wonderful and convincing indeed, but to us the buried Saviour, coming forth from the grave as "the Prince of life," is a sign more powerful and more inspiring. The men of Nineveh are to rise up in judgment with this and every generation. Their repentance ought to have awakened Israel when Jonah returned, and if it did not it condemned them and the perverse prophet with them. They will rise up in judgment against all sinners who have the greater sign and persist in their impenitence under the ministry of a greater than Jonah.

But will they not rise up in the judgment with us, and condemn us for our slothfulness and unbelief? Every instance of missionary success does condemn those who, by indifference or conviction, fail in supporting the great and vital work. The men of Nineveh deliver to us their testimony across the space of more than twenty-five centuries, and they are waiting for us in the judgment; but nearer and clearer is the note of warning and of awakening which comes from the fields of modern missions. The souls already plucked as brands from paganism prove that thousands and millions more would have been saved had there been no holding back, no unbelief, and no guilty indifference on the part of those to whom the Lord has committed his goods.

THE APPEAL OF MISSIONS.

FOREIGN missions are more nearly a work of disinterested benevolence than almost any thing we can take in hand. The money given does not come back to us directly and visibly. Those who build churches and schools at home reap the benefits at once in the enhancement of their property and in the improvement of the society which surrounds them. The gospel preached in a community or neighborhoed is worth a thousand times its cost in the improvement of public morals and in the promotion of the general welfare. The giver himself and his family are the immediate beneficiaries. The spiritual and the temporal interests are subserved. It is a provision for his own good, and contributes to his own comfort and enjoyment. The money given remains at home, is thrown into circulation, and scarcely leaves the hand that bestows it before, in some shape, it returns to the giver. The funds for foreign missions are expended abroad, and the end is to bless those who are far away—people of a different race, and perhaps living on the other side of the earth. If the bread thus cast upon the waters ever comes back it is after many days. It is this feature of missions which should most commend them to the Christian. Here is an opportunity to be unselfish, to do something for love's sake with no possible taint of low and unworthy motives. It is an occasion such as Mary coveted and improved when she broke the alabaster box and poured the costly nard upon the Saviour's head. What is often urged by a utilitarian covetousness as an objection to missions is, in truth, a singular and sufficient reason for them. Some measure for the crucifixion of self is needed, a test of genuine Christian devotion is demanded, and the devout soul longs for a duty that shall be stripped of every incentive but love. We have all of these in the appeal for foreign missions, because it is addressed to the purest and highest form of unselfish benevolence; and for this reason it is the queen of all religious enterprises.

Missions appeal most powerfully to the conscience. The command to go into all the world is explicit. The obligation might be inferred from universal provisions of salvation, from the scope of infinite love, from the breadth of the atonement, and from the ministry of the Spirit in all men. The matter might have been left to the benevolent impulses of the regenerated heart in view of the lost condition of the world without the gospel. It is not conceivable that those who have felt the peace and comfort of salvation and have realized the perils of sin should look upon a perishing race with indifference; but the Master's authority is directly asserted. We are commanded to do this thing—to preach the gospel to every creature. He calls his servants and delivers unto them his goods—the priceless treasure of the gospel—and will hold them to account for the sacred trust. Our marching orders are clear, and in conscience we must obey them. There may be other motives, but the cause could not be left to them, and hence we have the command. It is not for us to inquire into the reasons so much as it is to obey. The appeal is to the Christian conscience, to our sense of obligation to God, and to our recognition of the authority of Christ. It is God's appointed means of giving the gospel to the world. In his measure the commission is to every Christian man, and Christ expects him to do his part. It is not relevant, in this connection, to inquire how long it will take to Christianize mankind, or whether the world will ever be altogether brought to Christ. As a matter of conscience, we are to send the glad tidings everywhere, and see that the gospel is preached to all nations for a witness. Whether the heathen can be saved without the gospel is not the question. God has commanded us to send it to them, and our responsibility will be measured not so much by the extent of their danger as by our disposition and ability to fulfill the great commission. However it may be with the heathen, we shall ourselves be lost if we fail in our obedience to Christ's commands. It is not a question of sentiment nor of speculative theology, but of conscientious obedience to Christ. That must be a conscience grossly perverted or sadly in want of light that is not alive to missionary obligation. It is to conscience— the enlightened Christian conscience—that the cause of missions makes one of its strongest appeals. This is an element of value in it: that it addresses the conscience, that it quickens the spiritual nature, and that it goes down to the very root of religious principle. It breaks up the ground and enriches the spiritual soil of the Church, and thus contributes to her piety and power.

In another aspect of the subject faith stands out conspicuously. "Son, man, can these dry bones live?" The vision was to rebuke unbelief, and to illustrate the power of the gospel. Paganism is a valley of dry bones, and the world is a scene of spiritual death. What the gospel has done warrants the conviction that it will yet wave its victorious banner over every land. It has achieved enough within fifty years to assure us that erelong "the earth shall be full of the knowledge of the Lord as the waters cover the sea." It is written that the root of Jesse shall stand for an ensign of the people, and that "to it shall the Gentiles seek, and his rest shall be glorious." Christ saw of the travail of his soul, and was satisfied. The apostles believed in the gospel as the power and the wisdom of God. Those who have been born of the Spirit have in themselves the earnest of the world's conversion. Let the Church go forth at the divine command, prophesying in the name of Christ and calling for the life-breathing Spirit, and the result is not doubtful. Not to have faith in foreign missions is to confess our unbelief in the gospel and in Christ himself, and that we are profoundly ignorant of the history of Christianity. It is here that we ought to have faith and that we must have it. Faith in God, faith in Christ, faith in the Holy Ghost, faith in the gospel as the means of human salvation, is needed to encourage and strengthen our endeavor. It is an enterprise of love, of conscience, and also of faith. Here is a distinctive end and purpose for our faith, and according to our faith will be the progress of Christian conquest.

A capital excellence of missions is that in them we are in complete sympathy with the work of Christ. The Redeemer's heart is in this work as in no other. His mediatorial reign is directed to this object; his intercessions are for its accomplishment. It is of the travail of his soul, and the world's conversion is to be the crowning satisfaction of our crucified Lord. His love manifested on the cross is the supreme impulse in us. "For the love of Christ constraineth us; because we thus judge that if one died for all, then were all dead; and that he died for all that they which live should not henceforth live unto themselves, but unto him which died for them and rose again." All are dead, all are redeemed. Love gives us the cross and salvation through its awful agony. That love thrilled the heart of Paul, it fired the enthusiasm of Coke, Heber, and Judson, and it burns in the souls of our missionaries in distant lands today. If we all—the entire Church—could only feel the mighty argument of Christ's love, and yield to its constraining power! We shall hope and pray for the blessed consummation, for the baptism of Christ's love, that shall impel us no longer to live to ourselves but unto him that died for us.

AN OLD OBJECTION TO MISSIONS.

An article in one of our secular dailies recently called our attention to the old and threadbare objection to foreign missions—that these lead to the neglect of the religiously destitute at home. The tone of the article was fair and sincere, and doubtless expresses the convictions of many benevolent people who are friendly to the spread of the gospel.

An answer, in part, to this objection is that people in Christian lands have the gospel. There are what are called the neglected classes, and there are masses not much influenced by the direct teachings of the gospel; but the churches and Sunday-schools are open to them, Bibles and tracts are systematically distributed among them, and ministers, missionaries, and religious men and women are moving about in contact with them. If any are ignorant of Christ and of the teachings of Christianity, it is for the most part their own fault. All who desire a Bible have one; all who are willing to hear the gospel may hear it. With the heathen it is different. They have no Bibles, and they are without a divine revelation. If large masses of people at home choose to reject the gospel, this is no good reason why the Church should withhold it from the millions of pagans who have no gospel privileges whatever. Such a course on the score of benevolence would be criminal rather than praiseworthy.

We most heartily second all efforts to call sinners to repentance at home and to search out and urge the gospel upon the poor, ignorant, and vicious in our large cities; but at the worst their opportunities are incomparably better than those of the heathen. No amount of effort or expenditure can save all in any locality. The duty of the Church is, as far as possible, to give the gospel to all. It cannot compel nor assure its acceptance. It is manifest that, were we to wait until all the heathen at home were saved, we should never move beyond the limits of our Christian civilization. Had this principle been adopted by the apostles and the primitive Church, we should be heathen ourselves, and Christ would never have been preached outside of Jerusalem and Palestine. Paul, in that case, would never have set foot on the soil of Macedonia; Peter would never have gone to Babylon; and Rome, Greece, and Britain would never have heard of the Saviour. When the Saviour commanded his apostles and the Church to go into all the world, and to preach the gospel to every creature, he meant that they should go. As Peter, John, and Paul, under inspiration, interpreted this commission and went abroad before the people at home were Christianized, so may we.

What is possible may be done at home at the same time that Christ is preached abroad. The evangelization of the world is a work of time, and it is important that the work of preparation should be going on in many places at once. The gospel is as seed sown, and, being sown at home, it would be a cruel waste of time to wait for the harvest in one field before breaking ground and sowing in another. Our gardeners know that it would be folly to wait for the maturity of one vegetable before planting another. Between the one and the other there is no conflict, but each is coming forward in its own order and swelling the aggregate profit. Cotton-planters tell us that a fair amount of corn can be made without interfering with the cotton. While the cotton is being planted the corn is already up and growing, and the two cultures go on side by side without hinderance to either. The Church can do what is possible at home in both sowing and reaping, and it can at the same time be sowing gospel-seed in heathen countries.

The Christian Church is not doing its duty at home nor abroad, but there is no conflict between the two. It is a matter of fact that when the Protestant Churches had no foreign missions the masses at home were the most neglected. For proof we have only to compare the religious condition of England in the eighteenth century with its religious condition in the present century. The same life that stirs Christian men to seek the destitute at home also moves them to go to those who are perishing in heathen lands. It is a fact that the more the churches are imbued with the missionary spirit the more faithful, zealous, and liberal they are in supplying the people with the gospel at home. Some choose to explain that this is a reactionary influence that comes from the work of foreign missions. It may be so, but we account for it rather on the ground that all Christian work has its source in the one element of spiritual life, and that where this life burns in the heart the whole sphere of duty is embraced. If taught by the precepts and examples of the New Testament and imbued with the spirit of Christ, no Christian can resist the convictions and impulses of missionary work.

As for foreign missions being a failure, our answer in part is that the revival of religion at home usually keeps pace with our missionary zeal; and, further, that in proportion to money expended and all agencies employed, the success of the gospel is greater in foreign missions than it is at home. How can any one acquainted with what has been accomplished within the last fifty years say that foreign missions are a failure? A glance at the islands of the Pacific, Madagascar, India, and China, refutes the assertion. Within this period thousands and hundreds of thousands have been brought to Christ. But if this were not so, and if with little apparent fruit our mission-work were only a work of preparation and of seed-sowing, still it would be a great success as laying the foundations for the future conquest of the world to Christ. Foreign missions are successful; but if, according to our judgment, it were otherwise, still the duty of the Church is clear to go into all the world, and to preach the gospel of the kingdom as a witness to all nations.

DEAD AND BURIED.

AT the recent session of the Mississippi Conference, after a brother had represented the people of his charge as opposed to foreign missions, Bishop Keener related the following incident. Not long ago, while passing through a certain section in a private conveyance, his attention was drawn to a neat-looking church, situated in a pleasant grove, with a burying-ground contiguous. On inquiry he was informed that the church had only one member living. All the rest, of a once large membership, had died, and were buried in the adjoining grave-yard. It was an anti-missionary Baptist church.

Beyond the mere statement the Bishop made no comment, leaving the application to the Conference. To us it was about as startling and comprehensive a missionary address as we had heard in many a day. Our churches, to live, must be missionary. Opposition to missions, or indifference, is the certain precursor of death. That Church will die out that neither gives nor prays for missions.

Those charges that are without the missionary spirit are but half alive. They would be utterly dead if they did not form a part of a great connection from which some vitality is derived. Not many charges—perhaps none—are altogether indifferent to missions. Individuals are saved from complete inanition by the spirituality of those about them who feel the binding obligation of the great commission to preach the gospel to every creature.

But these dead branches—anti-missionary members—in any of our congregations are a weight and a curse to the general spiritual welfare. They infect the whole body to some extent, stand in the way of the pastor in his endeavors to raise the assessment, and join in the howl of worldlings and infidels against the folly of sending the gospel to the heathen.

We believe the anti-missionary Baptists based their opposition to missions on the doctrine of predestination and reprobation. God would bring in the elect somehow, and the result was certain. It is not easy to understand the ground on which an anti-missionary Methodist stands. It is as much as we can do to take care of ourselves—this is the usual plea. In some cases sincere and good people fall into this delusion, but generally opposition to missions is connected with lack of religious intelligence and utter ungodliness, or a very low type of piety.

Some of our pastors occasionally lose heart, and fear for their salaries when the missionary collection is to be taken. The more observant and enlightened, however, have learned that the spirit of missions is the spirit of life, and that where people give freely and gladly to send the gospel abroad they are most generous in its support at home.

A church that does not wish to die and be buried must wake up to the call of God to spread the tidings of salvation.

THE MISSION OF GOLD.

CHRIST OVER AGAINST THE TREASURY.

THOSE chests in the temple, with their trumpet-shaped openings, were suggestive to the throngs coming and going. To the Jewish worshipers they were not offensive, for it was a part of their religion to give. The offering of sacrifices, the prayers of the devout, and all sacred services might be going on near by, but the rattle of coin as it fell wrought no discord. It was in keeping with God's house, although that house was to be a house of prayer for all nations. Christ did overthrow the tables of the money-changers and drive out those who converted the holy place into a mart for buying, selling, and getting gain; but he looks with complacency upon this arrangement for the support of religion.

He is there over against the treasury, and as he rests from his recent conflict with the scribes and Pharisees there is something tranquilizing in the scene before him. Intent as he might be on the spiritual character and interests of the kingdom of God, the treasury and its contributors are worthy of his careful notice. His eye is upon those who come with their offerings, and he counts the pieces and accurately estimates the character of the givers. It was sheer and outright giving—the money was cast into the treasury. Nothing came back in the shape of prizes, confections, or spectacular entertainments. The money went into the chests, out of sight, and that was the end of it. It was for God and his temple, a gift out and out, with no discount taken off in the shape of fun and refreshments.

The poor widow is the central figure in the scene. The poorest of the poor, bereft and desolate, she throws in her two mites. It was but a farthing, but it was all her living. Many that were rich cast in much, but it was of their abundance. There might have been some conscience in their act, but there was no self-denial. It was less than convenient, costing no effort, and involving no loss of personal comfort. It did not even remotely touch their costly attire nor trench upon the delicacies of their tables. Their sumptuously furnished homes lost nothing of their splendor. They cast in much, but it was little for them. The only generous giver there was the one who gave a farthing. In her it seemed a reckless act, to be condemned rather than commended.

To have given nothing, when there were so many rich people able to meet the entire demand, would have been a plausible view of her duty. She should at any rate have kept half, dividing what she had equally between the Lord and herself. This would have more than satisfied the piety of most people. There is an utter abandon in this giving of all—a love and faith that is as unaccountable to us as it was surprising to the Saviour. So striking was this instance of consecration that the Master specially calls his disciples to contemplate it. It was a green spot in that arid waste of hypocrisy, ostentation, and covetousness. In an atmosphere of greed, self-righteousness, and malignant hatred of the truth, this was a relief and an object to dwell upon with peculiar pleasure and satisfaction.

Let us not mistake the lesson. It is the duty and the privilege of the poor to give. It is the privilege of the rich to give much, to build churches, endow colleges, and establish asylums; but the poor may give, and even exceed in their giving, though it be absolutely little. The farthing from those able to give dollars and thousands of dollars would be an insult to God, while it is commended in those who can do no more. A missionary hen may be much for a little child, while an elephant or a herd of cattle would be a meager offering for many well-to-do people. It was the farthing of the poor widow that Christ dwells upon with so much approval. It was an expression of love and devotion in her, and a blessing to herself. The temple was not built by the mites of the poor, nor do we suppose they went very far toward maintaining the services and supporting the institutions of religion. They helped, no doubt; but then, as now, the contributions of the more wealthy were the chief dependence. The world can never be educated and saved by widows' mites and farthing donations. God expects the Vanderbilts, Drews, Riches, Cornells, and men of large means everywhere, to consecrate their wealth to Christian enterprises.

But while this is so, it is the duty of the poor to give something. If the cause of Christ could do without their mites, they cannot afford to withhold them. The grace that is in them will seek this manifestation, and will be increased and strengthened by it. That poor widow might have truly said to herself: "These mites are much to me; they can be comparatively nothing in the great treasure, and the rich can easily pay it all." But this would never have satisfied her love, nor would her personal obligation have been met. There was a blessing in the duty. She performed it, and while she cast in all that she had she went away rich and content. It is not unusual to encourage small donations by arraying the fact that a dime will pay for a Testament, that fifty cents will give a Bible to some poor heathen, and that a nickel will buy one brick for the church wall. This is well enough, but we imagine the poor widow thought very little about the purchasing power of her farthing. She gave it to God in a way that was customary and open to her. It might go into the oil of the sanctuary, help to pay for the morning and evening sacrifices, or contribute to the adornment and glory of the vestments of the high-priest. She probably thought nothing of these things. Christ might have told her that the hierarchy was corrupt and about to vanish, and that her little store was as good as thrown away. It is the giving—the principle of it—that he scrutinizes and commends. Whatever became of the money, she did her duty and got her reward.

Christ is still over against the treasury. If he is present as an interested spectator anywhere, he is here. He beholds the givers, and weighs them in his balances. His eye is upon the rich and upon the poor. To him character is revealed by what men put into his chests. It is possible to deceive human judgment, and to make a show of piety where there is really no deep love. "The Lord shall judge his people." Christ is sitting in judgment on our collections. No man puts his hand into his pocket for Christ unnoticed by the Lord himself. He beholds *how* the people cast money into his treasury, what proportion it bears to what they have, the motive, and the sacrifice in the act. The responsibility is not relative as to what others do, but personal and absolute. The penuriousness of the rich does not excuse the poor, nor does the unfaithfulness of one release another. The poor widow may have gone too far, but Christ commends her devotion. She will, we fear, rise up in the judgment and condemn many, both rich and poor, of this generation.

COST OF SOULS.

Our China letter will be read with interest and profit. Up to date the converts have cost us about one thousand taels per head. The calculation is easily made. So much money has been appropriated to the China Mission, and so many persons have been converted. Result gives one soul for every fifteen hundred dollars expended.

We do not know the cost of souls in other missions, nor whether an estimate of the kind has been made. We might institute a comparison with our negro missions, or with the expenditures upon California of former years, if we had the figures at hand. Could not an approximation be reached of disbursements and returns in our regular work at home? How much money for every soul converted? Our gospel arithmetic might be carried up to the final application, How much for every convert since the day of Pentecost? Directly or indirectly what amount has been expended on our individual salvation? To answer this last question we should have to go a long way back, and the sum total might be no inconsiderable item.

Money in this connection has a peculiar attribute. So we thought in reading the China letter. Ordinarily it represents values. There is in a given sum so much food, a ship and its cargo, lands, houses, raiment, the capital of a snug business, or ten per cent. of interest. But here is a value of another sort. Money represents souls. In a given field of evangelical labor it is ciphered out to a cent. Every convert has cost about one thousand taels. These souls would have remained in their sins, and have been lost forever, but for this money. Without it neither missionary nor Bible could have reached them. Here is a new and peculiar value put upon what we possess, out of which grows a solemn and startling responsibility. The Christian's wealth cannot be divested of this fearful element of accountability. What has been expended upon our lusts, the extravagances of fashion, or hoarded in the grasp of avarice, represents souls which might have been saved had it been devoted to the cause of God. Our missions have always been straitened for means. Ten times the amount expended upon them would doubtless have secured a like proportion of spiritual results. Ten souls would have been converted where one has been. Who will be held accountable for these lost souls? It is a question for those to ponder who have kept back the tithes due to God's house.

Nor does this principle apply only to foreign missions. The money put in a Church represents the good that such a Church would accomplish; and that which is expended in keeping up the preaching of the gospel and sustaining missionaries in weak and destitute districts stands for the spiritual and immortal benefits secured by these instrumentalities.

Devoted men are necessary as missionaries; but these have been more easily found than the means for their support. Think of our *two* missionaries in China, with the field white to the harvest, and they compelled to curtail their labors for the want of a meager support which the Church at home withholds! There is need also of prayer, and the pervading ministry of the Holy Spirit; but neither of these will obviate the want of pecuniary aid. The grace of giving is as essential as that of faith. The salvation of souls costs money as well as labor and prayer. These souls in China have cost a great deal, but the missionary comforts us with the hope that the rate will soon be reduced from a thousand taels to one tael per soul.

That the larger figure is a high price depends upon such considerations as these: The absolute value of a soul saved in heaven—"What shall it profit a man if he shall gain the whole world, and lose his own soul?" Some of these fruits of our mission are now in heaven, and we are sure they do not feel that too much has been paid. Nor would those who remain on earth, rejoicing in the hope of glory, sell their faith for ten times the entire cost of our missions. The money would have effected more somewhere else. This is doubtful, unless it is clear that the money would have been directed to some other field. But nobody can suppose that the mere pittance we have been sending to China has lessened the contributions to other objects. On the contrary, the reflexive influence upon the piety and liberality of the Church has enriched and strengthened us at home. The souls saved in China are a clear gain, besides the benefits which giving and thinking and preaching about them have brought to our own doors. Missions are the life of the Church, and the farther from home the greater their power of reaction upon us. The good which flows from them depends greatly upon their cost. David would not sacrifice of that which cost him nothing. Neither should we. It is this which exhibits faith, and takes the churl out of the heart.

There is another view to which our correspondent refers—the prospective work in China. A large outlay at first, as in many secular enterprises, but there is a good interest in the time to come. The preparatory steps, it may be, have involved heavy expenditures and small returns; but now the prospect brightens, and the way is open to reach and save these benighted millions. Much of our impatience is due to our avarice. Suppose none had been converted as yet, is not our duty plain to give the gospel to every creature? Whether the people shall be evangelized slowly, rapidly, or not at all, may be no business of ours. Our responsibility begins and ends with doing our part. Here, however, we have assurance that nothing has been undertaken in vain.

The wonder is that so rich a harvest is about to reward the very stinted sowing. Events in China, under the hand of Providence, have long been shaping for a great triumph of the gospel. Fifty years hence a new estimate will have to be made. What will have been the cost of souls then, as compared with the present? If up to this time it had been ten thousand taels apiece, what will it be when the teeming millions of the East shall be born again? As Christians we ought to be thankful that such a chance for investment is afforded, and for this opportunity of making to ourselves friends of the unrighteous mammon.

ECONOMIZING FOR GOD.

The cheapness with which the present crop has been made is regarded as a hopeful circumstance. If the prices are low and the yield scanty in many sections, still if there has been but little outlay in the cultivation, the net results will be considerable. People who keep out of debt, and make a little, are well off in comparison with those whose obligations are more than the value of the crop. Economy is an excellent remedy for hard times, and a means by which the country after awhile will recover some degree of prosperity. It is a necessity with many who have already exhausted their credit, and it is a wise expedient where people would maintain their independence and recover from the financial prostration and losses which have befallen them.

Doubtless the exorbitant taxes call for retrenchment in other expenditures, as the taxes must be met or the property will be put under the sheriff's hammer. These are days of frugal expedients, of shifts in every department of expense. Luxuries, comforts, and conveniences once enjoyed must be dispensed with, that the things absolutely necessary may be secured. The old clothes, the last season's bonnet, the faded carpets, can be made to do somehow.

It is wonderful how many things can be done without when there is a strong compulsion.

But how is it with reference to economizing for God? The spiritual crop this year in our Southern fields has been more than usually abundant, and none has ever been made at a smaller cost in money to the Church. It has, however, cost much to the preachers in consuming what means they may have had in the destitution of their families and in the personal toils and hardships endured. They are not disposed to complain, and generally say but little about their privations; but we know that, as a class, they are greatly straitened. Are the people served by these self-denying men retrenching in other things that they may contribute to their support? Churches must be built and repaired, or the work of God will make little progress. Nearly every religious interest suffers, the annual collections—which are vital to our Connectional welfare—are reduced, and the Church in her missionary enterprises is brought to a halt, when the needed funds are withheld. The times are stringent with the most. If the gospel is supported, and the interests of the Church are kept up, there must be retrenchment in secular expenditures that there may be means to sustain the institutions of religion.

There must be economizing to this distinctive end—the foregoing not only of luxuries and expensive pleasures, but even of usual comforts. We imagine that it was in this way that the Macedonians did so bountifully in troublous times, so that "their deep poverty abounded unto the riches of their liberality." There must have been a great deal of self-denial, extreme frugality in living, and many sacrifices by those poor but devoted Christians of whom the apostle testifies: "For to their power I bear record; yea, and beyond their power, they were willing of themselves." It will not do now to go by the standard of ability as understood and practiced in the days of our prosperity. If people give of their surplus only, and according to convenience, as was the custom in former times, the gathering will be meager indeed. God's tenth is the same in proportion, whether we have little or much; but that tenth with many can hardly be spared in their impoverished condition. Let them save in some other way, even to the point of personal inconvenience, rather than withhold from God.

There will be a blessing in the deed, a blessing returning to them, and a blessing going out in manifold streams to gladden and refresh the Lord's heritage. We would only indicate the principle, and leave the application to every Christian's conscience. Let the devout woman consider wherein she can do without what she feels she really needs, in order that Christ's cause may be upheld. Let the man of God go over the demands which press upon him and the things which he desires, and mark some cherished object as taken from himself and given to his Lord. Save, deny yourselves, use every thoughtful expedient, that you may be able to aid in maintaining the gospel and in sustaining the enterprises of the Church. It is right that Christians should do this, and in these times it is absolutely necessary.

The falling off in religious giving is not so much with the poor, who have always been accustomed out of their deep poverty to contribute their mite, but it is rather with those who have been used to something like style in their living, and who have followed closely in the wake, if they have not kept fully up with the fashions. The sacrifice of mere appearances, the singularity of being behind the fashions, and of bringing their present style into contrast with the past, requires more courage than the surrender of actual comforts. They cannot give any thing for religious purposes and maintain the expenditures to which they have been accustomed. Their economizing for God would not touch the real comforts and needs of ordinary desire; but are they willing to give up the struggle after style and a sham respectability that they may be not liberal but just toward God?

There are of course some who have the means of giving largely even in these times of almost unparalleled pressure. The demand on them is more imperative than ever. Their stewardship involves a weightier responsibility, and they will be held to a stricter account by the Master. Economizing for God is not without application to them. In all their profits and investments, and in the use of their money, there is occasion for them to devise liberally for Christ. It is in their power to help the pastor and his family, to cherish every languishing interest of the Church, and to hold and extend the work of missions. Those that have money now, and hoard it, and speculate on it, and grow richer, while every religious enterprise is crippled and appealing for help, will have a sorrowful account to meet in the end.

SOWING MONEY.

GIVING to benevolent objects is sowing money. So Paul intimates to the Corinthians. Every dollar has a living germ in it that will sprout into new life and ripen into a harvest. Expended in other ways for pleasure, appetite, and avarice, it may bring temporary returns, but in the end it wastes and perishes. The result of fleshly sowing, in money as in other things, ends in reaping corruption. The dragon's teeth brought forth a crop of armed men. A bad use of money is sure to entail calamities and miseries. The only lasting and safe investment is in devoting it to God and godly enterprises. The only way to keep it forever and to have it always is to give it away. The reported declaration of a dying philanthropist is strikingly true: "What I have given I have, and what I have kept I have lost."

And yet the common conception of giving would seem to be that it is the alienation from ourselves of property and means, and that the giver dispossesses himself of that which he contributes. This is so not more than in the case of the husbandman who casts seed into the ground. He does not throw away his bread, but he makes it, and largely increases his store. The bread cast upon the waters is most wisely and judiciously disposed of to the advantage of him who finds it after many days.

That money sown comes back in kind may be true. There are promises which countenance the expectation: "Honor the Lord with thy substance, and with the first-fruits of all thine increase; so shall thy barns be filled with plenty, and thy presses shall burst out with new wine." Paul certainly intimates to the Corinthians that they should not be losers in a temporal way by what they gave in ministering to the saints, but that God would enrich them in every thing. There is a principle here which is taken into the account in the order of Providence, but it is not greatly emphasized in the teachings of Christ and the apostles, and for the reason that it might induce sordidness and covetousness in giving. The penalty of withholding may be impoverishment, and the reward of liberality may be increased wordly prosperity The pound improved secures the gift of more, while the pound hid away is resumed by the lawful owner. God is not indifferent to our stewardship of temporal things, and an even-handed justice is often exhibited in the condition of those who have abused or have been faithful to their trust.

But the temporal benefits of liberal giving are the lowest considerations in the Christian's mind. Except so far as these may affect his ability to give, they have a very subordinate influence. He looks not so much for the return of his money as for compensation of a nobler character. He would not be content to receive his money back again, if this were all, because he seeks higher and more durable blessings. Money-given is money sown, because the harvest is in spiritual blessedness here and in an eternal recompense hereafter. The actual good done is an element of satisfaction and exquisite delight; but even more gratifying is the sense of God's approval, and the consciousness that we have done all we could for the glory of God and for the happiness of men.

In whatever way we consider the results of giving—the temporal, the spiritual, the eternal—it has in it the analogy of sowing. In a lower sense—but in an accurate one—money, like the word, is the good seed of the kingdom. The analogy to nature is not pressed unduly when we say of this money-sowing: "That which thou sowest is not quickened, except it die." It must die to the giver before it can be quickened into a higher form of blessings for him; "and that which thou sowest, thou sowest not that body that shall be, but bare grain, it may chance of wheat or of some other grain." It is indeed a resurrection—something purer and better than that which is sown—for "it is sown in dishonor, it is raised in glory." Every farthing rightly given has this germinant nature. There is a fruitful life in it which can only be developed by sowing—that is, by giving it away. There is but one soil wherein money can be quickened and expanded into a spiritual and immortal harvest, and that is the good ground of religion and benevolence. Here it bursts forth into flowers most fragrant, into fruits like those that hang upon the tree of life, and into foliage whose every stem and leaf is full of healing balm.

Comparatively a small portion of the money in the world is sown. The most is expended upon self, the lusts of the flesh, the lust of the eyes, and the pride of life. It goes into railroads, into estates, into the investments of the stock exchange. It is consumed, wasted, lost in the attempt to keep it, while the consecrated use which transmutes it into imperishable treasure is the rarest of all.

The law holds good in sowing money as in sowing wheat —sparingly, sparingly; abundantly, abundantly. The farmer who sows sparingly reaps accordingly. He enriches himself by scattering his seed with a lavish hand. Few men are wisely liberal. They sow but little—they waste the most that they have. The money God has given them to sow is hoarded, or worse. The seed-corn bears no reasonable proportion to that which goes to the mill. They will reap sparingly—something perhaps—a few thin and blighted ears scattered over a sterile field. In grace and glory sparingly. Of the money we have spent, how much of it has been sown? And a few—passing few—sow abundantly. They are rich in grace, and in the great beyond they have a good reward for all their labor. They will come up in "that day" with joy, and bearing their sheaves with them.

What an auspicious hour is this for sowing money! How can we keep it back in this spring-time of godly opportunity when the world, so long fallow, is being broken up, and when mission fields, colleges, and churches, and the poor, are calling for liberal and open-handed devisings.

FROM GRACE TO GRACE.

THE BIRTH OF THE SPIRIT.

ONE of the greatest hinderances to the realization of this experience lies in its supposed identity or connection with outward rites and ordinances. If once persuaded that it is no more than baptism, or that it is conferred by the imposition of hands or the reception of a sacrament, the matter is forestalled, and an actual, conscious change of heart is no longer thought of. If ordinances are the channels through which the Spirit is communicated, there is no need of any further trouble. This is a delusion which blocks the way to a genuine scriptural regeneration with many. They have been baptized, they have received the sacraments of the Church, and in this they rest, persuaded that whatever is meant by the birth of the Spirit has been attained through the ordinances of the gospel. The very first step toward realizing the new birth is to get clear from this most fatal error, and to escape from this most foolish entanglement. Whatever the birth of water may mean, the birth of the Spirit is something distinct from it. The Saviour therefore declares: " Except a man be born of water *and of the Spirit*, he cannot enter into the kingdom of God." If the water necessarily involved the Spirit, or if its application secured the Spirit's operation, it was needless for the Saviour to add "and of the Spirit." The two births are as clearly separated and distinguished as it is possible. Water baptism is not enough; ordinances, in themselves, come short of the requirement; there must be, beyond and independent of it, the direct and transforming work of the

Holy Spirit. John the Baptist exhibits the same doctrine substantially when he contrasts his baptism with water with that higher baptism of Christ: "He shall baptize you with the Holy Ghost, and with fire." That Christ's purpose was to distinguish and separate the water from the Spirit is evident from the further fact that he contrasts the spiritual with the natural birth, and dwells with emphasis upon the necessity of being born of the Spirit.

If the inquirer is happily free from this confusion of ideas about the import of ordinances, he may find difficulty in distinguishing the birth of the Spirit from those conditions of mind and feeling which do not imply it. He is already leading a moral life as blameless and upright as was Nicodemus. Possibly he is a member of the Church, and instructed in the doctrines and practices of religion. Must such a one be born again, or is he already a subject of converting grace? Here, at least, was a good man and sincere who knew nothing about this birth from above. Nicodemus, with all his goodness, with all his candor and simplicity of mind, had yet to experience it. Precisely how good a man may be in amiability of character, in the performance of religious duties, and in concern for salvation, without being converted, it is not easy to determine. A man may be not far from the kingdom of God and not be in it. The kingdom may come nigh to us without coming in and possessing the heart. Doubtless there are multitudes who need the enforcement of this "must" upon their consciences, who are resting in the mistaken persuasion that they are all that God requires them to be. Nicodemus was a religious, a moral, an upright man, but the birth of the Spirit was for him something yet to be felt. It is a subject, therefore, for moral and religious people to ponder—a text to be expounded to Church-members as well as to others. That they are born again is hardly to be taken for granted, as there may be abundance of morality and religion without spirituality.

Then, again, the mystery connected with the direct operations of the Spirit is a hinderance in the way of some. This, however, is not so great a mystery as the supposed efficacy of baptism to regenerate, or that any moral change is effected by ordinances. The "how" is at least just as difficult and incomprehensible in the one case as in the other. But the direct operation of the Spirit is only one of countless mysteries. "The wind bloweth where it listeth, and thou hearest the sound thereof, but canst not tell whence it cometh, and whither it goeth; so is every one that is born of the Spirit." The supernatural is insisted upon. Illustrated perhaps by the natural, but supernatural still. The fact is matter of experience—something recognized in its effects to be perceived and felt in the spiritual nature as clearly as we hear and feel the movements of the air we breathe. Beyond this we are not required to go. The supernatural and divine are in religion, and their manifestations are in the wonderful change wrought in the soul.

As there is no abatement of the mystery, so there is none of the necessity of this spiritual birth. It is a marvel, and yet we are not to marvel at it. We can neither see nor enter the kingdom without it. Beyond the natural birth, beyond all ordinances, is this inexorable necessity. The new creature in Christ must be realized. Nor is this insisted upon without reason. It is no arbitrary condition, but of essential fitness for heaven. It is the supplement to the doctrine of human depravity, and the complement of our pardon or justification through faith in the blood of Christ. Pardon simply places us in a new relation to God; the birth of the Spirit is the production of a new character and nature suited to the new relation. "That which is born of the flesh is flesh." This sinful nature must be renovated. The natural man must give place to the spiritual. The carnal mind, with its enmity to God, with its rebellion and its earthly and sensual attributes, must be overcome and made pure. The necessity lies deep in our fallen nature and in the utter corruption of the human heart. The Saviour, in expounding the doctrine, sets it forth in its singleness and simplicity. He took down the old picture, stripped it of its framing, restored the coloring, and hung it out in the clear light of his own all-powerful rays. Divested of all types and symbols, the truth starts from the canvas: "Ye must be born again."

AFTER CONVERSION.

The converted man is a child of God. He is in Christ Jesus, and is born of the Spirit. Before conversion he was in a state of darkness and sin; but "there is, therefore, now no condemnation to them which are in Christ Jesus, who walk not after the flesh, but after the Spirit." Speaking of justification and peace with God through our Lord Jesus Christ, Paul declares: "By whom also we have access by faith into this grace wherein we stand, and rejoice in hope of the glory of God." The converted man stands in this grace of justification and peace—the state of pardon and regeneration—and rejoices in hope of the glory of God. "He is a new creature; old things are passed away; behold, all things are become new."

At the threshold of this new experience there is much ignorance in regard to many things—ignorance of many religious duties, of many of the precepts and doctrines of the Bible. It is a mercy that sinners may be converted who are ignorant; but to stand in the grace of conversion they must be instructed, they must grow in grace and in the knowledge of our Lord Jesus Christ. Without this, they will die spiritually as certainly as will a tree that has been set in a dry and sterile soil. At the beginning of this new life there is ignorance of many of the duties of the Christian profession. If these are not sought out and performed there will be an imperfect and weak development of spirituality, and possibly the loss of it altogether. A way to stand and to grow is to bravely take up the cross as a witness for Christ, and to work from life and also for it. The lack of the meditative element in piety is very serious, but at the same time spiritual religion thrives on exercise, and cannot well live without it.

If the glow of love does not at once incite to active endeavor and find something to do, it will soon pass away. The discharge of duty is generally the first and often the severest test of the new convert. Many never get beyond it. They fall at the beginning of the race. They resist the conviction that they ought to have family prayers, that they ought to pray and speak in the social meetings, or that they ought to work in the Sunday-school. Here they fall into condemnation, and by degrees the comfort of the Spirit is lost.

The new convert is familiar with the temptations that beset him as a sinner, but his probation as a child of God is something unlike what it was before. He is now tried as a Christian. His fidelity to Christ and to his vows is to be tested, and his love and faith and patience are to be assaulted. These assaults may come through the fleshly appetites, through the blandishments of worldly pleasures, through the allurements of wealth. There is special danger at the points where sin was intrenched and fortified by long habits. It may be in a temper long unbridled, in intemperance long indulged, in profanity strengthened by years, in avarice that has become the rooted habit of the soul. Ignorant as the young convert is in regard to the temptations which are to be encountered by him, there is for him a peculiar peril. It is well if he learns from his Bible and from more experienced Christians to be on his guard in time. The chain which held him a captive as a sinner is the one that Satan will likely use in his recapture.

While there is danger of falling into old habits of sin, the greater temptation with some may be to distrust their conversion, or to doubt the reality of a supernatural or divine work in the heart. The devil shoots arrows of fire at the believer. If he cannot seduce him by the enticements of appetite, the lusts of the eyes, and the pride of life, he will attack and endeavor to undermine his faith. The converted man is under conditions of temptation stronger and more subtle than those which surround him as a sinner. He was on probation as to accepting the grace of God; he is now on trial as to persevering in it. In the divine economy this trial, with its sufferings and afflictions, is calculated to develop character and to bring out the Christian graces in their harmony and perfection; but it may result in our spiritual overthrow.

It is remarkable how much attention is bestowed upon the converted by the inspired writers. It is not enough that men be converted. They must be instructed, nourished up in sound doctrine, warned, fed. "Feed the flock of God" is the inspired injunction. The sheep will perish if not fed. Converted though he be, a child of God and a new creature in Christ, the young convert is ignorant of the duties and dangers of the situation. The grace of Christ is sufficient to keep him holy and unblamable, but there is peril. It will take all watchfulness, all prayer, all Bible study, all the means of grace within his reach, to enable him to overcome. In some important sense the righteous are scarcely saved.

Many persons fall into sin after conversion; their consciences condemn them, and there is repentance and an immediate sense of the restoration of the divine favor. "He restoreth my soul" is a blessed truth, and there are few believers who have not had occasion to realize it in their own experience. If for any cause there is a sense of sin and condemnation, instead of covering our sin the instant duty and privilege are to fly to the fountain opened for sin and uncleanness.

There are also those who are permanent backsliders—dead branches in the Church. Their spiritual life is gone out, leaving nothing but the fruitless form of godliness. They are not led by the Spirit—the witness of the Spirit is lost; the traces of their conversion, as a spiritual change, are nearly obliterated. If finally saved, it must be by a fresh awakening, and by a renewed and deep repentance, and by faith in the crucified Redeemer. Fearful as the sin of backsliding is, the mercy, even the tender mercy, of God hovers over the backslider, and the promises of the gospel linger about him. Among the profoundest sleepers to be awakened are these backsliders—those who have a name to live and are dead. They were converted, but they are now fallen from grace. They need special attention and a special message. The devil's first lie to our race is the one he sticks to most persistently: "Ye shall not surely die." Beguiled by the serpent, and deaf to the divine warnings, the forbidden fruit is plucked, and the glory fades from the soul.

Neither sin nor backsliding, however, necessarily follow conversion. There are and have been many beautiful lives whose path is like the shining light—shining more and more unto the perfect day. The inward light has grown steadily brighter, and the outward life has risen higher and higher in its sublime purity and consecration. And, however it may be in regard to inward sins immediately repented of, the numbers who from the hour of their conversion live holy and exemplary lives are great. It is the Christian's duty and privilege never to lose the sense of acceptance with God, and never consciously to fall into condemnation. If we believe in a lower experience, we are likely to have it. If we go about disparaging the grace of God, expect nothing better than a perpetual backsliding and a perpetual repenting, and look for death to put an end to sin, we shall not taste the bliss of a full salvation. Christ came to save, and he is able to save. The converted man is a saved man, and it is his privilege to live with the sense of being cleansed from sin by the blood of Christ. This sense of entire cleansing, of near and unbroken communion with God, this rejoicing in hope and rapture of love, are a part of every-day religion.

THE SPIRITUAL FACE.

THE light in the soul transfigures the countenance. "A man's wisdom maketh his face to shine." In a literal as well as in a figurative sense, David says, "Who is the health of my countenance?" The inward change was manifest in the outward expression. The Saviour's countenance was ordinarily luminous, we may suppose, but the glory was obscured except in the solitary instance on the mount, when its complete effulgence was displayed to the wondering three. Moses exhibited the effects of near communion with God when he came down into the encampment with the divine beams playing upon his brow. It was the fullness of the Holy Ghost in Stephen that gave to him that heavenly light which arrested the attention of his malignant judges when they "saw his face as it had been the face of an angel." Phenomena akin to these are seen in ordinary conversions. The face before and after conversion exhibits marked contrasts. The moral change is written upon the visible features. The transition from darkness to light is seen in the outward expression. Peace and joy flood and irradiate the countenance which but lately was darkened and cast down by guilt and despair. In a revival meeting it is not difficult to pick out those who are still seeking from those who have found the pearl of great price. Ordinarily the face tells the story where there are no audible expressions of contrition or of rapture.

The countenance of the mature Christian bears in its lineaments the spirituality which reigns in the heart. There is a light and a sweetness in such a face which distinguish it from those who have never experienced the renewing of the Holy Spirit. In a mixed assembly, or in the throngs on the street, we imagine that we discern the mark which God has set upon his children. As in the prophet's vision the man with a writer's ink-horn set a mark upon the foreheads of the faithful, and as in the apocalyptic scene an angel ascending from the east "sealed the servants of our God in their foreheads," so it is now. Spiritual people have the seal in their foreheads. There is something in the face which answers to the purity and love glowing within. The power of grace to transform the face is something wonderful as seen in the conversion of adults. The marks of grossness and lust, the sharp, cold lines of covetousness, the ardent but unsatisfied desire of pleasure, the almost diabolical touches of selfishness and malignancy, the clouded and burning traces of fierce passions and unholy tempers, are swept away, and give place to a benevolent and sunny composure. It is the difference between the mountain rocked by volcanic throes, scorched by tides of burning lava, and covered with ashes and scoriæ, and the mountain whose base and sides are clothed with harvests, orchards, and gardens, and whose top towers in restful sublimity above the clouds. The beauty of childhood is greatly owing to the spirituality that is in it. Vice and ungoverned passion have not yet carved their ugly lines upon the face, nor stamped it with the dark and repulsive hues of conscious guilt. A congregation of children impresses us with the innocence and spirituality which speak in their happy looks. Such a scene of upturned faces is like a lake of rippling wavelets responding in manifold forms of beauty to the breeze and sunshine which play upon them.

The countenance indicates the various types and degrees of piety. The expression is often variable as the inward condition changes. It is often mixed in the conflicts, the depressions, and the triumphs of faith. The stern and ascetic, the deeply emotional, the cheerful and sympathetic, the peaceful and loving, like so many styles of art, put their several characteristics upon the canvas. "The Last Supper" is an endeavor to exhibit these types as they surround the great original and perfection of holiness. What the painter attempted with his pencil is in fact being done upon Christian faces. We have thought that denominational types are more or less revealed in the countenance. In a union prayer-meeting the faces, not less than the utterances, are tinged with the peculiar theologies. The stanch advocate of predestination, the conscientious stickler for immersion, the emotional Arminian, the lover of prelacy and liturgies, have their several creeds graven upon their faces, while the sheen of a common Saviour's love softens and subdues the rugged features of sectarian conviction. The Methodist, the Presbyterian, the Baptist, the Episcopalian, with good and wholesome faces all, have each their distinctive physiognomy. A Lavater or a Spurzheim might have seen this had their studies taken this direction.

The spiritual face is perhaps most marked in women. Naturally more beautiful and spiritual than men, they rightfully claim a nearer kinship to the angels. The higher and finer organization, with its deeper and truer intuitious, and with its more delicate and refined sensibilities, gives to womanhood this spiritual preëminence. The work of the Holy Spirit in woman is most perfectly reflected in her face. Her features are singularly plastic and mobile, and yield readily to the transforming power within. Her face to her spiritually is as the photosphere to the sun. Under the influence of religion it is not merely a beauty, but a glory. We do not hesitate to give Christian women the preëminence in all the attributes of real beauty; nor is there any doubt that this preëminence is due to their spirituality.

The spiritual face alone improves with age. The work is nearer completion as time advances, and the silvered head and the wrinkled brow have the gentleness and mellowness of the tranquil and golden autumn. We remember our sainted fathers and mothers as being lovely to the last. It was the spiritual in them shining more and more to the perfect day. Their decrepitude and decay were transfigured by the glory which, in angel forms, was about to be set free forever.

THE GLORY IN US.

The "far more exceeding and eternal weight of glory" is doubtless "the glory which shall be revealed in us." In both passages the glory is connected with "our light afflictions" and "the sufferings of this present time." "Revealed in us." There is a wide difference between what shall be revealed *to* us and what shall be revealed *in* us. What is out of us is clearly to be separated from what may be within. There is an outward and an inward glory. Material things—as the heavens and the firmament—declare the glory of God, and this exhibition of the divine handiwork is entirely external to ourselves. Whatever the things which are seen declare, are revealed to us. We may apply the same rule to the disclosures of the heavenly state. Even in material objects the present visible world is scarcely an earnest of the beautiful and sublime which invest the scenery of the incorruptible inheritance. Besides all the external adornments, there are manifestations of intelligence in the persons and forms of angels; and God himself is exhibited in the symbols of an indescribable splendor. The glory revealed to us is thus distinctly conceivable—something as much external to us in heaven as are fields and stars and mountains here on the earth.

On the other hand, the glory within must be removed from the sensuous and from objects and persons external to the soul. It is spiritual, and relates to the thoughts, tempers, and affections. It is a spirit divested of sin, disenthralled, and born from above. Here is something more beautiful than any landscape, earthly or heavenly—a soul reaching purity through the baptism of trouble and death, and renewed by the grace of the Holy Spirit. This defines the connection between present suffering and future happiness. It is not simply a contrast arbitrarily established, nor loss and compensation, nor reward bestowed, though all of these may appear in the result. Certain causes are described as associated with this gracious end. They work for us, and are the conditions of the glory to be revealed in us. We know that no such result is necessarily attached to affliction. The greatest sufferers here are not the greatest saints, nor are earthly troubles always followed by the rest which remaineth for the people of God. Submissive faith converts sorrow into a blessing and makes it the means of developing every Christian grace, while without faith the sorrow of the world worketh only death.

The glory in us is therefore a present glory, although not altogether revealed. It is perhaps incomplete—in the condition of being wrought, and preparing to break forth and cast off the shell of chrysalis. The finishing touches of a disciplinary providence are yet to be given, and the picture awaits the final pencilings which are to give it the stamp of perfection. While the believer is conscious of the great work which is going forward in the soul, the veil of incompleteness hangs over it, and he cannot now realize its nature and grandeur. The treasure is in earthen vessels, and the frailties of nature darken the luster of the inward life. Comparative obscurity invests the righteous as they are seen and judged by the world. It is in the final day that they shall "shine forth in the kingdom of their Father." But it is equally true that now the actual glory already in the soul is in a state of eclipse to our own consciousness. We can see in others qualities of virtue and excellence which they do not see themselves, and others may behold in us the exhibition of graces which we can hardly persuade ourselves to have any existence.

The sanctified cause throws over the soul a cloud which conceals from us what is being effected. Suffering depresses while it continues, and temptations excite self-distrust and humiliation. We are wrapped in the smoke and flame of the refining fire, and the present effect is to show us the alloy and drosses rather than the fine gold. It is perhaps God's wise purpose now to manifest in us what is evil and not what is good. Vile and sinful qualities are displayed to the conscience in the light of his countenance that they may be overcome and destroyed, while the surpassing attainments of holiness are shaded and placed in a subdued light for the present. If in this life there is a sanctified state wherein we emerge from this atmosphere of dust and smoke and conflict, and wherein we bask in the complacency of a pure heart, even here the fullness of the glory must be shrouded in a considerable degree. "Beloved, now are we the sons of God, and it doth not yet appear what we shall be." For the present our sonship is manifest, and we are assured by the Holy Ghost and confirmed therein by the witness of our own spirit. What we are we shall be, for death neither begins nor finishes the work of grace.

It is this revelation of the glory in us that is presented as a matter of experience in the future life. Now it may be neither expedient nor possible. There awaits us a wonderful inward as well as outward revelation—an apocalypse of the soul in the unfolding of the redeemed and sanctified powers and attainments to our own amazed consciousness. It is this fact which bridges over the apparently great and violent transition from earth to heaven. Without this inward glory the outward would oppress and overwhelm. Without it the fellowship of angels would abash and the divine presence would utterly confound. The glory in us is revealed just where it is needed to place us in accord with the heavenly state and to break the overpowering shock of what would be otherwise an abrupt and fearful transition. It is not unusual to find a certain sense of unreadiness in the most exemplary Christians, which yields to assurance and triumph only in the last hours of life. There the obscurity gives way, and the inward glory begins to brighten and to assert the presence of an adequate preparation for the final change.

The religion of forms and external rites vanishes before this conception of the glory in us. The kingdom of God is within us. It cometh not with observation, nor is it tied to visible temples and sacraments. Neither are the manifestations of heaven things to be gazed upon and wondered at as men now look upon the altars and frescoes of a cathedral. What is awful, spiritual, and divine is within. There will be nothing in heaven, apart from God, so glorious as the pure heart; and of all the revelations which shall come pealing upon the ear and flashing upon the eye, there will be nothing to compare with "the glory revealed in us."

SHINING MORE AND MORE.

THE path of the just, in a worldly sense, often grows darker as time passes on. Misfortunes and disappointments thicken around him. Death is a door opportunely opened, through which he escapes from earthly trouble. It is not the lot of the good to be eminently prosperous, nor is success in temporal affairs the sure sign and seal of divine favor. But in the spiritual sphere it is true that the path of the just shines "more and more unto the perfect day." Even in trouble and affliction there is a steadier and brighter light. These are better understood, and are sanctified, and there is greater strength and consolation attending them.

In no other respect is there more progress in the good man's life of faith than in the light which is shed upon his trials. Once they nearly overwhelmed him, staggered his confidence in God, and led him to think that he was mistaken in his religious experience. All was wrapped in mystery, and he walked in the darkness with a fearful heart and with trembling steps. The pathway of sorrow is no longer one of gloom and despair. The cloud has become luminous, and the Father's voice is heard speaking out of it in tones of assurance and love.

Things that in the earlier experience gave much anxiety and disturbed the repose of the soul are no longer sources of uneasiness and distrust. As the stream grows deeper it is less easily ruffled by the passing storm and less easily turned from its course by the obstacles which oppose its progress.

There is growth in this respect: that the religious life is

more uniform under the pressure of temptation, and that the peace of the heart has become too profound to be shaken by outward conditions and circumstances. It has come to be that peace which flows as a river, even the peace of God which passeth all understanding. When the affections have been set on things above, earthly things have lost their power to absorb and enslave, and also to bring anxiety and perturbation of spirit. The mature Christian looks back with wonder upon his earlier years and the many needless distractions to which he yielded.

In the substantial elements of religious enjoyment there is the growing brightness of truth and assurance. This is connected with a broader intelligence, with a more accurate knowledge of the word of God, and with a juster comprehension of the nature and reason of doctrine and experience. The Christian should become happier in his religion as he grows older in years. If converted in his youth, there were then no worldly cares, and many phases of temptation were unknown. As time wears on, occupation, contact with the world, the struggle for success in business, a dependent family, and accumulating labors and afflictions, all come to test the faith. The conditions are different in the outward life, but the inward power of grace is stronger than ever, and the path, however environed with earthly shadows and responsibilities, is in reality shining more and more.

The struggle with temptation is marked by increase of power over solicitations to evil. Instead of humiliation and defeat, there is victory. The temper is brought under control, the appetites are mastered, the affections are completely purified, and communion with God is close and habitual. There is a perfect day to the believing soul in this world—a progress which is unto it. Not the perfect day of heaven, but the perfect day of love; a heavenly-mindedness and a surpassing spirituality; a maturity of all the plants of grace and a sky of faith serene and cloudless. This is as it should be—as it may be. It is so with the faithful disciple of the Saviour. Christ is the light of the world, and if any man follow him "he shall not walk in darkness." Wrong living, neglect of duty, worldly-mindedness, may darken the path. Shadows projected by unbelief, deepened and perpetuated by sinful indulgence, may obscure the way which was once delightful and joyous. The darkness will grow thicker unless the cause be speedily removed. There is progress both ways—toward the perfect day and also toward the rayless night; unto the perfection of happiness or the depths of misery. One way or the other are we tending. It is well for us to pause and consider, to examine our reckonings and to take the sun. Is our religious life waxing or waning? onward and vigorous, or is it halting and feeble? Are we in the path that shines more and more, or are we in the road that thickens with gloom at every step? Religion begins with light and ends in light. Bright at first, it shines more and more.

THE LIKES OF THE KINGDOM.

INSPIRED COMPARISONS.

THE scriptural method of teaching is usually very concrete. Its historical and biographical scenes and sketches are to instruct, and its parables and metaphors make up no inconsiderable portion of the sacred volume. God, who made the soul and knows best how to move and inform it, has largely adopted types, symbols, and all varieties of figures. Such imagery as abounds in the most impassioned eloquence, and in the highest kinds of poetry, illuminate and embellish the inspired page. Abundant illustration characterizes the Saviour's teachings. He is at great pains to unfold what the kingdom of heaven is like. It is like leaven, like a grain of mustard-seed, like unto a man that is a householder. It is likened unto a certain king which would take account of his servants, and unto ten virgins which took their lamps and went forth to meet the bridegroom. In the exhibition of doctrine, in the delineation of character, and in portraying the future life, this process of comparison is freely used. The barren fig-tree, the rich man and Lazarus, and the Pharisee and the publican, are pictorial illustrations of the most startling and graphic nature. Things which in themselves are purely metaphysical and spiritual are made to appear to the eye as clearly as if spread upon the canvas or wrought in brass or marble.

With all their seeming plainness and simplicity, the inspired comparisons are often unfathomably profound. The careless and superficial, while delighted and attracted by the mere dress of the thought, may miss of the lesson intended. Hence, there is nothing contradictory in the declaration: "Therefore speak I to them in parables, because they, seeing, see not; and hearing, they hear not; neither do they understand." The mysteries of the kingdom are veiled or disclosed according to the character and spirit of the hearer. The Saviour's illustrations were so constructed as to become a test of character, shedding light upon those who are panting for it and leaving others to the darkness which they loved. Besides the quality of discrimination, this mode of presenting truth has the advantage of condensation. Seemingly diffuse, it is exceedingly compact. The parables are like gems which flash their colors from many sides, and like those supreme landscapes which display wondrous beauties from many different approaches. In the parable of the wheat and the tares, or in that of the ten virgins, it is difficult to conceive how so much could be told in so few words in any other form. The office of figure and all illustrative speech is really to condense. While it simplifies and embellishes, it also throws the subject in hand into the utmost compactness.

Plainness, discrimination, and attractiveness are qualities in the use of illustrations, but in Scripture are the further purposes of depth and brevity. This style is doubtless in keeping with the luxuriance of the Oriental imagination, and especially in accord with the genius of the Hebrew mind. But human nature craves it everywhere, and Christ spoke the universal language of man when he clothed the sublime truths of religion in imagery of the utmost grace and beauty. These likes of the kingdom are the most attention-compelling and the most awakening and enchaining of all the great Teacher's words. Many a careless soul has turned to repentance at that point in the discourse where the rich man and Lazarus are sketched; and many another has first yielded to the love and hope which the prodigal son inspires. The Bible is adapted to the human mind, and everywhere recognizes this need and appetite for illustration. Hence, we have the epic of Job, the pastoral of Ruth, the lyrics of David, and the surpassingly sublime drama of the Apocalypse; hence, also, the likes of the kingdom. The sensation created by the passion-play of Ober Ammergau indicates the strength of this craving for the scenic and dramatic. Truth is good in itself, but few like the raw material. To reach the popular apprehension it must be cooked, and seasoned with condiments to awaken desire. It must wear clothes, and this not for service alone but also for adornment. The eye drinks in color even as the thirsty stomach drinks in water. The mind hungers for rhythm and grace in forms and sounds as the body hungers for convenient food.

The old scribes illuminated their otherwise dry and turgid manuscripts and adorned their parchments with pictures which have outlined the text. Our own is eminently an age of pictures. Books, papers, and magazines are nothing without them. The style of writing and speaking partakes of this pictorial character. The pulpit glows more than ever with illustrations, and this demand of human nature is preëminently recognized in the forcible presentation of the gospel message. This is as it should be; only that there are dangers and excesses to be avoided. If we would attract and instruct, we must adapt our means to influence and enlighten men as we find them. It is safe to speak "as the oracles of God," and especially to draw our figures and illustrations from this inspired treasury. The analogies of the natural to the spiritual may, however, be easily misapplied; and there are no more fruitful sources of error than this fertility in the use of comparisons. In the fashion for object-teaching and illustrative preaching there is danger of such degeneracy as ends in the mere burlesque of truth. In the effort to simplify and popularize it is hard to avoid the peril of degradation. Talmage is frequently open to these objections; and Beecher, though a much superior painter, is not altogether clear of them. The likes of the kingdom are suggestive of matter and style, and to be sought and cultivated. All, however, cannot hold the pencil with equal skill, and for many to affect the pictorial style would be simply ludicrous. Then, again, the Bible is not all epic and parable, but there is a judicious admixture of lights and shades, such as the mosaics of art present.

Beyond what the inspired mode of instruction may suggest in reference to the methods of presenting truth, we are called to study and expound these resemblances, at least to ourselves. It is most important for us to know what the kingdom of heaven is like that we may realize its establishment in the heart and recognize it in the life and history around us. These portraits and scenes are to be placed in every possible light, and to be looked at and analyzed and reëxamined. If they may not teach us to preach, they will assuredly tell us how to live and what to be. Studied with the light of the Holy Spirit shining on them and us, we shall be rewarded by a thousand surprises. New merits and hitherto undiscovered expressions will burst upon us, and we shall find in our experience what it is for those to whom it "is given to know the mysteries of the kingdom of heaven."

LIKE PASSIONS.

The example of eminent and holy persons is weakened by the disposition to regard them as somehow removed from the ordinary sphere of human experience. They are like the fixed stars—so amazingly remote that we have scarcely a spectroscopic hint of the fact that their elementary constitution is like our own. Distance heightens the impression of their grandeur and stability, while it conceals the perturbations and convulsions which are going on within them. Take up almost any of the great characters of the inspired history, and this tendency to place them in orbits very different and very far from those in which we move is apparent. Such patience as Job had, such faith as Abraham illustrated, such love as John attained, such zeal as Paul exhibited, are regarded as exceptional and as connected with conditions which can be realized by few.

The opinion was common a century ago, and has always obtained to some extent among religious people, that the assurance of pardon is given to only a favored few. So thought Susanna Wesley's father; so thought Dr. Samuel Johnson. Paul may have enjoyed the witness of the Spirit, and the participators in the scenes of Pentecost had in them the Spirit of adoption, crying, "Abba, Father!" But there are abundance of people who never think of bringing these comforts and blessings home to themselves as a part of their spiritual heritage. To them they are things as far off as the fires of Sirius, and as little known as the chemistry of Aldebaran. To them that brilliant galaxy of heroes and heroines displayed in the eleventh of Hebrews, as stretching across the entire firmament of inspired history, is an unresolved nebula of luminous but impracticable coruscations. These illustrious names are hardly conceived of as standing for real human creatures, and as representing men and women constituted like themselves.

To be profited and encouraged, we must bring these examples of piety and faith near to us, and look upon them as moving in our own plane of experience. The impartiality of the divine record is helpful in this respect, not only vindicating the truth of the narrative, but revealing the likeness of those celebrated men to ourselves. The little lines which tell us that the sun and stars are made of the same materials as the earth are not more instructive than are those occasional strokes which afford glimpses of human passion and infirmity in those we have been wont to place above the condition of ordinary mortals. It is something that James thought worth while to tell us in connection with the story of Elias's faith that he "was a man subject to like passions as we are." The history shows this as it describes him in his flight from Jezreel, in his vexation and despair by the way, and in the cave of Horeb. But we might forget all this in the affair with the priests of Baal and in the singularly glorious scene of the translation. When he shut the heavens, when the clouds came at his bidding, and when he was about to step into the chariot, he was all the time "a man subject to like passions as we are" —naturally weak and infirm, but exalted and glorified by the grace of God.

It shows not what God can make out of angels, or what he might have made out of sinless and perfect men, but what he can make out of our fallen humanity. As modified by circumstances, it exhibits a standard of common attainment in which the weakest and humblest has a personal concern. Longfellow has rendered the lesson in its less important application:

> Lives of great men all remind us
>   We may make our lives sublime,
> And, departing, leave behind us
>   Foot-prints on the sands of time.
>
> Foot-prints that perhaps another,
>   Sailing o'er life's solemn main,
> A forlorn and shipwrecked brother,
>   Seeing, shall take heart again.

It must have been an incident of peculiar comfort to

John when, amidst the unfoldings of the apocalyptic vision, his act of worship was arrested by the admonition: "See thou do it not; I am thy fellow-servant, and of thy brethren that have the testimony of Jesus." Here was one who had been like himself already invested with shining robes and gloriously resplendent in the world of light. It is of such humanity as ours, with its frailty and infirmities, that saints are fashioned here and upon which a crown of glory is placed in heaven. What the grace of God has done for others it is able to do for us. We may follow in the footprints of a greater than Elias, and sit down with him on his throne at last.

CHILD-LIKENESS.

The evangelical prophet, in his vision of Messiah's kingdom, describes the greatest triumph over most discordant characters when he tells us that "a little child shall lead them." The wolf is to dwell with the lamb, the leopard is to lie down with the kid, the calf and the young lion and the fatling are seen in companionship, and a little child leads them all. The child leader is in the foreground of this sweet picture, and is in strong contrast with the turbulent and rugged forms which quietly submit to his guidance. The dimpled arm is laid upon the lion's mane, and the leopard and the wolf yield to the soft caress. Savage malignity and the mightiest forces of cruelty and hate are held in abeyance by the fascinating spell of innocence. All these symbols of lordly power and all-prevailing discord are held in complete subjection by this type of humility.

The prophet's vision and the Saviour's symbolical action are in perfect harmony. The little child which Christ placed in the midst of his disciples carries our minds back to the imagery of Isaiah, and we see in both the exhibition of the same great essentials of the gospel kingdom. In both it is the little child that leads—that "is greatest in the kingdom of heaven." The only greatness is humility; the only real strength is meekness and docility of mind. Christ insists that without this child-likeness entrance into the kingdom is impossible. It must be received as a little child; and "except ye be converted, and become as little children, ye shall not enter into the kingdom of heaven." Doubtless one of the chief hinderances of many unconverted people is their pride. But for this they would have sought and found peace long ago. They are unwilling to be led and taught of God, and to yield implicit obedience to the demands of the gospel. They are too wise in their own opinions and conceits, and trust too much in their superior cultivation and intellect. The deep self-abasement of repentance and the entire self-renunciation of a thorough spiritual awakening are far from them. The difficulty in their case is to get low enough—in a word, to receive the kingdom "as a little child." If it could be obtained in a learned way, in a dignified and philosophical manner, with no sense of sin and with no confession of guilt, the matter would be settled. Pride of intellect, and the fancied possession of superior parts and attainments, keep many from that spirit of inquiry which would result in their speedy salvation. Candor and simplicity are associated with humbleness of mind. Thorough honesty with himself is rare with the sinner. He may be honorable and upright in his social relations, but he is not true to himself. He persists in disguising the guilt and corruption of his heart, and clings tenaciously to the notion of his own righteousness. He is wanting in integrity in dealing with God and his own soul. He is a sinner, a great sinner, but unwilling to admit in the secret thoughts of his heart that he needs the mercy of an offended Lawgiver. The great obstacle to entrance into the kingdom is this self-exaltation. He would receive it as a man of learning, as a man of wealth, as a scholar, thinker, moralist, and gentleman—in any way except as a little child. Docility and transparency of mind and thorough honesty of soul are the sure precursors of the new birth.

If the spiritual kingdom is entered as a little child, it is also maintained in the same manner. The maturest Christian life is noted for its profound humility—not the affected humility of cant and hollow profession, but that lowliness of mind which sits in the dust before God. Faith is always humble. The Syrophenician woman and the centurion were distinguished by this trait. Such faith had not been seen in Israel, nor such humility. We cannot conceive of faith as separated from this deep self-abasement. In such characters as Moses and Abraham—men of princely greatness, and possessed of the loftiest attributes of mind—humility is the inseparable attendant of their faith. Evangelical faith embraces perfect teachableness, unquestioning obedience, and unfaltering trust. We may be tempted to enter the regions of speculation and to wander in the mazes of skeptical philosophy; we may endeavor to construct a religion of science, and to affect a higher wisdom and a better understanding in theological lore than others, but we shall be compelled at last to come back to the starting-point of simple reliance upon God. After searching through the universe for something more satisfactory, we come back to the feet of Jesus and return to God as the rest of the soul. After all of our efforts to be great and wise and knowing, we find that the highest and divinest life is to be converted and to "become as little children."

All genuine growth in grace is in this direction, wherein simplicity, transparency, and humility more and more invest the character. The politic, the worldly, and the ambitious are far removed from this description of true religion. These qualities are near neighbors to hypocrisy, and sometimes mar the Christian profession. How that little child must have rebuked the self-seeking and ambition of the disciples who had just inquired, "Who is the greatest in the kingdom of heaven?" The child was the gospel of unworldliness, of lowliness and sincerity, while in the hearts of the disciples was the budding of a carnal and selfish ambition. That child in the midst is our lesson and our rebuke—warning against a tendency which has outlived the group which then surrounded the Master. The seeking of great things for ourselves, the persistent angling after public commendation, and the indulgence of a politic and restless ambition, are in profound contrast with the spirit which Jesus demanded. The child illustrated the divine kingdom, but it took the grace of Pentecost to set it up in the heart. Nothing but that baptism of fire can cleanse the fallen soul of its duplicity, conceit, and vanity. Nothing less can cure it of pride and inordinate affection, and bring it to that child-likeness which is at once the loveliest and sublimest of all our religious attainments.

PLANTING AND TRANSPLANTING.

PLANTED IN THE HOUSE OF THE LORD.

SUCH are to flourish in the courts of our God. They are to be fat and flourishing, and to bring forth fruit in old age. We would put the emphasis on "planted." This is more than merely to be in the house of the Lord. It is something different from transplanting. Generally, this cluster of promises is dependent upon the planting. The psalmist must have had in view the religious training of children, the conversion of the young. Special blessings rest upon them. Old sinners and middle-aged transgressors, and those who have ripened in worldliness, may be saved. In some instances they may be more than saved—helping to save others, and doing a great work of usefulness. But those who start early have many advantages—they hold out better; they are more fruitful. Samuel may have been an eminent illustration of this planting, and the original of the portrait. Literally he was planted in the house of the Lord—placed there in his childhood, and kept there.

Home influence and religious instruction are of course necessary, but the Church aspect of piety is here set forth. The children are connected with the house by their public baptism, by the enrollment of their names on the register, and by recognition as the subjects of pastoral as well as of parental oversight. But this process of planting in the house of the Lord embraces also the habitual attendance on public worship at a very early age and participating in that worship. The child is to be taught the duties and truths of the gospel the practice of religion, and the need of personal experience of the work of the Holy Spirit; but besides he must also be instructed in regard to his relations to the Church of Christ, and that he is called to identify himself formally with the people of God.

The Sunday-school in a measure meets this demand, as it is a school of public worship, of prayer and praise, as well as of religious instruction. Its services are usually in the house of the Lord, and the Church idea, with its institutions and ordinances, is exhibited and impressed. Still, the Sunday-school does not meet the full requirement. The child must become a part of the congregation, hear the word from the lips of the preacher, and form a part of the assembly that may be described as the Church and as the house of the Lord. Religion may be taught at home, in the school, and by various agencies; but something would be lacking if there were no public ordinances, no social worship, and no training in the duties of God's house. Conversion is the main thing; and yet, to secure a thorough religious education and to develop and give permanence and usefulness to religious character, there must be this planting in the house of the Lord. There must be an early induction into the public worship of God and early instruction in the nature and obligation of the ordinances and institutions of religion.

In our dealing with children this is a serious defect: that we do not, even with sufficient literalness, plant them in the house of the Lord. We do not instruct them clearly in regard to the import of their baptism and concerning the open profession of Christ and the duty to claim the privilege of recognition as members of the visible Church. Besides Christian morals and doctrines, this special phase of religious training requires more than incidental attention on the part of parents, pastors, and teachers. There is a partial neglect—often entire neglect—of the Church discipline and training; and the result is that children, as they grow up, practically repudiate all outward ties to the Church and all obligations to conform to its rules. With some notions of religion, and with imperfect conceptions of the nature of the Church, they drift away from the house of God and cease to regard themselves as in any way connected with his people. In childhood they have not been impressed seriously with the fact that they sustain any real relation to the Church, and their presence in the congregation has not been insisted on as a matter of any moment. It is not strange that when they become older they should regard themselves as still free to neglect the house of God and to keep aloof from its services.

It is a sad and yet not very uncommon thing for parents advanced in years to sit alone in the house of the Lord, while their grown-up children have become indifferent to the exercises, privileges, and instructions of the sanctuary. Their children have not been wholly neglected; there have been religious instruction and example, but the failure has been to plant them in the house of the Lord. The children went to Sunday-school perhaps, but they did not attend preaching. It was not impressed upon them that they were to worship with the congregation. They were practically taught to consider the prayer-meeting as exclusively for the older people. Thus they have come to years unconverted, without the habit of worship, and with no taste for the service of God's house.

Is it possible for religious parents to so attach their children to the Church, and to so imbue them with the love of it, that they shall cling to its worship as long as they live? Not in every case, probably, and yet much can be done to secure this result. If care is taken to plant them in the house of the Lord, the presumption is that they will grow and flourish therein.

TRANSPLANTING.

In spiritual as in natural husbandry this is a critical operation. Many trees and plants die under it, many more are withered and stunted and are sickly and unfruitful, while a few are improved and do better for the change. The same is true of the spiritual process. Members of our churches are moving from one section of the country to another. What effect have these changes upon their religious welfare? Some are culpably negligent about taking their letters, and others who take them fail to hand them in and to unite with the church where they have taken up their residence. This is a common and great evil, a sin not of small magnitude—this negligence and indifference about their relations and duties which those who were members of the Church exhibit in their new homes. We have known instances where the interregnum between taking a certificate and depositing it has been used for a little relaxation—such as theater-going, and other diversions and practices incompatible with the Christian profession and discipline.

Sometimes people defer uniting with the Church on the ground that their sojourn is temporary, or from other flimsy reasons it is delayed until the certificates of membership are worn out or lost, or become so old that they are ashamed to produce them.

The experiment of living out of the Church for ever so short a time is dangerous. It is like taking a tree from the soil and expecting it will retain its life without being immediately reset. If life is preserved, it has sustained an injury that may never be wholly cured. How much harm negligent Christians sustain by the presumption of living for a time out of the Church cannot be estimated; and the loss to them is greater from the fact that the restraints and helps of their old associations are broken off and they are now amongst those who do not know them as the children of God. In their old homes they were known as members of the Church; the watchful solicitude of pastors and brethren were thrown around them; but in their new domiciles they are not recognized as of the household of faith, and cannot be until they exhibit their credentials and publicly connect themselves with the people of God.

It is here that many have fallen and have been lost to the Church and to heaven. They have been torn away from long-accustomed religious associations, and before new ones are formed the sap and life of their religion are gone. All the records of backsliding and apostasy attest the fearful danger of delay in renewing our fellowship with the Church. However specious the reasons for it, and plausible at the same time, there is serious risk in it. It is a temptation of the devil, and the disposition to yield to it forebodes shipwreck and ruin. From long and careful observation, we are convinced that many souls are lost from this single cause, and that multitudes of members are lost to the Church by changes of residence and the failure to promptly renew their religious communion.

But where the letter is duly deposited, how often does it prove to be a nominal thing? We watch the result very much as the gardener watches a tree that has been taken from some other soil. Will it live? and will it flourish as it once did? It is not uncommon to see those who in their former homes were pillars of the Church—the backbone of its enterprise, and active and zealous in every duty—become cold and useless in the Church whither they have removed their membership. There are reasons for this in the fact that they are strangers, and that time is needful for the growth of new ties and even of Christian friendship and sympathy. Every thing at first is strange, cheerless, sometimes repulsive. A religious homesickness comes over the soul, and great spiritual discouragement.

These disadvantages would be much lessened if the pastors and most experienced members of our churches better knew the "heart of a stranger," and would exhibit peculiar interest in those who come from other and distant charges. In most of our churches there is a lamentable defect in this respect. Pains are not taken to make the new-comer feel at home, and to supply the society and sympathy which are so needful and which his heart is yearning for. This consideration, which ordinary courtesy not less than Christian benevolence would seem to require, is often utterly wanting. Nobody takes the stranger by the hand, nobody visits his family, and it requires a wonderful amount of faith and self-assertion to maintain the old standard of spirituality under such untoward circumstances. Of most of our charges the confession is a true one, "We are very guilty concerning our brother." Often do we leave choicest and most sensitive spirits to languish and struggle in unfriendly neglect, when a little genuine kindness and encouragement would have cheered and saved them.

The jeopardy of the process would be diminished by more love and faithfulness on the part of the pastors and people, but it would not be altogether removed. There is danger at best, and he who changes his membership must be on his guard. He must become rooted and grounded as soon and as thoroughly as possible. Watchfulness and diligence and prayer are needed more than ever. Temptations to neglect Church duties will be strong and in alliance with the shock which the disruption of old habits and associations has occasioned. Where we are not so long and well known there may be a tendency to relax in circumspection toward the world, and the social enjoyment which is not immediately found in the Church may be sought in the world and its unlawful pleasures. The only safety is in a most hearty entrance upon the duties and service of God and the diligent improvement especially of the social and devotional meetings of the Church.

By this process of transplanting we have seen the most vigorous and fruitful dwindle and lead a half withered and barren life. It is with prayerful solicitude that we notice the process and look after the result. Does the transplanted member take vigorous root and deep hold of the soil? Is there no sign of loss or blight? And how great the relief when at length the crisis passes and there is a healing and knitting of all the fibers, and the member enrolled as having "joined by letter" becomes as a "tree planted by the rivers of waters." At a time when there is so much shifting and changing of both temporal and spiritual homes, the effect upon our religious interests and welfare should be carefully examined, and the dangers to which we are exposed should be exhibited and averted.

TEACHINGS OF THE CLOUDS.

CLOUDS WITHOUT WATER.

THERE are few things more tantalizing or more keenly disappointing in a dry time than to see the clouds roll up with promise of a plentiful shower, and then to pass over our heads without giving so much as a drop to the thirsty earth. So full of blessings apparently, and so near, and yet failing to discharge the coveted store. There are clouds that drop fatness in their grand march across the sky, dispensing fruitful harvests and bringing refreshment and gladness to man and beast. There are clouds that float high and thin, that spread out widely, and that are utterly empty. They sail across the horizon to awaken expectation, and then to disappoint.

That "certain men" should be described as clouds without water is suggestive. As applied to the ungodly in general, the figure is forcible. Our end and mission are to carry blessings to the world. But the wicked, whatever their pretensions, are like the vapor that never condenses. The earth would become as iron, the streams would dry up, every thing beautiful and useful would wither, if the world were left to the ministry of the unbelieving. They contribute nothing for the relief of a race stricken with sin. Touching our moral and spiritual needs, how vain are the systems of skeptical philosophy and science! They boast a great deal of culture and of the refining influences of material discoveries. Infidelity, like that of Voltaire, claimed to overthrow superstition and to enthrone liberty and reason. Positivism and all the self-styled idol-breakers—the materialistic atheists of the day—have set aside the notions of a personal Creator and of man's conscious immortality. They claim much, but they have done nothing for the welfare of society. Men are athirst for spiritual consolation, for the waters of life, but these pretenders leave them to cry in despair for peace and satisfaction. The world—for any thing that they can give—remains a moral desert, swept by burning winds, and parched and withered by a dearth that knows no alleviation. The hell of the rich man has its counterpart in a world that looks to the rejecters of the gospel for its guidance and instruction. One drop of water is more than these swelling clouds can bestow. Amidst the tormenting flames of doubt and guilt and affliction they offer nothing for the relief of human sorrow and misery. Their books, their lectures, their theories, and their personal influence are all alike empty and worthless.

But the figure as applied by Jude would seem to refer to some who have "crept in unawares." Assuming to belong to the company of the good, and yet "turning the grace of our God into lasciviousness," and denying both God and Christ. A Christian without Christ, a religious man without God, or a hypocrite who wears the form and denies the power of godliness, is a cloud without water. This is the worst aspect of the illustration—a godless godliness, fleshly riot in holy places, a frocked and mitered infidelity. The Church in the time of Leo the Tenth, and at the breaking out of the Reformation, was at its center much in this condition. Pontiff, priests, and people were covered with the leprosy of licentiousness, simony, and the disbelief of the truths of the gospel. Clouds without water are Churches thus corrupted and debased. All depends upon their purity and spirituality, whether they shall refresh God's heritage with fertilizing showers or leave it to blight and desolation. There are Churches like these empty clouds. They claim to be the elect, they promise great things, but there is no balm in them, and the plants that look to them for life are not watered. The early and the latter rain does not come down from them upon the fields of God. The dark picture drawn by the inspired writer need not exist in all its features in order that this single touch may have application to men and things of the present day. There are Churches not corrupt, and Sunday-schools mainly well conducted, that ought to yield a large result and do not. There is a vast deal of ecclesiastical vaporing, counting the people, boasting of progress, when the net result in Christian achievement amounts to little. There is wide margin between a sprinkle or drizzle and a good rain. That is a good cloud that hangs low and condenses copiously. How shall we do that our Churches, our Sunday-schools, and all our religious organizations may condense more freely, and pour rivers of spiritual water upon the people?

The description has reference mainly to persons—very bad persons—as the drift of the epistle shows. But the negative side of bad people and of the tolerably good is much the same. The sin of omission may coincide in both. A cloud with thunderbolts and storm in it may be without water, and a cloud bright with sunbeams, and sailing noiselessly across the sky, may be without water. One does much mischief and no good, the other simply does no good. There are these men of negative goodness—waterless clouds. There are the bad, the sensual, the heterodox; and there are the well-behaved, the inactive, the unspiritual. Sometimes there are great pretensions, but little results. There is the profession, but nothing follows to correspond. There is no active work, no leavening influence. The family, the Church, the community, do not feel the power of a new life. It is a profession, and nothing more. There should be water in every Christian cloud, and it should fall like rain upon the mown grass. It should not be light, and carried about of winds to no purpose, but big with the riches of grace, and filled with the precious influences of a spiritual and zealous faith.

The preacher may be a cloud without water. His business eminently is to pour refreshing streams upon thirsty souls. The Church is the garden, the congregation is the field, and he is the ordained means through whom these are to be blessed. Is he full of Christ? Does the word of Christ dwell richly in him? Is he dripping with unction? Such a cloud will be sure to revive the weary and bring joy and fruitfulness. Pulpit vaporing is the sorriest of all vaporing. Who has not heard preachers whose windy and frothy utterances have recalled the pertinent words, "Clouds without water?" After all the seeming promise, and the long and weary waiting, the serious hearers go away as thirsty as they came. The preacher was not a beneficent cloud, but merely an empty vapor.

CLOUDS AFTER THE RAIN.

CLOUDS returning after the rain is the Preacher's description of old age. It is as if sorrow were to come upon sorrow, trouble upon trouble. There is rain at all seasons; but there is a season—the winter-time of life—when the clouds come back upon us with all the gathered volume of a whole life of misfortune. Very few comparatively become old, and yet a considerable argument of the royal Preacher for early piety is based upon its necessity as the support and comfort of age. Youth has health and hope, middle life has strength and abundant occupation, and in both there are conditions of pleasure and enjoyment somewhat independent of religion. But to the old, in whom desire has failed, and for whom youthful pleasures and the employments of mature years are no more, what is there left if the comforts of religion be not theirs?

The sorrows of old age are partly in the ties of domestic affection that have been severed. The wife or the husband is long since gone; some or all of the children have dropped into the grave. Parents, in the order of nature, have passed away, and the friends and associates of youth have nearly all disappeared. Old age is almost necessarily a state of loneliness, and stands apart and solitary, though surrounded by the younger elements of society. Nothing is more common, and nothing more pathetically true, than the plaint of age, "I am left alone"—alone, although jostled and crowded by the living, restless throng. Then infirmities of body have usually so increased that positive pleasure is lost, and hours free from uneasiness and pain are rare. The fresh, clear eye of youth is dimmed. The soul can never more look out upon the forms and colors of this beautiful world as it once did. The exquisitely tinted clouds and sky, and the varied landscape, wear a subdued and faded aspect. The ear has parted with its fine sense of sound, and the rapture of melody is a thing of the past. These avenues of so much delight in the earlier years are partially closed, and the sensations which they yield are stripped of the zest which they once possessed. The touch has lost its delicacy, the smell can no longer regale with the breath of pleasant odors, and the taste has lost the nice discrimination which detected the savor of the choicest food. It is the lot of the aged to be thus in a large measure shut out from the material world, and to live and move in a world but half open to the physical senses.

If poverty comes, there is this aggravation in it: the absolute impossibility of restoring the broken fortune. The tree is not quite fallen, but it is so nearly down that "there it shall be." It is so nearly prone that nothing can ever lift it again to its place. As far as this world is concerned, there is no future of restored prosperity and activity. Life, with its opportunities and possibilities, is left behind, and the soul is confronted with the labor and sorrow of a few brief years, and then the grave and eternity. Life in all of its stages has its storms and tempests; in every period of infancy, youth, and maturity there are sufferings and afflictions; but old age is marked by the return of the clouds after the rain. After the period of vicissitude, of alternate light and shadow, of rain and sunshine, comes the unbroken, the settled, and somber winter of our years.

As religion is the preparation for death, it is also the preparation for old age. In the Preacher's estimate of the matter we must remember God in our youth if we would be sure of his favor in old age. When the clouds return after the rain, and the pitiless tempests beat upon us, it will be too late. Aged sinners seldom seek God; they rarely turn to Christ. The near approach of death and accumulating infirmities do not usually turn the tide of unbelief and indifference into the channels of penitence and faith. If the winter come upon us without religion, its days of darkness will be without relief. There will be no spiritual comfort, no blessed hope, no light from the throne above. Old age without Christ is the most dismal, the most forlorn, the most fearful condition that is conceivable in this world, and separated but by a very thin partition from the outer darkness of the final catastrophe.

With a sure hope of eternal life, with the comfort of the Holy Spirit, and with the heart throbbing with love, how different! The clouds that return after the rain are then lined with silver, there is a bow of promise upon the darkest, and none is without its rift through which the light of heaven breaks upon the believing soul. It is a somewhat somber picture which the Old Testament preacher draws of old age, but it is accurate and to the life of the average experience. There is in it, however, the assurance that godliness brightens up the scene and imparts a peculiar glory to that period which is most encompassed with infirmity and sorrow. Aged Christians are almost uniformly happy. Gradually and leisurely they are disrobing—throwing off the earthly—that they may be clothed upon with the house which is from heaven, and that mortality may be swallowed up of life. Cut off from the outer world in a great measure, they have resources within themselves—the recollections of a devoted and useful life, communion with God, and an eternity of blessedness opening before them.

The eye is dim, and the ear is dull, and the heart beats slowly and wearily; "but as it is written, Eye hath not seen, nor ear heard, neither have entered into the heart of man the things which God hath prepared for them that love him." In old age especially are these prepared things revealed by the Spirit. The winter's store has been gathering, and there is abundant cheer for the days when leaden skies and howling blasts are without. The clouds that return after the rain, however dark and tempestuous they may seem, bring no evil to the children of God. Rather they afford occasion for the revelation of peculiar mercies and for the most striking illustrations of infinite tenderness and faithfulness. In no other circumstances do we realize so fully that time predicted by the ancient seer, when "the man [Christ] shall be as a hiding-place from the wind, and a covert from the tempest."

THE WIND AND THE CLOUDS.

THERE is such a thing as too much caution. It may be carried so far that all effort is paralyzed. The wise man thought so when he declared: "He that observeth the wind shall not sow; and he that regardeth the clouds shall not reap." The wind would blow away the seed and hinder the sower in his work; and cloudy and rainy weather would damage the grain in the reaping. And yet the husbandman who pays no attention to the weather would be considered as lacking in common sense. Our weather bureau and the appliances for weather forecasts have come in since Solomon's time. Planters and farmers are not indifferent to the value of meteorological science as it is now developed and applied.

But within certain limits it is true to-day, with all the advantages of modern science, that men must move forward with their sowing and reaping, and that where no risk is incurred nothing will be done. The season for each kind of work is brief, and there cannot be much delay without losing every thing. There may be failure anyhow, but there can be nothing but failure if we do not strike out, and do the best we can. Some labor will be lost, some seed blown away, some of the ripening harvest injured, in almost any average season; and it may turn out even worse, so that all shall be blighted. The tiller of the ground must be hopeful, brave, and have faith in his work and in his God. He cannot wait till the time of sowing is past; he cannot be idle in reaping-time till he is sure no foul weather will come. Besides, he must often go forth to sow even when the wind seems to be rising, and he must thrust in his sickle when the clouds are gathering. The result may be better than he feared, and, sowing with tearful apprehension and reaping with a dismayed heart, his garners, nevertheless, may be filled.

Some people are always watching for the open door of usefulness. They would do something in the way of benevolence. But circumstances seem to discourage effort.

There is sure to be something in the way. Some obstacle to success is suggested as often as the desire to perform any good work comes upon them. Thus they spend their lives observing the wind, regarding the clouds, and they die before the favorable time arrives. They neither sow nor reap.

Better is that disposition for active usefulness which impels us to be ever doing the good that is nearest, helping the afflicted, working for Christ in humble ways every day, without stopping to ask whether it will come to much or little. It may be much, little, or almost nothing, but it may grow like Robert Raikes's Sunday-school. Sow in the morning, and also "in the evening withhold not thine hand." "Give a portion to seven, and also to eight." As the husbandman, dependent and short-sighted, must trust in Providence, and do his work without too anxiously regarding the weather, so must we work for Christ and for human welfare.

People eminently useful have had credit for sagacity and foresight when, in fact, they did not look ahead at all, but simply went about their Master's business, and doing with their might what their hand found to do. They builded better than they knew, or rather they did not know that they were building any thing. They wrought at no problem. They were neither inventors nor discoverers, but users of implements already provided, and doing precisely what earnest souls had always done. Columbus stumbled upon a new world while seeking a path to an old one. Methodism is called a child of Providence because it has grown without a plan and with little provision on the part of its master-workmen. Wesley saw the world around him going to perdition, and dead Churches sunk in formalism and in spiritual decay. We dare say he looked neither to the right nor to the left. He observed neither wind nor clouds, but went forth to sow and also to reap. He did not dream that a great Church would come out of what he was doing, nor did he stop to consider what might be the results. He snatched the brands from the burning where he could find them, called sinners to repentance, put his converts in societies, and left the matter of Church-making to God.

The preacher may be overcautious about casting the gospel net, or he may doubt at the point where he might have had a revival. The signs are not propitious, as he thinks, for church-building. A domestic mission is needed, but there are winds and clouds. The wise ones thought the pioneer missionaries were beside themselves, but such men as Carey, Judson, Heber, and Morrison went forth leaving the weather to Him who governs the winds and the clouds. Even now there are weather-wise Christians who shake their heads and say, "Beware," when any forward movement is broached.

The true missionary spirit is not that of cloud-watching. The heathen are perishing, and we can reach them with the message of salvation. It is not necessary to inquire when the millennium will come, or whether it will ever come. Nor need we calculate how long it will take to convert the world, or whether it will ever be converted. It is the time of sowing, and the ground is fallow. It is the time of reaping, and the fields are white to harvest. There are winds adverse and wasteful and clouds dark and ominous. But it matters not. We must work now, and do our best, and perhaps leave to future generations the knowledge of what has been done.

There is a cautiousness that works more harm than recklessness—a conservatism that does not conserve, but rather tends to decay and to death. There is a divinity that shapes the end of the real and irrepressible toiler for

Christ. Men marvel at his temerity when he begins, and are struck with wonder at the success that crowns the endeavor. Let us move on, and let God take care about the weather.

DAYS AND SEASONS.

THANKSGIVING.

THE chief truth underlying the appointment of a day of thanksgiving is the recognition of the existence of God and that he is our Creator and Preserver. This is not all that the Christian would like to have, but it is even more than forty millions of people can agree upon. The materialists would rule out any mention of God and fail to see any thing but an absurd superstition in the whole affair. People of deistical notions, after the fashion of Hume and some of his contemporaries, can find nothing in their conceptions of God to warrant gratitude or thankfulness at one time more than another. Our Hebrew citizens can consistently thank God, but they cannot tolerate the name of Christ in connection with a presidential proclamation or in worship. In their own way, and in accord with their several convictions, people will give thanks. Prelatical, High-church folks, Catholics, and some others, will look upon the appointment of a day by the President as interfering with churchly prerogatives—as a high-handed usurpation.

The majority of Protestant Christians, however, will not stand much upon the order or form of the matter, but will pray and give thanks "through Jesus Christ." Neither will they stumble at the fact that the proclamation comes from no very devout source and that they are called to give thanks at a time when it would be more appropriate to put on sackcloth and devote the day to fasting. It is well always to give thanks, "and praise is comely for the upright in heart." God has done his part toward making us a great, prosperous, and free people, and if we are not all of these it is no fault of his. Thousands of people are this day without bread and raiment, and the country was never more sorely pressed and straitened in its business and finances; but so far as this state of things is due to political causes, the nation has itself to blame. The present crisis—which has unsettled every thing, and is entailing distress, bankruptcy, and want upon multitudes—is the result of years of oppression and despotism which the majority has left unrebuked. God is not the author of sin. He has not made the corruption, dishonesty, and moral pollution which stalk abroad in society and rule in high places.

God has done his part for our welfare in that he has given us fruitful seasons and has sent his rain and sun upon the just and the unjust. No general visitations of pestilence have been among us; there have been no overwhelming earthquakes, no far-spreading and devastating storms. The miseries that are upon us and those that threaten are of our own making as a nation. The people, as a people, must condemn themselves for the misfortunes they suffer, while they have God to thank for all the blessings they enjoy. Virtue and piety are the only roads to national prosperity and happiness. Without these, good crops, benign seasons, good health, and inexhaustible material resources will be in vain.

Attributing as we do our sufferings to the vileness of man, we do not doubt that God in his providence will somehow overrule the strife and wickedness of men for good. He is ever educing good out of evil, and mercifully guides the storm which human passion and selfishness raise. We must not, in our painful consciousness of political abuses and a limited commercial prosperity, overlook the many blessings given in our domestic relations, in our deliverance from famine, and in at least the moderate supply of things necessary. Under the rank wild grass and beneath the dark forest branches there are many humble but beautiful and fragrant flowers. Beneath this frowning autumnal sky there are some hardy blossoms of rare brilliance and splendor. People happy in their homes, without luxuries but with many comforts, should not crush the bloom at their feet while gazing with troubled brows upon the general troubles of the land. Let us be fair and honest, and give thanks for the things we have.

If we cannot give our gratitude a national turn, we can as individuals give glory to God for his providential care; and the more heartily that in the midst of national disturbance and financial distress we have had preservation and things necessary. The Christian dwells apart; he walks with God. The secret of the Lord is with him, and he finds occasion for thanksgiving and praise where other souls are only given to distrust and murmuring. The nation has held together a hundred years, and we as individuals are yet alive, and the Lord reigneth. Let us thank God and take courage.

CHRISTMAS GREETINGS.

THE day has come again, and we wish our readers joy. The world has a Saviour. He came into the world, and he came to stay. His birth has made a new world of the sin-cursed and death-stricken earth. The mystery and the glory of the incarnation stirred the universe. The wise men of the East were drawn to the spot where the holy child was, the heavenly powers broke into song over the event which was to rise above all epochs in history, and we may well believe that Satan was startled by the long-predicted advent.

Christ in the world! This is the import of our Christmas. He came, and his work of redemption is going forward. The babe is now the crowned and mighty King. His kingdom is come and is coming. His presence is felt in every land, and every year increases the number of those who join in the anthem of praise. A world without a Christ! Could any thing be more drear and dark than life without the consciousness that he has come and that he came to be with us forever? In spite of its tears and sorrows and death, life is grand and beautiful as it stands lighted up and transfigured by the Sun of righteousness. The general joy is from this great fact. It may have a low expression and be often perverted to base and sensual gratifications, and the most of those who join in the annual festivities may have little apprehension of the indescribable glory of the redemptive plan, but the sentiment has become rooted and universal that a Saviour—God's only-begotten—was given as the manifestation of infinite wisdom and love.

Happy for us if we may realize to-day that we have a Saviour in our homes. Christ is in history; his gospel has entered into the civilization, the thought, and the worship of the world at large. But we must bring the child Jesus into the family circle and into the domestic gladness and reunions which mark the occasion. Parents and children and household associations are drawn around this consecrated center of all love and happiness, and all should feel how completely their sweetest pleasures and brightest hopes grow out of him who was born in Bethlehem of Judea and whose infant form was laid in the rude manger. Let the children be glad. And yet it should not be a Christless Christmas, as is too often the case. It is peculiarly their hour, as the Redeemer was a child and as they are in a special sense the objects of his love. Their joy is due to Jesus, and Christian childhood is invested with a happiness unknown to the childhood of heathen and pagan lands.

The blessings which the gospel brings to little children are among the most wonderful and striking of all. They ought to cry "Hosanna!" and to be first to bring their tribute of praise and to crown the Saviour Lord of all. The child Jesus was a gift to the childhood of the whole world, and therefore let the children sing and let them be glad. Christ in the family, at the fireside, at the well-spread board, and amidst the groups of reunited kindred! So it should be. Not revelry, dissipation, and sensual indulgence, but a sense of Christ's presence at the feast and as the revered and honored guest of every house. He stands at the door and knocks, and most happy is that home to which he is admitted.

Christ in the heart! This should be the crowning experience. Always in the heart, but especially to-day. His felt presence and grace in the soul are essential to our happiness, and are also needed to keep us from the hurtful and silly dissipations so prevalent. The devout believer will not be in sympathy with the reckless merriment and intemperate reveries which too much characterize the holiday season. He will, however turn more than ever to Jesus as his hope and consolation; and while others are exclusively making provision for the flesh to fulfill the lusts thereof, he will be careful to put on the Lord Jesus Christ. Christ will be in him the hope of glory, and his heart will be in unison with the wise men who brought their precious gifts and their grateful worship to the newborn Saviour; and his soul will be in most perfect accord with the angelic song: "Glory to God in the highest, and on earth peace, good-will toward men." Christ in the world, in the family, in the heart! May this be the direction of our meditations and the ground of our rejoicing. We wish our readers joy in the social amenities and intercourse of their homes, in the happy companionship of friends and kindred, and joy in Christ—the Child that was born, the Son that was given.

NEW-YEAR.

A LIFE without dates, and with nothing to mark the lapse of time, would be highly unsatisfactory. Gray hairs, wrinkles, and bodily decay might indicate the fact that we are growing old, but we like to know how old the world is and how old we are ourselves. There is a certain beneficence in the existence of dates, of epochs, and definite way-marks in the journey of life. It is well, in many respects, that the year has a recognized beginning and end; that there is this mile-stone to remind the traveler of the ground he has passed over, and of the lessening distance between him and "the house appointed for all living." Time passes inexorably and swiftly. It can neither be arrested nor retarded, but the motion seems accelerated by every revolution of the earth, so that as our days decrease in number they appear to grow more rapid in their flight.

We may pause to speculate upon the years that remain and where we are in reference to the entire measure of our probation. Have we but fairly entered, have we reached the meridian line, or are we near the night which sooner or later shuts down upon every mortal life? In many instances it is more than a mere conjecture that this new year shall be the last. The extremely aged do not look beyond it, the hopelessly diseased are waiting the final summons, and many who in health are passing out of middle life are reminded by the lengthening shadows of the nearness of eternity. With thousands, however, who are in the bloom of youth "the morning cometh, and also the night." Instead of the gradual and mellow tints of the sunset, their end will come with the suddenness and gloom of the solar eclipse. Their sun will go out without going down. Death's harvest of the past year is sure to be repeated in the present, and among those that fall will be representatives of every age and condition.

New-year's-day is not, therefore to be a time of gloom because an occasion of serious reflection. Those who have a right to be joyous under any circumstances may be so to-day. To the Christian there is nothing saddening in the brevity of life, nothing calculated to cause gloom in the lengthening shadows. With him "to live is Christ, and to die is gain." He is one year nearer home; and if this year be his last on earth, it will record his entrance into the rest of God's people. The impenitent sinner has no right to cheerfulness at any time, and never less than the very time which he most devotes to thoughtless mirth and extravagant demonstrations of joy. To him the past is one of condemnation, and he is a year nearer the judgment—a year nearer hell! He is a guiltier being than he was twelve months ago, and the time to come only deepens that guilt. Of the Christless soul, even in the holidays, we may adopt the inspired words: "I said of laughter, it is mad; and of mirth, what doeth it?" What greater madness than laughter, mirth, and reveling whilst men are "without God, and having no hope in the world?" What place is there for mirth when the fleeting years are only hurrying them unprepared into the presence of an angry God? What doeth it, this unseemly and incongruous mirth, when there is but a step between the soul and eternal death? The one condition and element of real happiness is wanting, and it is a farce, a mockery, a solemn delusion, to think of its possession until we have given up our sins and surrendered all at the Saviour's feet.

By many the beginning of the new year has been looked forward to as the occasion of carrying their good resolutions into effect. Christians have purposed to enter upon a closer walk with God, and to give more attention to their religious duties. The unconverted have set it apart as a time for their entrance into the visible Church and the beginning of their religious profession and practice. It is the appointed day for reformation, the breaking off of bad habits, and the inauguration of a new and better order of living. But will these good resolutions be kept? If the believer has felt the need of a deeper work of grace, why has he put it off until this day? How has he dared thus to limit the Holy One of Israel, and to defer what duty, conscience, and reason demanded at once. The serious-minded sinner will find no mystical or talismanic spell in the day which begins the calendar of another year. The self-renunciation will be harder, the conflict with the corrupt nature will be even more difficult than six months ago. The act in every case should be contemporaneous with the serious conviction and purpose. The resolve was a bribe to conscience, and the performance is easily postponed. Every thing is lost when men consent to defer an obvious present duty, and especially when they brace themselves with the obligation of a definite day. There was sin in the postponement, and it will not be wanting in most cases when the set time arrives. The probabilities are strong that the Christian who has been waiting for the new year in order to realize a higher type of piety will continue to live in a low and declining state. It is almost certain that the majority of those who have determined upon moral and religious reformation will pass the assigned limit and go on in their sins. The very worst use of the day is to make it the axis and target of good resolutions. The same influences that led to the putting off of the call of God will carry the procrastinator beyond the prescribed limit, and launch him upon another year of unbelief. To resolve to be a Christian, or to resolve to be a better Christian, at some future day is a most heinous sin. It is trifling with God, and insulting his goodness and authority. It can only be done by resisting the Spirit and by deliberate rebellion against the divine government.

The voice of the old year is a sermon of manifold instruction and application, calling for gratitude for mercies temporal and spiritual, for humiliation and self-abasement, for penitence, and for honest searching of heart. Above all its lessons is the importance of an immediate and decided choice of "that good part." In view of the failures and sins of the past, the waste of time, the perversion of opportunities, we shall do well to adopt the psalmist's prayer: "So teach us to number our days that we may apply our hearts unto wisdom." If we have come so far without having enlisted for Christ, by all means set up the tabernacle "on the first day of the first month," and let this be the glad day of our espousals. A happy New-year it will be if it marks the beginning of a new life, or if it is signalized as its triumphant end. Toil and care, poverty and suffering may be in store, but it will be a happy year if God go with us. Doubtless the year dawns gloomily upon many. The earthly outlook is most disheartening, and they venture forth with fear and trembling; but it may be a happy year, nevertheless, if Christ's footsteps are on the billows, and if his form moves amidst the tumult of the elements. Through all the weary pilgrimage, through the waste, howling wilderness, and in the face of the mightiest enemies, the ancient promise stands: "My presence shall go with thee, and I will give thee rest."

THE GOSPEL OF SPRING.

THE language of the season, when devoutly interpreted, is full of profitable lessons. All nature is now reviving from its temporary death and starting into new life. The vegetable kingdom is awaking from its winter's slumber and entering upon a period of renewed activity. The mighty forces that have for a time been held in torpid silence begin to assert their power, and the hidden life is bursting forth into manifold forms of melody and beauty. The foliage of the trees and the music of the birds, the fragrance of the flowers and the hum of insects, are the heralds of the refulgent summer. "Awake, thou that sleepest," is the message of spring to the soul. The season not only calls the husbandman to fresh and vigorous activity, but it reminds us of our spiritual vocation to higher experiences in the kingdom of God. While it is a type of the better resurrection which awaits the body after the winter of the grave, it is also an illustration of those blessed renewals of the Spirit which come to all that patiently wait upon the Lord. The universal awakening in nature finds its archetype in the revival of grace in the heart and in the times of refreshing which visit the churches.

The spring, with its ever-surprising and wondrous phenomena, is one of the grandest apologues that can be applied to spiritual things, and especially as it exhibits this aspect of a renewed and more vigorous life. Its voice to the slumbering Christian comes up from the forest and the fields, and from the buds and blossoms of the orchard and garden. Its notes of promise and encouragement sound from the groves and hills and overflowing streams. Zion is admonished, by the attire of verdure and bloom with which the earth is invested, to awake and to put on her beautiful garments, while the believer is to put on the Lord Jesus Christ, and to be clothed with salvation. To many the recent past had been a time of guilty repose, a bleak and cheerless waste without warmth or gladness; but there is a renewing power to bring back the times of joy and singing. The sinner has been dead long enough. The gospel of spring to him is to warn and to invite. He must feel the power of a spiritual resurrection and experience the creative omnipotence which quickens the death of winter into vernal sweetness and exuberant life. The change from nature to grace is as marked and extraordinary as that which indicates the transition from the gloom of December to the brightness of May. The unconverted and careless soul may thus hear the voice of awakening and promise. This activity and irrepressible energy in the lower forms of life, and this reänimation of dead things in the earth, the waters, and the air, should be as a sound from heaven arousing the unbelieving heart to earnest concern for salvation. A winter without a spring is simply death everlasting, and a soul unawakened and unrenewed necessarily sinks into the blackness of darkness forever. The gospel of the written word and the gospel of the season are in harmony. Their common message to saint and sinner is one of a reviving and an awakening realization of our religious privileges and responsibilities.

And what more strikingly illustrates the change in conversion than the contrasts between winter and spring? Spring is the world regenerated, and is as the babe in Christ, embracing the possibilities of the coming seasons, and having substantially in itself the germs of all glory and of all perfection. Nothing in nature is so like a birth from above as the transformations which take place in this period of boundless and startling changes. If any man be in Christ he is a new creation after some such manner as the material world is when it feels the renovating and vital breath of spring. The old things of a state of unbelief have passed away, when the sinner is delivered from the power of darkness, very much as the last vestiges of wintry desolation have retreated before the sunshine. The light and warmth which have given health and life to vegetation are symbols of the Sun of righteousness, whose healing wings bring peace and comfort to the contrite spirit. As we look upon the earth and sky, clothed and garnished in the radiance of the cloudless morning, and exclaim, " Behold, all things are become new!" so is it when the mourner in Zion enters into the marvelous light of God and feels the love of God shed abroad in his heart by the Holy Ghost. Like the transition in the seasons, conversion is life from the dead, the passing from death unto life, and a translation from the power of darkness into the kingdom of God's dear Son. The gospel of spring is not only a call to awake out of sleep, but it is also to arise from the dead and to become the children of light. It coincides with the central and overmastering necessity of our natures: " Ye must be born again." The voice that wakes up and revivifies the world of nature must be heard in the depths of the soul, and the dead spirit must be raised and changed.

It will be well if the season of blossoms and melody is allowed to impress us with the character of true religion. The garment of praise is given for the spirit of heaviness. All living nature—animate and inanimate—accords with the prophetic evangel which promises " beauty for ashes, and the oil of joy for mourning." The visible and material mirror those images of the inspired pen which stamp a *present* blessedness upon the religious experience. Religion is clad in singing robes, such as the spring wears in her exhaustless wealth of radiance and harmonies. It is an epithalamium, and not a dirge. God clothes the world in forms of grace and in the richest colors, and decks the hill-sides and gems the meadows with flowers of the gayest and most brilliant tints. He has made every thing beautiful in its time, and thrown over all his creatures the spell of a jubilant and tuneful inspiration. Christ in the heart is a feast of delight, a spring breaking forth in the desert, and a garden in the wilderness. His is not a religion of cowls and sackcloth and cloisters, but a praise and a joy forever.

This inspiring season reminds us that the present is the period of preparation and of seed-time. Grace is glory in the bud and the earnest of the heavenly inheritance. Now the sower goes forth to sow, and an all-gracious Providence is watching over every form of embryonic life. "Thou makest the outgoings of the morning and evening to rejoice. Thou visitest the earth and waterest it; thou greatly enrichest it with the river of God, which is full of water." Under the genial influences of the divine mercy we labor in anticipation of a golden harvest. The germs of life are springing and the buds are unfolding—prophetic of the final result. The beginnings of an endless life are in the still and unseen processes which are going forward in the heart. The believer is in all things working for eternity; he is working together with God, improving the season and making the most of its sun and showers. Wonderful and satisfying as are the present experiences, there is in them this character of preparation, and this looking to something beyond, of which they are but the promise. "It doth not yet appear what we shall be," but the believing heart rejoices in the conscious foretaste of a measureless good.

We do no violence to the analogies of the natural and the supernatural when we assert that the gospel of spring embraces the resurrection of the just. Not that other resurrection which is to shame and everlasting contempt, but that which is to everlasting life. The sleep of the grave is at length to give place to the last and crowning miracle of our faith. As yet, "since the fathers fell asleep, all things continue as they were from the beginning of the creation," even as in midwinter, when nature gives no sign of her approaching life. But we know that the sun, in his appointed time, will retrace his path of fire, and that this apparent death shall yield to life. The generations are waiting for this manifestation of the sons of God, and all the plans and purposes of the Redeemer are moving toward this stupendous consummation. The season of returning life and joy joins its voice to that of a more sure word of prophecy: "Awake and sing, ye that dwell in the dust; for thy dew is as the dew of herbs, and the earth shall cast out the dead."

THE FALL OF THE LEAVES.

THE season has come again when the leaves are dropping into their autumnal graves. It seems but yesterday that they opened out of the spring buds and spread their soft green palms to the sunshine. But it is months ago that they were born—a life-time in the vegetable world has nearly passed, and, having served their generation, they are now about to fall on sleep. Many have fallen prematurely; and herein they are a type of human mortality—fallen, while yet green and unwithered, by the hand of violence or torn by some rude blast. Thus perish the young and the strong—dying without fading, and preserved in memory, as in an herbarium, ever young and beautiful.

The prelude of death in the leaves is wonderfully gorgeous and impressive. All the brilliant tints are lavished upon them. All the splendors of coloring are displayed in the forests as they are about to be unclothed. The death-robes, woven of purple and gold, far surpass the liveries of spring and summer. They seem to be clad for a glorious translation rather than for a bed in the dust. They are arrayed in royal apparel as if enjoying a triumph and as if marching in the pomp and grandeur of conscious victory. Fading "as a leaf" brings with it other thoughts than those of mere frailty and decay. The revelation of life and immortality invests old age with a peculiar glory, and the spiritual life in its maturity glows with a light of supernal radiance. The frosts of age, like those of autumn upon the foliage, beautify while they destroy, and life winds up in a blaze of manifold colorings which neither spring nor summer could produce. The fall of the leaf is often tranquil. Its hold is released by the gentlest zephyr, and no torn and bleeding fibers indicate that nature has sustained a violent shock. It is death in its gentler aspects, coming when expected, and in harmony with all the moods and aspects of the world around. The breeze that severs, like unseen angels' wings, bears it softly and slowly to its resting-place.

The fate of the leaves, however and whenever they fall, is the type of a universal mortality. They all go sooner or later, and the evergreens differ from others only in this: that they are ever dying, just as the human race is ever wasting and renewing its life. Some autumn leaves, though withered and sear, hold most tenaciously to the bough, resisting the storms which have scattered all their companions; but they yield at length to the inexorable law. The hour comes when not one of these myriads which came forth with the spring buds is left. It is even so with man. The falling leaves are rehearsing in his ears the lesson of his mortality, and in their quiet way are telling him what he likes not to hear or heed. Archetype, type, or parable, their language is plain. With no clamorous voice, and with no vociferous cries, like the stars, only with another mission, "there is no speech nor language where their voice is not heard." The fall comes to us with this among its other annual sermons. It speaks in the pomp of its unapproachable hues, the serenely ebbing life of all the wealth of foliage with which the trees of the grove and wood are adorned, and in the sure but beautiful death which is overtaking every leaf.

There is a moral leaf that does not wither, a spiritual tree that is planted by the river of waters. But as to our material life, in this world "we all do fade as a leaf;" the marks of decay are upon us, and the touch of autumn's breath tinges every face. It may not have been so with the trees of paradise, and it will not be so with those trees which grow upon the banks of the river of life. There is a land where the falling leaves and their lessons have passed into history, and where there shall be no more death. It is to our world of sin and death that the fading leaf is confined, where the symbol is realized, and where the warning is needed. And thus, while it preaches death, it leads our thoughts farther, to a blessedness and life altogether in contrast with the brevity and vanity of the present. The peroration glides unconsciously and inevitably into the realms of life eternal.

> There happier bowers than Eden's bloom,
> Nor sin nor sorrow know:
> Blest seats! through rude and stormy scenes
> I onward press to you.

BIRTHDAYS.

To every one these days come with incentives to serious thought and meditation. The birthday of another may awaken a degree of interest, but there is something more serious and intensely personal in our own. It has been the occasion of feasting and rejoicing, especially among the great and royal in all times; and it is, among humbler folk, an occasion of friendly congratulation. Why our friends should notice the day is perhaps to be thus explained: They mean not to say we are glad you are growing old, and that you have left another mile-stone behind you on the road to the grave. If this should sometimes be the secret feeling, none would care to express it. What then? This perhaps: We are glad that you were born, and that you have lived so long. It is well for us and for the world that you are still alive. The door is open also for that kind and well-meant flattery that tells how gently time is dealing with us, how young for our years, and for the expression of wishes that many and happy years may be added to the earthly term.

The day is all one's own, as other anniversary days are not. In them all the world seems to be growing old together, and the things commemorated belong to the joy, sorrow, and instruction of multitudes. Other people may have been born on the same day, as many were; and other events happened, as great and decisive battles, important discoveries and inventions, revolutions for freedom, earthquakes. These coincidences do not invade our domain nor interfere with our proprietorship. To him who was born it was a very momentous day; even to the most obscure it was a more important day than that which dates the rise of empires or the crumbling of thrones. To be or not to be—or, rather, to have been or not to have been—that is the question. He might not have been, but he was born; and with the birth have come all of life, all of time, and the eternity beyond. The most are glad to be. They are thankful that they were born, to look out upon the universe, to see the light of the sun, and to be as a part of the life and the intelligence that throb and glow in the creation. And with the devout this sense of gratitude swells unutterably, since to be born opens to the soul the blessed consciousness of God and the boundlessness of the everlasting. Not to have been born is the next most fearful thought to annihilation. The one is what might have been; the other, to the doubting mind, is what may be. Our life given, we cling to it, grateful to have escaped from nothingness, and more grateful that we live for evermore.

It is perhaps a little humiliating to consider that the world did very well without us when as yet we were not. Nearly all history was made before we came into the world, and creation itself, with all its beauties and wonders, was already old. The light, the flowers, the spangled frame of the skies, the Bible, and redemption—all were perfected without us. Laws were framed, freedom fought for, society organized, printing, gunpowder, the mariner's compass invented, and the Copernican system accepted, and we were not here to help. It would have made but little difference if there had been this one name less. Now and then is one born whose not being would seemingly have been an irreparable loss. How could the world have done without Paul, Luther, Calvin, Wesley, Kepler, Newton, Shakespeare, Washington? But it is only a few stars of the first magnitude that we should miss from the multitudinous hosts of the sky. What the birthday is to him who is born may not be much in the seeming to the great universe into which he comes, and if we were to go out of it only the smallest neighborhood would know that any thing had happened. But there is a mission even in this momentary flitting across the horizon of time. "It doth not yet appear what we shall be." We are born to an inheritance in nature, and with the possibilities of a heavenly throne. Of him who is born we may say, All things are his; he is heir, if he will be, of all things, even of God himself. Even the capacity of being lost marks the dignity of the being and the worth of it.

Probably the birthdays remembered in heaven are coincident with the dying-days of earth. The years as numbered here are not counted there. The emergence from the mortal into the immortal is the epoch from which the personal history dates in the eternal world. There must be a celestial calendar of some sort, a dial-plate upon whose golden face no shadow needs to fall, or the revolutions of some mighty sphere by which the years and cycles of heaven are noted. In the long hereafter the few fleeting years of earth must fall away as mere specks or atoms in the retrospect. In the depths of eternity they would not be worth counting in answering the question, "How old art thou?" We must start from a new point, and have ample measures of duration.

The last birthday comes to all. Friends and kindred may prolong the remembrance after we are gone, but in time the memory of it fades out, and the passing generations sweep on, removing every trace. As between the great and famous, and the little and obscure, it is only a measure of time. Pharaoh's birthday was notable and grandly celebrated thousands of years ago, but when he was born is a mere conjecture now. As far as this world is concerned, the difference is almost nothing.

And as to length of days, the difference between youth and old age becomes a point invisible at last. The birthday with the young is brightened with health and worldly hope and with the consciousness of increasing strength and wisdom; that of the aged is sometimes clouded with the infirmities of years and with the feeling of regret that life has been spent to so little purpose; but we cannot tell which is nearer the last. It would seem to be an incongruous combination which the preacher has framed for our learning, but the lesson applies, in all its parts, to the birthday of the good: "A good name is better than precious ointment, and the day of death than the day of one's birth."

LIGHT OUT OF DARKNESS.*

OUT OF A DARK ROOM.

"TRULY, the light is sweet, and a pleasant thing it is for the eyes to behold the sun;" but then the eyes must be sound and healthful, otherwise the light comes to be regarded as an enemy, and is the occasion of the most exquisite torture. Under such circumstances the deepest night is most agreeable, and darkness lies upon the sensitive organ as a soothing poultice. We observe with what pertinacity the sunbeams struggle to penetrate our seclusion. In spite of shutters and curtains, here and there a fugitive ray comes in as a painful obtruder. We pursue it as if it were a serpent rather than an angel, and seek to stifle it by deeper shade. We are conscious of an outer world of surpassing glory whose effulgence presses and knocks for admittance, and yet our chief care and study are to suppress the faintest glintings that strive for admission. We know full well that without is the world of beauty—scenery of gorgeous coloring, and a landscape that imbibes and reflects the unceasing streams that flow from the golden sun. From this prison of gloom we can only think about it. There is neither desire nor capacity to look upon it. The one and

---

*The occasion which gave this article to the *Advocate* was an attack of inflammation of the eyes, painful and tedious, yet borne with such gentle, cheerful patience and consideration for the one who was blessed with the privilege of sharing the darkness of that sick-room as nurse and amanuensis, that she found it the brightest and sweetest spot in her home—the home that was never dark while the radiance of this strong, pure, beautiful life shone therein.—E. K. P.

only fear is lest any particle of this brilliancy should invade our retirement.

Perhaps this whole experience gives us some clew to the phenomena of a soul diseased—to that aversion to light and to that shrinking from revealed truth which, under certain conditions, are exhibited by the conscience. Light is come into the world, and men love darkness rather than light. The most beautiful and beneficent is hated. The condition fitly represents that state of soul which belongs to the natural man. It is not utterly dark. There is some diffusion and reflection of light in spite of the barriers to admission. We seem to see very well, and it is only when a shutter is turned that we become aware of how little we do see and of the darkness in which we abide.

Our dark room, in comparison with the brightness of the outer world, is what our present state of being is to that which is to come. Friends coming in are to us as angel visitors, and yet they stumble and grope as if in pitch darkness. The transition from a brighter atmosphere unfits them to move in this. We can imagine that the descent of an angel from heaven to our earth would be indeed as a leap in the dark were it not for their self-contained illumination and for the possession of senses of supernatural power. The bar to knowledge and intercourse between the saints in glory and the good on earth may be only a wall of supernal light on the one part and of a cloud of darkness on the other. We cannot look up through the brightness; they cannot pierce the veil that overshadows us. They are shut in to "the inheritance of the saints in light;" we, in the shadows of our mortal home, await the epiphany that shall restore us to their companionship. These goggled eyes remind us how we "see through a glass, darkly"—how subdued, ill-defined, and limited is all our vision here in comparison with that day when with open face "we shall see the King in his beauty, and behold the land that is very far off."

And yet our imprisonment may be but temporary, and to a gracious end. It is for a healing purpose—that we may be prepared for the light. The eye must be restored, that it may bear the sight of the sun. God has placed us in comparatively a dark room. There is balm in Gilead and a physician there. Restored faculties is the preparation which enables us to appreciate the light we have, and prepares us for glory that is to come. It is well for a world of sinners that God has so attempered his revealments to their purblind condition, and that in mercy to human weakness only the skirts of the awful form are seen in its majestic march. He places us in the cleft of the rock—throws over us the shadow of a living as well as omnipotent hand —while his goodness passes before us. What seems to be an imprisonment and restraint, which limit our movement and vision, are in reality those contrivances and conditions that are necessary to our present healing and to our final liberation..

We observe, as the vision clarifies and the engorged eyeballs cease to throb, that the light becomes more tolerable, and we begin to feel that "truly the light is sweet, and a pleasant thing it is for the eyes to behold the sun." We can look out somewhat now. There is no longer any attempt to crush the straggling rays. They are rather welcome, and come to us as the tokens and earnest of a blessed deliverance. Instead of striving to exclude the sunbeams, we rather pray for their ingress. Surely "the earnest expectation of the creature waiteth for the manifestation of the sons of God." We are being called out of darkness into "his marvelous light." Somewhat after this manner is the progress of a soul from sin to righteousness and from righteousness to heaven. There is a gradual inflowing of light as the spiritual cure goes on. The love is for light rather than darkness. The senses are adjusted to the ever-increasing splendors of truth, and the whole nature is brought into accord with that which is luminous with spiritual beauty. "Old things are passed away; behold, all things are become new."

There comes, as the completeness of convalescence approaches, a strong yearning after more light and a sense of sufficiency to emerge into the glowing day—such desire as the heart sometimes feels to break through the vaulted blue and gaze upon those splendors that suns and stars but dimly reflect. The cry of the pure heart is, "I beseech thee, show me thy glory!" It longs through a clearer medium to look upon "the light of the world," and to gaze upon the Sun of righteousness.

In our dark room there are ministering spirits—eyes that see for us, hands that deftly anticipate the needs of the helpless. Some, if not all, in this earthly prison-house have their guardian-angels—angels neither winged nor invisible, but, what is far better, incarnate in woman's form. Who can tell the unseen ministries that attend us all, and that beyond our recognition aid and supplement those we see? And through all and in all the remedies and cares of earthly skill and love is it not the hand of Him who gave sight to the blind that gives the efficacious and healing touch?

NOT ORPHANS.

"COMFORTLESS" is a comment rather than a translation. "I will not leave you orphans" is the literal meaning. Orphanage is indeed a comfortless condition. In its spiritual sense, it is to be "without God in the world." Wycliffe hit the sense precisely—"fatherless." Atheism is orphanage in regard to the divine fatherhood, and so are all apprehensions of God which exclude his personality and goodness. But, more than this, to be without Christ is to be orphans without the comfort and presence of the Infinite Father. Christ alone shows us the Father, and manifests him as the Father to the believing heart. Our sonship is based upon faith in Christ: "But, as many as received him, to them gave he power to become the sons of God, even to them that believe on his name." In contrast with the orphanage of the soul is the spirit of adoption: "And, because ye are sons, God hath sent forth the Spirit of his Son into your hearts, crying, Abba, Father!" Whatever speculative or theoretical notions we may have about God, the cry of "Abba, Father," in its deep, heart-penetrating sense, never springs from a mind estranged from Christ.

Strauss, as quoted by Taylor Lewis, says: "In the enormous machine of the universe, amid the incessant whirl and hiss of its jagged iron wheels, amid the deafening crash of its ponderous stamps and hammers, in the midst of this terrific commotion, man, a helpless and defenseless creature, finds himself placed, not secure for a moment, that on some unguarded motion a wheel may not seize and rend him or a hammer crush him to powder. This sense of abandonment is at first something awful." The fearful desolation of the skeptic is well depicted in this honest utterance. Having rejected Christ and the supernatural, there is nothing left but blank despair. In contrast with this dark and rayless night of unbelief is the spirit of adoption in the children of God, the love of God shed abroad in the heart by the Holy Ghost, and the sense of security as the believer nestles in the arms of an almighty and loving heavenly Father.

Orphanage rightly describes the abandonment, the helplessness, the hopelessness of those who have drifted out into the black and fathomless waters of atheism; and all systems of religion and philosophy that reject Christ tend to atheism, and ultimately reach it. A weak and ignorant child, left parentless in the world, and thrust out upon the current of society without sympathy, love, and wisdom to guide and shelter it, only faintly exhibits the melancholy state of the Christless soul. To such a one there is no personal wisdom, mercy, or goodness, no justice, truth, or righteousness, in the ordering of events. There is a blind, inexorable, unfeeling force and a material fatalism in the sweep and movement of nature. There is no God, no pitying Father, no beneficent power to whom helpless creatures may appeal and in whom they may trust. Man is a stray and parentless waif, a something in which intelligence and consciousness have been evolved to perish in death or to pass into other conditions and forms as inexplicable, and perhaps more miserable than the present.

From such dreary views of the world, and of man and his destiny, the hungry soul turns with relief to the revelations and privileges of the gospel. Christ does not leave us in this horrible and repulsive orphanage, this utter loneliness of spirit, this state of severance from a love which the soul instinctively craves. He comes to us. God comes to us in his Son, and the Spirit of his Son in us cries, "Abba, Father!" Man is not a mere lump of matter, drifting we know not whither, but an immortal spirit made in the divine image, redeemed by love, and guided through sorrow, temptation, suffering, and death to the everlasting mansions.

There is nothing so utterly alone, so absolutely helpless, so surrounded with unmitigated gloom, as the human spirit without God. The companionship and sympathy of our fellows do not help us, since they are in like case as miserable as ourselves, and powerless to avert disaster or to secure good fortune. Our earthly parents have brought us into a world of trouble, but they cannot guide us through it nor give us hope in passing out of it. As to all higher relations, and as to the interests and destiny of the soul, our orphanage is absolute and appalling until the divine fatherhood, the infinite tenderness, the far-reaching mercy, shine forth in Christ. Comfortless because of our orphanage, all comfort breaks upon us through the sonship in Christ. In him "the Eternal God is thy refuge, and underneath are the everlasting arms."

Christ found the world in a state of orphanage, alienated from God, and with dim conceptions of his paternal love and compassion. He left his disciples trembling and doubting, and with feeble conceptions of God's care over them. He looks upon struggling, tempted, agonizing souls everywhere, tossed and worried by doubt and sin, and hungering for a strong consolation. He comes to us all to reveal the Father, and, in the place of the spirit of bondage to fear to plant in us the spirit of adoption. He comes to break off the chains of darkness, to open the prison doors, and to thrill the longing heart with the one cry which ends our banishment from the infinite and eternal love. He comes in the power and joyousness of his own Spirit, crying "Abba, Father" in the orphaned soul.

GOD'S CHASTISEMENTS.

THE afflicted are tempted to distrust the paternal goodness of God because they are called to suffer. The very opposite conclusion, however, is the true one; "for whom the Lord loveth he chasteneth, and scourgeth every son whom he receiveth." This is a peculiar stamp of acceptance and seal of sonship. God is dealing with us as with sons, not as with enemies and rebels, when he permits the rod to fall upon us. Great trials and sore tribulations are therefore to the Christian full of comfort, since they indicate God's fatherly love and their own filial relation to him whose throne is in the heavens.

A common mistake made by suffering believers is in their estimate of the results of affliction. We frequently hear them declare that they get along better in religion when in prosperity and health, and that pain and trouble only bring darkness and dissatisfaction. They do not propose to deny the scriptural teachings that benefits most important and glorious flow from the afflictions of the present life. They only propose to constitute themselves exceptions to the general law. David was right when he said: "It is good for me that I have been afflicted, that I might learn thy statutes. Before I was afflicted I went astray; but now have I kept thy word." Paul was not beside himself when he gloried in infirmities and tribulations, and with a towering faith exclaimed: "For our light affliction, which is but for a moment, worketh for us a far more exceeding and eternal weight of glory." Generally true, they are the exceptions. There are those who take this view of the subject: that it is better for them to be exempt from trouble, and who really think that the tendency of sorrow and trial with them is to depress their faith and to mar their spiritual life.

This is a very natural mistake, and one which Paul anticipates: "Now no chastening for the present seemeth to be joyous, but grievous; nevertheless, afterward it yieldeth the peaceable fruit of righteousness unto them which are exercised thereby." The present seeming is grievous indeed. A fierce struggle is aroused; the soul is overwhelmed, and tempted to rebel. Faith, so far from being strengthened, wavers, and the buddings of doubt and distrust appear. It is afterward that the peaceable fruit of righteousness is yielded. Submission may not be reached at once, but the opposite, self-will, and even defiance, awake as never before. There is no clear vision. Clouds and darkness are round about. The spirit is broken, hope almost gone, and faith in God is shaken. But afterward the victory comes out of this fearful conflict, and all the graces are refined and perfected by the ordeal through which the soul has been made to pass. The peaceable fruit is after the smoke, dust, and din of the battle-field are over. A present joyousness is not the sign of profitable chastening. Here we run into the error that affliction is not good for *us*, however it may benefit others. The seemingly untoward effects really are the precursors of the good. The present grievous aspect of God's dealings, the cheerless and terrible upheaval, the stirring up of rebellion, doubt, and other repulsive sediments of the corrupt heart are to be followed by the calm of a resigned and submissive spirit.

It is a dangerous condition to be in when a man concludes that he is an exception to the law of suffering, and that his religious welfare is best promoted by prosperity. The peril lies in this: that when the trial comes he will fail to see the Father's hand, and will miss the blessing which infinite love and wisdom have designed for him. Because the present seeming is grievous he resents this mark of his sonship, and the peaceable fruit is never realized. While God has dealt with him as with a son, he has alienated himself from this dear relationship, and by his willfulness that which would have proved the peaceable fruit of righteousness is blighted in the bud. The course of safety and comfort is to surrender ourselves to the inspired teaching and to cultivate subjection unto the Father of spirits. Grievous as is the present, and as it must be to do us good, there is the joyousness of the afterward. How long sorrow may continue, how long the pain and the travail, we may not tell; but the afterward, even in this life, is blessed. The peaceable fruit is sure to come out of this tearful sowing. In this life, but certainly and completely in the life to come, will the fruit appear. "For I reckon that the sufferings of this present time are not worthy to be compared with the glory which shall be in us."

THE DISCIPLINE OF FAILURE.

"THE man who never lost a battle" is a rare man in the world. The greatest successes have been preceded by what seemed to be disastrous defeat. In proof, we might recall the careers of Peter the Great, of Russia; of Frederick the Great, of Prussia; and the struggle of our own country under Washington for liberty and independence. If Napoleon had not been uniformly a conqueror at first, it is not unlikely that he would have ended his days as "head of the army" and ruler of France. In war the defeated general may learn more than the one that overcomes, and the victor is often demoralized and fatally damaged by his temporary triumph.

It may be so in the battle of life for bread and fortune. It has been said that the best merchants are those who have passed through the trying ordeal of business embarrassment and failure. In it they have learned such lessons of sagacity, prudence, and economy as enable them to guard against like miscarriages in the future. In a certain sense it may be true that the highest ultimate success in secular affairs sometimes comes out of the training and experience of failure. It may not be quite true of the navigator who has lost a ship that he is more to be trusted than one who has not, but under some circumstances it might be so. Some men would be more vigilant after such a misfortune.

However this may be, there is a moral discipline in our temporal reverses, so that what we call failure leads to the highest of all success. The uniformly prosperous man is not usually the most spiritual. The rich merchants, bondholders, and capitalists seldom help to swell the prayer-meeting, nor are they usually overmuch occupied with their religious devotions. There are exceptions, but riches securely held are generally unfriendly to piety. The true riches have come to many only after the mammon of unrighteousness has been lost. To them a great success would have been ruin everlasting.

But in the spiritual conflict—the fight of faith and the effort to lay hold on eternal life—does the finally successful soul universally win? In this most important of all soldierships, are there many who can boast that they have never lost a battle? Conquerors and more than conquerors at last, there has been defeat and even rout in the march. They have been flanked and ambushed and overcome by the deceitfulness of sin. But the tyro in religion becomes acquainted with the tactics of Satan. He discovers his wiles, and learns his own most vulnerable points. He need not have yielded for a moment. He ought to have had on the whole armor of God, and he might have come out of the conflict without a scar. But his errors and false steps, if wisely laid to heart, have opened his eyes to his peril, and they have driven him to the tower of his strength. He sees now how backsliding came about, how the easily-besetting sin found a foot-hold, and how utterly weak and defenseless he is when unbelief separates from Christ. Humility, watchfulness, and a deeper love may thus flow from the conscious failures which have more or less marked almost every Christian life. It is under such discipline as this that the soul cries out for the living God, and seeks for the perfect cleansing and the completeness of grace to overcome all sin and the power to walk in the light evermore.

The consciousness of failure in any direction entails suffering, but it ought not to drive us to despair. It is humiliating, disappointing, discouraging; but God is the God of all grace, and "if any man sin, we have an Advocate with the Father." The sense of past defects and unfaithfulness should quicken our steps now, and lead to an immediate and unreserved consecration to Christ. If life in its secular aspects seems to have been a failure, the purpose and the result may be a wonderful success in the spiritual achievements gained through suffering. If our great Exemplar learned obedience "by the things which he suffered," much more may we. What men count the greatest failures may be the grandest of successes. If there be mortifying failure hitherto in our religious lives, there should now be the resolve of new and fresh endeavor and the determination to live nearer to God.

Let us not be discouraged by the oft-repeated reference to "the man who never lost a battle." That man is not often met with in war, business, or religion. Defeat has its lessons for us all, and after defeat and through defeat have come the permanent and final successes of almost all great careers and noble lives. The successful man is he who wins the last and the best things.

THE LIFE THAT NOW IS.

AS A TALE THAT IS TOLD.

SO to the inspired poet it seemed. "We spend our years as a tale that is told." As the most exciting story comes quickly to an end, and all its scenes and incidents fade with its closing words, so is it with our years. Or, as some explain, our years are as a thought, a transient ejaculation, a momentary utterance that dies on the lips. Adam Clarke insists that the Hebrew has a sadder meaning: "We consume our years like a groan." He says: "We live a dying whining, complaining life, and at last a groan is its termination." All of these conceptions of life apply to it as a whole and to the end of our earthly being, and in many respects they describe each single year that passes. The tale is told as far as the past year is concerned. We can recall its events and muse upon its scenes, but we cannot make it other than it is. Whether a thought, an ejaculation, a groan, it has been uttered, and we cannot arrest its flight. We can now see how the story might have been better, how it might have been illuminated with nobler actions, and how it might have been illustrated with brighter colors. If we had it to tell over again, we would try to make it worthier, and have it rounded with more satisfying results. The record, however, is made, and it cannot be recast.

The meditation dwells upon the shortness of life—a brevity that fails to impress us until the tale is ended. As life proceeds, with its absorbing occupations and varied pursuits, we are not conscious of the lapse of time. It is only when we pause at the end of a year that we partially realize how short it is, and only at death shall we feel the full force of the declaration that "our days are as a handbreadth." The individual life is as a moment in comparison with the life of the race; and in our relation to the general progress we are but madrepores in the building up of the ages. The vanity of life is most apparent in our personal insignificance and in the mortality that bounds our earthly career. And yet the drop, as part of the ocean, is invested with an importance and sublimity which belong to the entire sea. The atom partakes of the grandeur of the mountain of which it is a portion. A year well spent contributes something to the general store, and a life finished in goodness and usefulness is a legacy of price left to coming generations. When we turn from the earthly and mortal side of our being, the vanity of life disappears and its true purpose and surpassing glory are manifest. This is the import of these sad and depressing views of man's earthly lot. They are indeed somber and humiliating if this world were all. A pensive and melancholy shadow rests upon all sublunary things until the light of heaven shines out. If life's story ended here, and if there were no immortality to follow, then the picture could not be too dismally drawn. As a preparation for another life the present is long enough, and all its sorrows and toils have their explanation in the discipline that is needed to fit us for a higher and happier state.

The tenor of the psalmist's reflections is admonitory. It is so in fact—that we consume our years as a tale that is told. We permit them to slip by without improving them as we should, content to be entertained as they go, and having no adequate conception of their precious and irrecoverable opportunities. Diversion and entertainment have been the chief desire, rather than earnest work and a great purpose. We have built castles in the air, wasted our time in reverie and dreams, dallied with superficial pleasures, and made life a worthless fiction instead of a grand reality. We have moved amidst the clouds of the unreal, the fantastic, and have lost ourselves in bewildering speculations, while we have banished all serious thought from our minds. Life has been a tale of plots, episodes, and romance to amuse, rather than a school for the formation of character. We have reveled in it as a novel when we should have studied it as a sacred history. It is this misinterpretation of our years—the careless, dawdling, and frivolous way in which we consume them—that calls for the censure of the inspired sage.

The levity of men in their retrospect of the year is well described. It is something to be rehearsed with the lightness and thoughtlessness of a story that is told. We forget that the dead year will have a resurrection, that it will meet us in the judgment, and that the impress of it must remain with us forever. People drink, dance, and make merry over the grave of the old year. There is infinite jest in its dying-hour, and a rare humor in the conviction that it is gone. This is our crazy way of estimating life and celebrating its epochs—verily as a tale that is told. It is a solemn thing to live; and, if in our right minds, we cannot be otherwise than serious when we meditate upon the year that is past.

It will be to the thoughtful a history of the divine providence and grace, a journey wherein the pilgrim's feet have been under heavenly guidance, and wherein a beneficent hand has led the weary and perplexed traveler into the paths of safety. To such it may be also a poem of epic power, interspersed with odes and hymns, and filled with the sweetness and harmony of a faith kept and of duty performed. And it may stand out to our view as a work of art hewn from the great quarry of time and wrought and polished into a form of imperishable beauty and grace.

That we *consume* our years in any way is enough to arrest the attention of the most careless. The flame of life is devouring the taper. The years are taken up into ourselves, and we are giving them out in various forms of personal influence and carrying them with us to the eternal day. As to us, it is as if so much of time were burned up, or as if it were drowned in a deluge. What we have saved from the flame and the flood may not be much, but it is all that is left us. Whether we have been prodigals or dutiful sons, whether we have spent to waste or to save, is the question to be answered.

Sincerely do we wish our readers a happy New-year. Some of you have spent the past year well, and this gives promise of a happy year to come. Some of you have consumed the past year in vanity—perhaps also in sin. You have lost much that cannot be retrieved, but through infinite mercy you may have a happy year too. Would that we could for once reach the ear, the conscience, and the heart of all who have thus far neglected the great salvation. We would point them to Christ as the refuge, and beseech them to make sure at once of the blessed hope. Let the new year be begun aright. From henceforth live for eternity, live to be useful, and dedicate your body, soul, substance, and time to Him who came into the world to redeem you. With the new year the tale of our earthly life will indeed be told with many of us. May it be the portion of such to enter into the Master's joy.

"I WOULD NOT LIVE ALWAY."

THE good Dr. Muhlenberg, author of the hymn "I would not live alway, I ask not to stay," is dead, aged eighty-four.

He lived long enough to hear his hymn sung for half a century, and hear of it as being sung all over the world. Middle-aged people who have been accustomed to the hymn from their childhood supposed, for the most part, that the author, whoever he might be, must have lived and died long ago. A man of such a mood, one would think, ought to have died young, and thus, in some sort, to have illustrated the sentiment of his song. His years, however, stretched beyond the allotted span, and he who "would not live alway" went far beyond the measure of days which fall to the most of old men.

We doubt not his old age was sunny and joyous, and that he took in the blessings and beauties of the outer world as only Christians can. In temporal things Providence was kind to him, and his was a complete, well-rounded, and happy life. He never took back his hymn, or the sentiments of it, that we know of. Whether it was sung at his death-bed or funeral we do not know; but it might have been with propriety. It is such a hymn as we should naturally suppose only an old man would write, or one in great affliction. But Dr. Muhlenberg must have been comparatively young when he wrote it, and as yet little acquainted with the greater sorrows of human experience. As years multiplied and old age came on apace, he must have felt that this early effusion wonderfully anticipated the longings of the aged saint. What the younger Christian could write only the aged believer could completely feel.

The text is taken from Job, but the sermon is from John. The old patriarchs felt the weariness of life, but they could not have written this hymn. They had the theme, but the song must wait until Jesus and the resurrection should be more clearly manifested. The stringed instruments of the Old Testament can be touched and all their music brought out of them only by the masterly skill of gospel faith and assurance. Neither Job, David, nor Isaiah could have written the song that Muhlenberg did.

In many respects religion makes the present life more tolerable than it would be without it; but with all of its consolations and joys the blessed hope of a brighter world draws the believer away from it. The routine of daily affairs, the pettiness of employments that occupy the most of our time, the staleness, flatness, and tedium of the work we must do, drive us to think of better things and to wish for them. Mr. Jefferson, in his old age writing to John Adams in this mood of weariness, speaks of the labor of putting on and taking off his shoes. What a large part of every life is consumed in these details, and how the soul comes at length to fret with its chain and to loathe the conditions of its earthly captivity! If there were no sharp pain and no rooted sorrows, this would be so; but when these are added, what wonder that men tire of life? Given these circumstances of earthly experience in connection with a hope of heaven, and the utterance of the patriarch and the Christian's song are easily comprehended. They are not adapted to every phase even of religious experience, but there are few devout souls who cannot at some period of their history adopt most heartily all they contain.

It is well for us that the inevitable hour is looked forward to with something more than mere resignation. Providence and grace work together to this end, so that the Christian not only submits to the divine dispensation, but he rejoices in it as the crown and glory of infinite mercy.

THE DUTY OF LIVING.

FEW men in their senses are willing to take the responsibilities of deliberate suicide. There are many—more than is ordinarily supposed—who would choose to die rather than live. The troubles of life go very far toward reconciling people to death. The grave to many is less dark and repulsive than life.

The Christian's apprehension of the subject may be defective. The natural instinct, which is strong in brutes as well as in men, leads us to cling to life. The objects of affection and dependence strengthen our hold upon it. The instinctive love of life and the ties of natural affection constitute usually the main incentive of living. To leave a dependent family seems to be the uttermost of death's calamity. Where the natural desire of life is overcome by the vanities and failures of it, and where life does not appear essential to the maintenance and happiness of kindred, there would seem to be no adequate motive of continued struggle here.

It happens, with these inadequate views, that life is held very cheap. Readiness to die is judged by the state of reconciliation with God, by the absence of any fear of death, and by those longings after immortality which are intensified by present sufferings. To depart and be with Christ is far better, doubtless; but does the work of God come in as the real and potent reconciling tie to life? We would ask as many thoughtful Christians as may read these lines whether, in their reflections upon their own living and dying, this highest and truest of all motives has entered much into the account. In view of the probability of departure from earth, has not the chief and only concern been about wife and children and unsettled temporal affairs? These interests lie near to the hearts of all, and they are not only natural but right. Is there not something wrong, however, when these are the only concerns, and when the service of God is left out of our valuation of life? Many insure their lives for the sake of their families and their creditors, but we have never heard of any one insuring his life for the support of the gospel or the extension of Christian missions. Such instances may be, but we are not able to recall them.

The highest value of the Christian's life is in its relations to our Father's business. To live is Christ, and living unto the Lord is the real converse of living unto self. To live for wife and children merely or chiefly is an elongated selfishness. To live simply in obedience to natural instinct is brutish. The duty of living grows out of a higher conception of life as the talent to be improved for Christ's honor and the furtherance of his spiritual kingdom. The Christian, with his readiness for death and his longing for heaven, is bound to earth by the strongest of all ties. Beyond those other considerations which are common to all, he values his life for what it may be worth to the cause of religion and the general good that he may do. It may happen that he is called sometimes to take his life in his own hands, and to choose between a present martyrdom and a prolonged life of devoted toil. The point is determined by which is likely to accomplish most for God.

Life becomes a high religious duty in this aspect of the subject, not only in the sense of working while we live, but as it is a duty to live. The idle servant is guilty of moral suicide, but the reckless servant is not less to be condemned. It is a Christian duty to live, and to live long. It is better neither to wear out nor to rust out, but so to husband and distribute the strength as to secure the greatest longevity and the longest usefulness.

The Scriptures certainly make long life a boon. To the worldling it appears so, but not less is it desirable to the Christian. The "good old age and full of years" is the exultant crowning of the Old Testament obituaries, and some of the promises hold out long life as the greatest blessing. Godliness is profitable, "having promise of the life which now is." Parents are to be honored "that thy life may be long in the land," and a psalm of promises concludes, "With long life will I satisfy him, and show him my salvation." It is the curse of the wicked that they "shall not live out half their days." If long life were not a thing to be desired, and upon the highest grounds, these scriptures would be misleading and contradictory.

To the good man long life is desirable on many accounts, but chiefly for the maturity and perfection of his usefulness in the militant kingdom of Christ. Time is short—too short to do much in, it may be—but every year is of untold preciousness to the earnest worker in the vineyard. The elder years are also of increasing value, in which the accumulated capital of wisdom, knowledge, and piety is expended upon fresh and larger enterprises. Generally people look for retirement just where their capacity for greatest usefulness begins. To expect early retirement from active and devoted labors in religion, and to count upon an early death, are much the same thing. To live long, and to labor long, is the duty to be set before us. Long life is a blessing to us, that we may attend to the nurture and care of our families and see our children settled in their chosen pursuits. But it is a blessing for another and better reason, that it affords the completest and fullest scope for the accomplishment of the greatest good.

Nor ought any underestimate of our powers and opportunities to be allowed to break the force of this motive. The most inferior talents, amidst the most unfavorable circumstances, will accomplish a great deal if they have time to work in. Every life is important to God and to his work, and every life has a mission which is essential to the cause of Christ. You may think it matters little when you die or how long you live; but if you feel that you have something to do and a part to contribute to the great evangelical whole. it matters much. It behooves you to live, to live to be old, and lay the completest offering possible upon the altar. Our old Christians are precious to the Church; and our aged ministers, full of years and labors, how could we do without them? These gray-headed men and women in our congregations and our church-meetings are now doing their greatest and best work. To the believer there is a blessing in living as well as in dying, and we think that too much stress cannot be laid upon living as a duty we are called upon to cherish.

There is a great deal of unwholesome cant about the vanity of life and the blessedness of death. In God's order and providence death is a blessing at any time to the good, and we are grateful for the light which providence and immortality shed upon the problem of early dissolution. But, for all this, there is a beauty and love and godliness here; and, beyond the material and social aspects, living and living long assume the character of a sublime and sacred duty. It cannot be a matter of indifference to the believer whether he lives or dies. If instinct were gone, and social ties all severed, and the way to heaven unclouded, his Christian work and mission would suffice to make life valuable and to be retained to the latest hour.

NOTHING TO LIVE FOR.

THIS expression has often fallen from the lips of the pious, and yet we question the considerateness and the truth of it in most cases. We can scarcely imagine a situation in which it is justifiable. With no higher views of life than those which are held outside of the Christian faith and revelation, there are many circumstances that lead to this utterance of despair. A man whose interest in life terminates in himself, or in his own immediate family, or to whom the end of living is in physical enjoyment or the pleasures and successes of business, politics, or literature, may arrive at a point where these objects are utterly and hopelessly gone.

If mere enjoyment and happiness, in its common acceptation, be the absorbing pursuit, these may be exhausted long before the appointed years are numbered. It happens that the individual is bereft, in the summer or winter time of his age, of those for whom he was living—flower and leaf and branch are lopped off. Or, he has reached an age when the physical senses have lost their delicacy as avenues of grateful sensations. Contemporary men and women have passed, and he is left alone in a young world with which he finds little that is congenial. The fortune he has sought has eluded his grasp or has melted away from his possession. He finds himself without a country after long years and prayers for its welfare. He feels himself to be disinherited and ejected from the world in which were all his hopes and joys.

A Christian is not insensible to these influences, and, under stress of affliction and disappointments may feel that he has nothing to live for. The words are unadvised and the sentiment false. We are supposing that things have come to their worst pass; that disappointment is at every turn; that we are so bereft and stripped that the worldly eye sees not a vestige of inducement for continued existence here. In fact, so desperate a state is seldom reached where even the unbelieving and carnal heart will not find something amongst the ashes and cinders of its broken and devastated temples. But we suppose and admit the reality of the worst that can be stated or felt. Here the afflicted soul comes to the conviction of an aimless life. And so it would be if there were no world to come, no spirit within us to be purified by fire, and no millions of human and redeemed creatures to be helped by us.

Allowance should be made for the hour of paralyzing and

alienating grief, and for the shock and fury of the overwhelming storm. But does not this feeling of uselessness grow out of narrow and selfish conceptions of what we live for? The snow-shoe, by placing the weight on a broader surface, sustains the wearer. We sink because the base is narrowed to a point. The heart has lavished its affections exclusively upon a single group or speck, instead of taking in its affluent sweep the races and generations of men. The elements of happiness have been gathered around self. Our earnest prayers, and our fervent love, and our tender sympathies have scarcely extended beyond the circle of family ties and personal friendships. It is a shell of narrowness and selfishness in which we have been living, even religiously living. The feeling that we have nothing to live for reveals this terrible defect. If our world and our religious affections have been pressed into this limited compass, it may often be deeply and sadly felt that life is left without an object. You are living for your children, or for an only child. They are taken, or the idol in which your being is engrossed is removed. You have been absorbed in the attempt to realize some ideal of earthly happiness, and it is now shivered into pieces. What is there left? If, on the other hand, your life, its purposes, plans, and ends, had been projected upon the broader catholicity of Christ's life, and your mind had been "the mind that was in Christ," how different and how much more cheerful the conclusion that would have been reached!

Self-love, temporal enterprises, kindred ties, and the temperate pleasures of life, are allowable ends if held in connection with and subordinate to the claims of Christ. It is the limited and imperfect notion of duties confined to our nearest relations and inferior interests that makes it possible for any one to say that he has nothing to live for. Surely, if we are crucified with Christ, our sympathies and love are expanded with his. The natural affection which commended Mary to the care of the beloved disciple did not exclude tender solicitude for the world. Neither did devotion to Jerusalem swallow up that wider concern for all the ages and races. The cross is the exponent of an unselfish benevolence whose universality stretches so far beyond humanity even as to bind and reconcile the things in heaven. There is nothing sectional in Christ. His name and spirit rebuke it. To put on Christ is at the same time to put off self and to be emancipated from sectionalism and from the bondage of "inordinate affection." In Christ there is neither Jew nor Greek, male nor female, bond nor free.

The scope of redemption embraces all relations and conditions, and gives its own breadth to those who are imbued with its spirit. The heavenly citizenship breaks over all domestic and geographical boundaries, and carries us wherever men and angels live, and beyond them to the Universal Mediator and the one God and Father of all. It is only when our existence and its objects have been shut in to the merest atom and molecule of the great universe that this conviction of having nothing to live for is possible. It is really the hell which selfishness and idolatry have kindled about the soul. It is a death and despair for want of enlargement and the liberality of the Lord's Spirit. When God in his providence takes away the objects around which our affections have been gathered, he evidently designs to liberate and to lead out into other and wider fields of usefulness. The odors of the broken vase are not lost, but set free. There is something to live for so long as the world stands and we remain in it. This we shall realize when the narrowness of self and its near modifications are crushed out of us and we attain to the mind of Christ.

We know of devoted believers who for years have kept their beds unable to feed themselves. Are such examples of patient suffering without their value to the Church and the world? There are those whom age and infirmity have retired from active exertion of any kind, but they are not shelved so long as prayer remains to them and they can bear witness to the faithfulness of the promises and the comfort of the Holy Ghost. We have seen believing men and women, bereft and sorely stricken, thrust out into greater usefulness and exhibiting the power of the gospel to sustain and comfort as they never did before. When we have reached the point where it seems that we have nothing to live for, we have really come to a vantage-ground of usefulness. The loss to ourselves is a gain to Christ, and we are now furnished for earnest work.

How can any Christian be without something to do in a world like this, full of suffering and sin? The thing that is next to us invites effort. Reduce the misery in your own neighborhood and increase the comfort and happiness. Take hold of the most homely of opportunities and be content and thankful for any open door, so it enables you to do a kind and helpful office to the body or soul of one for whom Christ died. Especially let us sometimes go beyond the limits of kindred and the tether of self. True benevolence may be hatched and nurtured by the affections of home, but it must not always abide in the nest. Our religion is unfledged as yet, unless our love dares a wider flight. If God has shaken and thrust you out, accept the lesson and apply it. If he has not, do not wait for the storm or the bolt that shall shatter the bough. Flight strengthens the wings and gilds the plumes.

THE GRAVE AND BEYOND.

THE DEATH OF FRIENDS.

THE death of those with whom we are most intimate, and who are snatched, as it were, in a moment from our sight, is attended by sensations such as no other event excites. We part with friends continually who are moving to distant places, and whom we scarcely expect to meet again in this world; but we may communicate with them, and we still think of them as breathing the common air and moving amidst the sunbeams which play around our own footsteps. In these separations there is a sorrow, a sadness, and a tearful regret; but we are consoled by the reflection that the absent are in the body, and are partakers with us of the nature and conditions of the earthly life. We may meet them again in very much the same state in which we parted, and, if they are still alive, our conceptions of them, however far away they may be, are of the familiar forms and voices which linger in the memory. We follow our friends about in their journeys and homes and employments here, and have some satisfaction and pleasure in picturing to our own minds just how they are, what are their thoughts, and what may be the visible and tangible surroundings—the earth, sky, and people amidst which they dwell.

Death is of tremendous significance, and the effect upon us is without comparison. What it is to the one called away—something so fearful, so glorious, and yet so incomprehensible—we can imagine, and it is this which separates and secludes it from all other experiences. As it relates to the living the sensation is new, and at the same time solemn and most mysterious. For this world and for the remainder of this life we know the separation is absolute. No message can be wafted back, and no post will ever bring us tidings. No cable can span this deep and bring us word of those who have gone to

> The undiscovered country, from whose bourn
> No traveler returns.

Enoch was not, "for God took him." Thus, as respects any further communication, our most intimate friends, our dearest kindred, are not. They have vanished from us while walking by our side, in the midst of discourse unfinished, and while we had no thought of their taking away. They have completely dropped out of the affairs and associations of time, and so absolutely that they no more exist as a part of this earthly system. They are not on the earth, they no longer breathe this air, nor do they inhabit such bodies as they once had. Nothing so prepares us for their death as to relieve it of all seeming violence, and as to save us from the inevitable shock. In most instances the warning is very brief—a few days at most; sometimes there is none at all. But where age or long illness has led to what we supposed was a calm resignation, the moment which marks the last pulsation and ends the earthly pilgrimage overwhelms us with a grief and a desolation which it would seem impossible to anticipate or prevent. In this state, and altogether as they were in the flesh, we shall see them no more; and when we do meet again, how different the circumstances from those which have attended our associations here!

The death of any one—even a stranger—as announced in a morning paper, sets us to meditating; but the death of one we know and love starts a peculiar train of thought and reflection. Memory is quickened, and the associations of the past, the history as it has been connected with our own, the wrongs and negligences in ourselves especially, and our failure to improve more fully the precious communion, come up with an almost preternatural vividness and rapidity. It is a time for self-reproach when we feel that reparation is impossible; and the negligences, omissions, and inconsiderateness of days gone by have a sting which cannot be extracted. But we do not dwell on the past alone. In such a lame way as is in our power, and doubtless with manifold misconceptions and errors, we follow the departed, trying to realize what death is, what are its physical and mental phenomena, and the emergence, from earth and flesh, of the immortal spirit. We must think of them in some way, and have some sort of conception of their being and of their employments. For their sakes, as well as for our own, we rejoice that life and immortality have been brought to light, and that we can think of our dead friends as helping to swell that great cloud of witnesses which surrounds us. They are "saints in light," and they are still, in character and in consciousness, such as we have known them on earth.

Every tie and relationship has a distinct effect as realized in the death of kindred. In the bereavement of parents, children, husbands, and wives there is something which distinguishes each separate sorrow. The death of parents awakens feelings unlike those excited by the death of children, and so of other relationships. Different chords are touched by these various ministries of grief, and a different class of emotions is stirred, according to the character of the affections upon which the blow of affliction falls. In reference to all it is true that these bereavements have a peculiarly mellowing and refining influence upon those who yield submissively to the dispensation. No other trouble— as, for example, those of bodily suffering, or the loss of property, or the disappointment of our plans in life—yield results so beautifying and enriching to the soul as those wherein the tenderest and best affections are for the moment bruised. A death in the household points, as no other means can, to the unseen and eternal world, and helps to a strong realization of the nearness and certainty of the heavenly and the spiritual. There is surely no other form of sorrow that is so effectual in loosening our hold upon temporal things and in exposing the emptiness and vanity of worldly success. The disruption of all ties, the breaking up of the associations and pursuits, and the sudden ending of all, stamp the earth as an empty and worthless thing apart from its relation to the future life. As men advance in years their path becomes more and more thronged by the images and memories of those who have put off the mortal tabernacle. In early youth we scarcely know any who have passed the solemn boundary; but every year adds some friends to the heavenly company, and as the years advance the number is greater and their fall more rapid, until at length we seem to live almost exclusively amidst the recollections of those who have passed away. The aged survivor especially feels that he is nearly alone, and that his comrades and fellow-travelers have been, for the most part, transferred before him to "the land that is very far off."

The death of friends and relatives ought to affect us deeply and in a manner most salutary. But the sorrow should be such as consists with a clear apprehension of immortality. If there were no affliction there could be no sanctified application, and the blessed and golden fruits of this peculiar chastening would be lost. It is in the full blaze of life and immortality brought to light that this sorrow purifies our earthly and sordid natures, and lifts the soul to heights and glories hitherto unknown. It is useless to prescribe the bounds and measures of the anguish. He who is "the resurrection and the life" wept over the form of a dead friend whom he was about to raise, and his sympathy comprehended and fathomed all that the stricken sisters felt. As Christians, however, we should not sorrow as those who have no hope. Our dead are in Christ, and our mourning should be such as consists with an unfaltering confidence in him who has "the keys of hell and of death." All mystery will soon be explained, and the conditions which separate the living and the dead will presently cease. The longest life is but a hand-breadth, and the months or years that remain will be passed as a dream. Happy for us if we may fully appropriate David's words of faith and hope: "As for me, I will behold thy face in righteousness; I shall be satisfied when I awake in thy likeness."

DYING AS A LITTLE CHILD.

AGED saints in their dying-hours often seem to return to the simplicity of their childhood, and their faith and trust have the sweetness and dewy freshness of their earliest religious experience. It was Dr. Guthrie who in his last hours called for a song, and when asked what they should sing, replied: "Give me one of the bairn's songs." Dr. Paxton, in his address at the funeral of Dr. Gardiner Spring, stated that in his last illness, when disease was added to the infirmity of age, he seemed to be taken back to his childhood, and on one occasion, after repeating a child's hymn, Dr. Spring repeated also the evening prayer of early days—"Now I lay me down to sleep"—and added: "God bless me, and make me a good boy, for Jesus' sake. Amen." It was truly a divine scene, this aged and learned theologian entering heaven as a little child. There is something not only sublime and touching but instructive in such facts as these. They may help us more perfectly to understand and appreciate the Saviour's emphatic declaration: "Verily I say unto you, whosoever shall not receive the kingdom of God as a little child, he shall not enter therein." It would seem that not only are we to receive the kingdom of grace as little children, but the kingdom of glory also. The child-likeness which constitutes so important an element of conversion and Christian character comes out in its greatest clearness and beauty at the end of a long career, and just as the immortal crown is be obtained.

The humility, the sincerity, and the unquestioning trust of our earliest years are often marred by contact with the discussions and skeptical thought of maturer years. Unconsciously a taint of self-sufficiency and pride of intellect have been permitted to soil the spirit, and the soul has gone out of Christ somewhat to wrestle with problems of theology and philosophy, and to grapple with secret things too high for human comprehension. For the earlier and truer processes of faith there has been an attempt to reach satisfaction and assurance through the investigations of science and criticism, and by the unaided powers of reason. Some of the loftiest and most erudite minds have retained the child-like spirit through all the labors and attainments of a life of study; but with many this dew of youth and this precious aroma of the opening flower are lost.

Contact with the world and the maturing of the appetites and passions have a tendency to stain the innocence of our first experience, and to darken, where they do not altogether obscure, the soft and pure light of life's morning. Happy are they who pass through the robust period of passion and active life, and meet and contend with the cares, business, and trials of the world without ceasing to be as little children in their thoughts of God, and in their trustfulness respecting Christ and his promises! The religion of childhood is the true religion of the whole life, and the conditions of conversion in the young are the same as those which meet men later in their history. Learning, experience of the world, matured mental powers, and a wider field of knowledge contribute nothing to the ability to apprehend Christ, and to believe with the heart unto righteousness. However old and wise and learned, the impenitent sinner must get back to the point of tenderness and humility, where the operations of the Holy Spirit were first consciously felt. The repentance will be more bitter, the awakening more terrible, the change more violent and demonstrative, but the humility and simplicity of the trust in Christ must be that of childhood.

The Christian life is a growth and a perfection, but its strength and ripeness are in this direction of likeness to a little child. It is the wisdom, the safety, and the glory of the mature man to return to it, and to keep the heart in this atmosphere of gentleness and transparent love. The hours of birth into the earthly life, the spiritual, and the heavenly are doubtless related. The birth of conversion is invested with the attributes of a simple and trusting spirit; and these same qualities are present and prominent when the soul struggles into the glory of its immortal inheritance. If there has been a certain hardness about the religious temper, and a certain finish and gloss of culture and learning in the opinions, these give way at the last to the meekness and single-mindedness of the first love. The spirit, weary and baffled with its efforts to attain to wisdom and understanding, comes back to the point where all true greatness resides.

The aged believer throws off the gathered stores of all the years of riches, honor, and learning, and rejoices to get back to the mother's knee, and to close a long life of devotion with the infant prayers and songs with which it began. This unquestioning confidence, this pure gold of faith separated from the dross of skeptical doubts and intellectual pride, and this absence of all fear concerning the life to come, are as a balm to the parting soul. No elaborate liturgies are then desired, and no masterpieces of poetry and music are asked for. "A bairn's song" suits best the soul that is near to the melody of heaven, and the prayer which infant lips have uttered is the most fitting close to a life which now glides gently into a world of perfect and endless praise. Dying as a little child is, after all, only to die the death of the righteous.

WHAT WE SHALL TAKE WITH US.

"SHALL we take our memories with us into the other world?" Our correspondent might as well ask whether we shall take ourselves thither. That is a very dubious and modified immortality that strips us substantially of all conscious identity, denies the recognition of friends, and leaves us almost as ignorant of our past existence as if we had not lived in the present world. If we do not take our memories with us, what do we take with us? If our entrance into eternity be like our birth here, with no sense of preëxistence and with no felt relations to the past, what is there left of immortality worth the name?

We take ourselves into the world to come, and this means our souls, with such mental faculties and spiritual powers as we may have. With no recollection of the earthly life there would be no continuity of existence to us, and the notion of accountability would be an absurdity. "The things done in the body" are to be received in the judgment, and the whole process of reward and retribution implies the most vivid and complete remembrance. Death will not break the thread of mental and spiritual life. Consciousness may be momentarily suspended in the transition, but the spirit wakes in possession of all the attributes of its personal and intelligent nature. "Son, remember," were the words addressed to the rich man. They are at least significant as indicating the activity and uses of memory in the retribution of the wicked, and we may well suppose that this faculty will perform an important office in the blessedness of the glorified.

We shall leave many things behind us—our earthly friends, our temporal pursuits, our property. "We brought nothing into this world, and it is certain we can carry nothing out." The miser must let go his money-bags; the millionaire must give up his stocks, bonds, mortgages, and real estate; the devotees of pleasure must part with their dissipations and revelry. The earthly work of the Christian ends with his life here, and the goods which his Lord delivered to him to be improved must be surrendered and accounted for. When we go away we take ourselves, the characters we have formed, the natures, good or bad, which have been developed under the conditions of human probation. The school and its appliances are left, and the pupil goes forth having in himself the results of his fidelity and diligence, or bearing the mortification and bitterness of neglected opportunities. "As the tree falleth, there it shall be." "Whatsoever a man soweth, that shall he also reap."

Death severs our relationships; it takes us away from our temporal enterprises; it dissolves our hold on property, and separates us from the conditions of mercy which surround us here. But it makes no essential change in character. This goes with us, with all that character implies. Death does not destroy it, judgment only recognizes and defines it, and eternity affords scope for its development. What the outward circumstances of the other world may be are comparatively unimportant now. The great determining principle is in ourselves, what we are, and what our relations to the infinite and holy God. The pure in heart shall see God. Sowing to the flesh will surely be followed by a harvest of corruption.

It is well to ask what we shall carry with us, and then to live in view of the obvious answer. Let men make to themselves friends of the mammon of unrighteousness; let them lay up treasure in heaven; let them so use the temporal that they shall be rich eternally. "For where your treasure is, there will your heart be also." If we make an idol of wealth, and live merely for selfish and worldly ends, we shall find ourselves poor indeed when the final hour comes. Conscience, memory, and all the endowments of intelligence, all the capabilities of the soul, will only contribute to the supreme misery if the spiritual part has been neglected. The surprising thing in death to many will be that it has not touched their characters at all, and that it lands them on the eternal shore as to their moral and spiritual natures just as it overtook them amidst the pursuits of life.

A circumstance connected with our question, and to be seriously pondered, is the fact that the most die at a time unexpected to themselves. "For man also knoweth not his time; as the fishes that are taken in an evil net, and as the birds that are caught in a snare; so are the sons of men snared in an evil time, when it falleth suddenly upon them." This is true especially with the unconverted. They fall in the midst of their plans and before they have given earnest attention to the interests of the soul. "Death took him by susprise" was the remark concerning a prominent citizen who died a few months ago. A surprise to his friends it was, but this did not matter; but to be surprised himself had to us a very solemn and startling meaning. How com-man this experience must be! Men, women, in their prime, and young people in the freshness of their years, falling ing sick, or by violence taken off. Unexpected blows of misfortune may fall upon us, but we can recover from the shock; but what is it to die before we have thought about it, and to be suddenly confronted with the dread reality? Truly, what shall we take with us when the Son of man comes as a thief in the night, and when, without warning, the soul, unprepared, is hurried into the spirit-world?

HEAVEN A CHARACTER.

THE most important and practical conception of heaven is that it is a character. It is a state the elements of which are not gained after we get there, but are attained here, and carried with us into those regions of light. The apostle gives thanks unto the Father "which hath made us meet to be partakers of the inheritance of the saints in light." The atoning blood not only delivers from condemnation, and from the curse of the broken law, but it is represented as cleansing from sin. It not only satisfies the divine government and vindicates the holiness of God, but it saves the soul from the dominion and pollution of sin. It declares the righteousness of God, and also through faith purifies the heart. Both as a legal ground of condemnation and judgment and as a possible defilement was sin to be taken away by the Lamb of God. Hence the washing and purifying power of the blood. "The blood of Jesus Christ, his Son, cleanseth us from all sin." Of the same import is the inspired exclamation: "Unto him that loved us, and washed us from our sins in his own blood, and hath made us kings and priests unto God and his Father: to him be glory and dominion-forever and ever. Amen."

A present holiness and a personal is contemplated in

these and in many other exhibitions of the sacrificial death of the Son of God. Pardon is but a part, although the head and fountain of all spiritual life and experience. The work of inward holiness is connected with the remission of sins, and is most emphatically declared to be essential to the heavenly life. It is holiness without which no man shall see the Lord, and the blessedness of the pure in heart consists in this: that "they shall see God." To be saved in heaven we must first be saved from sin on earth. It is true that "it doth not yet appear what we shall be," but there is no uncertainty about what we must be in order to enter the heavenly kingdom. The new birth is absolute, and without this birth of the Spirit no man can either enter or see the beatific inheritance. As to place, in its relation to the present world we inhabit, or in its relation to the vast system of material bodies which stretch beyond the reach of the most powerful telescopic reflectors, it is a matter of curious and unprofitable speculation. What the raised body will be, what the mind in its attainments and powers, and what are to be the splendid and sublime accessories of scenery, employment, and society, are pleasing themes, but their practical importance is less than nothing in comparison with the character which constitutes our fitness for the heavenly home.

Christ is the foundation of all our hope, and it is through faith in him that we are to be saved; but then it is through faith in him as a Saviour from sin. There is no other way by which his atoning merit can bring a soul to glory except that which regenerates and purifies the heart. He is the ground, the procuring cause, the meritorious means; but there can be no heaven for any unless they have attained to sanctification of the Spirit, and have believed with the heart unto righteousness. It is this conception of a gracious meetness for heaven that stimulates the healthful

Christian life, and inspires it with the earnest and heart-searching pursuit of holiness. "And every man that hath this hope in him purifieth himself, even as he is pure." There is nothing more contradictory or absurd than to talk of holiness in heaven while the attainment here is neglected or ignored, unless it be the thought of the irreligious mind that heaven can be any thing conceivable apart from the spirituality of those who compose its society.

The greatest comfort and glory of the gospel are the freeness and fullness of a present salvation from sin which it proclaims. Heaven, as the object of hope and pursuit, is always connected with the purity which the blood of Christ secures to the believing heart. It is needful and profitable that we should look at these subjects as thus related. Holiness and heaven—the work of sanctification, " perfecting holiness in the fear of God," and the city which "had no need of the sun, neither of the moon, to shine in it; for the glory of God did lighten it, and the Lamb is the light thereof."

MISCELLANEOUS.

ONE OFFICE OF THE SPIRIT.

GEORGE MULLER says that "one office of the Spirit is to bring things to remembrance." The reference we suppose to be to the words of Christ: "He shall teach you all things, and bring all things to your remembrance, whatsoever I have said unto you." The teaching and the bringing to remembrance are two parts of one process and operation of the Comforter. What Christ had said to his disciples was to be vividly and accurately recalled, and the meaning was to be made clear. They had heard much that they did not understand. The Spirit, when given, would bring to remembrance and also explain. The memory and the understanding were both to be quickened and acted on. The promise was fulfilled in the inspiration of the apostles, but does not the promise also point to some of the ordinary operations of the Holy Spirit in the experience of all who are brought in contact with revealed truth? While there is no proper inspiration, there must be a divine illumination in order to the apprehension of spiritual things. As Paul declares, God must shine into the heart "to give the light of the knowledge of the glory of God in the face of Jesus Christ." A great deal that Christ had delivered to his disciples was neither remembered nor comprehended until after the Pentecostal baptism. It remained dormant in the mind, and out of the sphere of consciousness until the power of the Spirit brought it forth.

Something like this seems to take place when those who

have long been familiar with the words of Scripture are awakened and brought to repentance. Promises and warnings that had long been forgotten come thronging into the mind, and they come with a force and meaning that they had never had before. In the hour of conversion the soul is often flooded with light, and Scripture that had previously been distasteful and mysterious is called up and made attractive and luminous. In times of trouble and great emergencies passages that had hitherto excited no particular notice, and that had no apparent lodgment in memory, came forth with amazing clearness and promptitude, and with a new meaning, to meet the needs of the tempted and distressed soul. But with reference to the unconverted who have been religiously instructed in childhood or have been hearers and not doers of the word, is not the Spirit busy with them in waking up the memory? For long periods there may be utter forgetfulness of the early lessons of piety, and the scriptures committed and the sermons heard may appear to be buried in oblivion. More than this— there may be the purpose to forget and to banish all serious convictions. Impressions are sought to be overcome and driven out by absorbing pleasures, vicious indulgences, engrossing business pursuits. And thus for years the seed sown is apparently lost, and no trace of the truth is to be discerned. But every now and then comes an awakening; the prodigal comes to himself, and he remembers his father's house, and the long-forgotten lessons come teeming in upon the heart with overwhelming freshness and power. Such instances reveal an important fact in reference to this one office of the Spirit in bringing to remembrance the things we have heard and which we are disposed to neglect.

Not in all cases does this work of the Spirit end in the repentance of those in whom it is felt. The Spirit may be resisted until he takes his departure; but, nevertheless, he strives mightily and long to clear up the clouded memory of sin and to restore the convictions that have well-nigh faded out forever. There is this ground of hope for parents who see little immediate effect of their painstaking instructions. Their children may forget and they may not now comprehend, but they may prayerfully count on the Holy Spirit as their ally in the endeavor to bring their children to Christ. Thousands who hear the word carelessly and casually, and who pass out from the house of God and from the preacher's sight and knowledge, carry with them that upon which the Spirit fastens, and which he wields with power and persistence for their salvation. It is a ground of hope that Christ's word has been lodged in the mind. The Holy Spirit will look after that word and watch over it ever afterward, and when long forgotten and obscured and overlaid by years of neglect, will bring it forth as the battle-cry of an aroused conscience and make it the instrument of a moral revolution. "The just shall live by faith" struck Luther on the stairs of the Vatican, slew his self-righteousness, and made him a new creature in Christ. It was through the teaching of the Spirit that Wesley, after ten years of perplexity and struggle, got his first clear conception of faith and experienced that amazing change in which he felt his "heart strangely warmed."

This office of the Spirit has much to do with the growth and progress of the spiritual life after conversion. All truth cannot be present to the mind at once, nor can it be fully displayed in a moment. The Spirit is continuously bringing to remembrance and teaching. Duties are recalled, privileges exhibited, doctrines explained, experiences cleared up. There is no inspiration of new truth, no revelation apart from the written word; and yet there is a wide and wonderful field of divine illumination, by which the memory is acted on and the spiritual understanding is quickened.

How prone we are to forget and how slow to understand! These are among the infirmities of believers, and out of them arise their greatest perils. As it was at first, so is it now; and the Comforter is promised to us to teach us all things and to bring all things to remembrance. This office was not limited to the inspiration of apostles, but it has a continual use and exercise in connection with the ministry of the word and with the experience of all who are brought into contact with the gospel. It lies at the foundation of our hope of the world's salvation and of the final triumph of Christ among the nations. Only by the Spirit can Christ be glorified in the heart or made glorious in the world. But for the Spirit operating with freshness and power everywhere and always, the gospel would be preached in vain. It is because he teaches and brings to remembrance that we are sure that the word of the Lord shall abide forever

GOLDEN VIALS FULL OF ODORS.

In the gorgeous vision of one section of the Apocalypse, prayer is mentioned as connected with the opening of the book that was "written within and on the back side, and sealed with seven seals." None but the Lamb could open and read that book, and in the opening of it the prostrate and adoring living creatures and the four and twenty elders "have every one of them harps, and golden vials full of odors, which are the prayers of saints." The same lesson is presented in another scene representing the opening of the seventh seal, in which "another angel came and stood at the altar, having a golden censer; and there was given unto him much incense, that he should offer it with the prayers of all saints upon the golden altar which was before the throne." The symbolical import of incense was recognized by the worshipers in the olden time: "Let my prayer be set forth before thee as incense, and the lifting up of my hands as the evening sacrifice."

In the vision it is the prayers of saints which the incense represents. We may well believe that no other prayers ever ascend before God so as to influence the arm of God and so as to bring blessings down upon the world. The cry of penitence is heard, the prayer of the publican for mercy is answered; but as an intercessory power and as a means of opening the gospel to the world, it is "the effectual, fervent prayer of the righteous man" that availeth much. The prayers of saints are in those golden vessels. They are diffused as an aroma about the throne, and are precious and acceptable to him who sits upon it. It is in the degree that men are holy that their prayers are recognized in heaven and that they are interwoven with the dispensations of mercy and salvation. The prayers of saints are ever present, and are intimately connected with the opening of the book and the loosening of the seals both in the sphere of providence and grace.

The value of prayer is exhibited in the preciousness of the incense made of the most fragrant and costly materials and in the costly golden vessels filled with odors. Prayer, thus represented, is no common or mean commodity. The opulence of the vessel indicates the richness of its contents. There is nothing about the throne, save the Lamb himself, that seems to be more esteemed. The harps are in the same hands with the golden vials, and yet the song must follow the answered prayer. "There was silence in heaven about the space of half an hour," and that silence seems not to have been broken until much incense, with the prayers of all saints, was offered upon the golden altar. The seven angels, with trumpets ready, were waiting, but no one was sounded until "the smoke of the incense, which came with the prayers of the saints, ascended up before God out of the angel's hand." We may not penetrate in detail the import of these stupendous events—the trumpets and the seals— but the connection of prayer with them is clear. God's praying saints on earth are among the most conspicuous and potent actors in these mighty movements which are directed from the throne of God. The book is not opened, the seals are not loosened, the trumpets are not sounded, without prayer. God, angels, the living creatures, the symbolical elders, the elements, all seem to wait for the incense of prayer from the golden vials.

We might further gather from this imagery that the prayers of saints are carefully preserved and their power is felt long after they are offered. They are treasured up in the golden vials—kept, and not lost. These golden vials are so many depositories of life and mercy, vigilantly guarded by the golden-crowned elders. The precious vessels are full of odors, to be set free as burning incense when occasion calls. Prayer in heaven's charge will keep. The answer may be long after the praying saint has passed to his reward. If the prayer of a saint and according to the will of God, it must sooner or later ascend as incense and be offered upon the golden altar. These golden vials are many—the prayers of every branch of Christ's Church on the earth and of the individual saints of every Church—but they all reach their common destination, and blend in one cloud of incense before the throne. What a single saint has contributed to the grand result we may never know, but each prayer helps to open the books and to break the seals of salvation to a lost world. As there are no individual discords in the song, and as the harps are touched by many hands with a perfect diapason, so there is oneness and accord in the prayers of saints. The precious gums may be gathered from a thousand different trees and may be compounded by a thousand different hands, but all are blended in one cloud of burning fragrance.

These vials of prayer are vials of mercy. The same vision that tells us of the golden vials full of odors has also its vials of wrath. How much the world is indebted to the prayers of saints for God's forbearance and long-suffering we cannot now tell. We do know that God heard Abraham's prayer, and that the presence of ten righteous men in Sodom would have saved it. But for the prayers of the saints that are in the world the divine judgments would be far less restrained than they are; and but for these prayers it is not unlikely that the day of wrath would have come long ago. The vials of wrath are filled by the wickedness of men. The ungodly are treasuring up wrath against the day of wrath. They are, by their unbelief and disobedience, tempting God and inviting their own ruin. One of the same four living creatures who at one time had a harp and a golden vial full of odors, is at last represented as delivering to the seven angels seven golden vials full of the wrath of God. When prayer has done its work for the world—its work of mercy—then wrath will come upon men to the uttermost. The vials full of the sweet odors of love and compassion, and freighted with the incense of life to the lost, give place at length to those of doom. If men do not repent, if prayer for them prove in vain, then the vials of wrath must be poured out.

Meanwhile the vials of mercy—the prayers of saints—are before the throne. These prayers bring blessings upon all. They stay the hand of justice; they prolong the sinner's space for repentance; they enrich the Church with copious showers of grace; they open the gospel to those who are in the shadow of death. It is not a vain thing to wait on the Lord—for a whole Church to unite in special prayer. The prayers of saints are in the golden vials full of odors, and the fragrant incense rising from tens of thousands of pure hearts ascends and fills the heavenly place. Doubtless the new song has swelled afresh from the hosts above on this account, and we may look confidently for the outpouring of mercy upon the fields of our earthly Zion.

THE HEATED TERM.

THIS is the sun's triumph. The clouds seem to have hidden themselves, and the sky, from dome to horizon, is all ablaze. During these longest days the sun does not waste, but grows stronger and fiercer. He rises early and sets late, and greedily covets every moment. How grandly and irresistibly he begins his burning march, and with what lavish glories he adorns the scene of his evening adieu! He "rejoiceth as a strong man to run a race." How he seems to gather about him the glowing vestments of the morning, and at evening covers himself with the heat and splendors of the long, long day! Blessed sun!

And yet shame on us to say we are almost sorry when his burning eye looks in upon us in the early morning, and right glad we are when he goes down. To be rid of him for a few brief hours is an unspeakable deliverance. If he were to shine here all the time, at night skirting the northern rim of the earth with only half his fiery disk in view, how should we live at all? The midnight sun! We want none of it. It is not the perfect day that we long for, but the perfect night rather. Even if the stars were to disappear for a time, it would be a relief; and the comet now flashing in the north-eastern sky is a most repulsive visitor. With the thermometer up in the nineties, a glow-worm or a lightning-bug is an unwelcome intruder.

How inevitably, in this season of fervid heat, everybody thinks of cool things and calls up every scene and object and experience associated with flowing brooks and living springs and deep, deep wells, out of which come the overflowing bucket covered with dripping moss! The forest dells and ravines, through which rivulets gurgle and in which the notes of the birds are fresh and liquid, how vividly they come to us! We have some heart now to think of arctic explorations, and almost wish we were in the haunts of the walrus and the white bear, moving amidst the floes and icebergs, and well on our way to solve the great problem and to discover the Open Polar Sea. Open Polar Sea! Would it not just now be a satisfaction to know that there is none, and that there is at least one spot that is perpetually frozen up? Arctic voyages are better summer reading than "Through the Dark Continent." We are almost tempted to think lightly of the fate of Sir John Franklin, and to regard it as a most rare and desirable euthanasia.

We would stand on the Alps, on the Apennines, but not with the thunder talk. We would climb to the regions of perpetual snow, and stay there until this torrid heat be overpast. Our walls, if it were possible, should be hung with pictures in which winter scenes predominate—fields covered with the drifted snow, an atmosphere flecked and dappled with the falling crystals, forests bowed beneath the weight of their snowy mantles, streams locked in icy repose, and railroads, towns, and hamlets completely snowed in. It is thus that in sickness we dream of health, in poverty that we covet riches, and in delirium that the thoughts dwell upon the fountain.

The mercy of mercies under this brazen sky is the ice we have. The new South is in our ice-factories. Who would not be fraternal, seeing what a surpassing blessing and comfort there is in Northern ice? Better than its politics, better than its literature, even better than much of its religion, is the ice. We are brethren, frozen together and indissolubly united. Under the grateful influences of the music of the ice-pitcher and the generous cooler, how our hearts warm toward our Northern brethren! Its effects are more magical than those of open purses or the most gushing declamation. For the sake of a cooler climate, we might be reconciled to a three months' sojourn in the White Mountains or the Adirondacks. We are free to confess that the North is the better country in the summer-time, and that during the summer solstice their civilization has a better chance than ours.

The problems of the two civilizations are different. The one is how to estivate, the other how to hibernate; and this seems to be the point of contrast the world over—how to get through the winter, how to get through the summer. The easier task is ours, and yet it is not without its dangers and difficulties. The crops are growing, and the bread and raiment and wealth of the country are in the silk of the corn and the bloom of the cotton-plant. The sun is making the sugar, the wheat, and the rice. He is making all; and while we swelter in the city and toil in the field, malaria is brewing, and there is death in the pot. God is over all. He has appointed the bounds of our habitations, and there is good in all and blessings always for them that love him. In this melting and death-dealing heat let us think of him who is "as the shadow of a great rock in a weary land."

THE TWO MARVELS OF JESUS.

IT is recorded that Christ marveled on two occasions— once at an instance of unbelief and again at a display of remarkable faith.

It was in his own country, and among his own kinsfolk and acquaintances, that he was the greatest offense and where he met with an unbelief which astonished even him who "knew what is in man." He was not amazed so much at the general unbelief prevailing in the world, nor was he unprepared for the doubt and enmity of the Jewish people; but that those whose privileges and opportunities had been greatest, and who were familiar with his life and wonderful works, should reject him was a thing surprising to him. "He marveled because of *their* unbelief." The Jews in general did not excite his wonder by their malignant treatment and blind opposition, and the reception which the gospel would meet with at the hands of unenlightened heathen was foreseen with calmness and equanimity.

It was unbelief under peculiar circumstances of favor, in the presence of evidences which ought to have been convincing if not overwhelming, that wrung this note of astonishment from the Master's lips. If faith could have been reasonably expected anywhere, it was there. We do not know that he ever marveled at any other exhibition of unbelief. There was something so exceptional in this—it was such a manifestation of prejudice, of willful enmity against truth and righteousness, of persistent error and sin in the midst of the brightest displays of truth and goodness—that it called for this disclosure of wonder on the part of the Son of God.

For him to marvel at unbelief was far more significant and a much more striking fact than if it had been related that any of his disciples had been thus affected. Good men may marvel at such unbelief as would have drawn no comment from the Saviour. Knowing the heart as he did, there was to him nothing surprising in the usual manifestations of depravity. We may be dumbfounded and perplexed where Christ would only have seen those depths of hardness and sin with which he was most familiar. Cases of impenitence which provoke Christian people to impatience and despair are seen by him with forbearance and hope. When Christ marvels at unbelief the case must be far out of the common range and of the most serious and desperate character. Unbelief in Nazareth was a different matter from unbelief even in Jerusalem or Samaria.

The type of unbelief at which Christ marveled was very nearly that which men in Bible lands and in Christian communities entertain. It is that practical rejection of the Son of God of which men are guilty who are surrounded by the most convincing evidences and demonstrations of the divine nature and authority of the gospel. Here, under the very walls of the churches, within the sound of Christian teaching and song, and amidst lives and examples which witness for the truth, is the phase of unbelief which assumes the nature and proportions of the marvelous in the mind of Christ.

From the astounding unbelief of Nazareth we turn to a marvel of a very different character. A centurion, a man of war, not even a Jew, comes to obtain the healing of his slave. "I am not worthy that thou shouldest come under my roof; but speak the word only, and my servant shall be healed. For I am a man under authority, having soldiers under me; and I say unto this man, Go, and he goeth; and to another, Come, and he cometh; and to my servant, Do this, and he doeth it." Here was faith of the very highest degree in a man whose life was apparently unfriendly to religion and whose surroundings were of the hardest and most worldly character. He who had declared his astonishment at the unbelief of the Nazarenes is now surprised by a most wonderful faith. "When Jesus heard it he marveled, and said to them that followed, Verily, I say unto you, I have not found so great faith; no, not in Israel." The faith of the leper whom he had just healed was nothing in comparison, though that was great indeed. It excited no remark whatever. He was a Jew, acquainted with the law and the prophets, brought up in the knowledge of the miraculous and the supernatural, and in a condition to understand and appreciate the claims of Christ as the promised Messiah and the Son of God. But for this Roman soldier, this man of war, this heathen born and bred, what could be expected of him? Faith in him, and such faith, was something wonderful. Christ marveled at this faith even as in the other instance he marveled at their unbelief.

Something akin to this type of faith may doubtless be found in those who believe amidst the lack of helpful conditions, and who exhibit a confident reliance and an unshaken trust in spite of the discouragements and hinderances which beset their path. "So great faith" anywhere would have been extraordinary; but so great faith in this man, and in his circumstances, astonishes Christ himself. Such phases of faith now and then appear in Christian experience in the man of business, in the sailor amidst the rudeness and profanity of the forecastle, and in the trials and adversities of every-day life.

Here are the two marvels of Christ: An unbelief which seems to have shocked and astounded him, and a faith which awakened his wonder and admiration. One was the very opposite of the other. One was the extreme of sin, a guilt and corruption from whose terrible depths Christ shrunk back with startled wonder; the other was the extreme of grace, a loftiness of trust, and a degree of humble confidence which excites amazement in him who demands the faith of all men. Either would be a fruitful study by itself; but when the two are thrown together the contrast helps us to measure that emotion of the marvelous which both alike excited in the mind of the Son of God.

OLD AND NEW METHODISM.

Our people are often sharply lectured for their departure from the old paths, and some writers and preachers are always ringing the changes upon the defection of this generation from the stricter practices of the fathers. We have need, no doubt, to go back occasionally to the primitive days, and to mark and pattern after what was most excellent. But, after all, we do not think the former times were better.

In our doctrines we are the same, our pulpits and press mind the same things and walk by the same rule. The necessity of the new birth, the witness of the Spirit, and going on to perfection are fully exhibited. Class-meetings may have fallen off in some sections, but in many churches, and, we trust, in the most, they are kept up, and the love-feasts, we believe, are everywhere observed. The old times certainly had no advantage over us in prayer-meetings. They were not more regularly held, nor more spiritual. Then it must be remembered that sixty years ago there were no Sunday-schools to speak of, Methodist schools and colleges scarcely existed, and the subject of foreign missions occupied but little attention in comparison with the present magnitude of this enterprise. Sunday-schools, education, and missions are the achievements of new Methodism in the main. We might also point to the enlargement of our publishing interests; to the better support of the ministry, although still below the standard of ability and justice; to the improvement in church-building, and to the general advance in the grace of giving. These things should go for something surely when the mood is on us to censure and scold the Churches as we find them now.

In religious experience the measure of numbers is greater, but we doubt whether the proportion of chaff to the wheat is greater than formerly. The demonstrations peculiar to what is called "the old-fashioned conversion" were most natural and common in those days when the mass of the converts were without Sunday-school privileges, or religious privileges of any kind. The gospel came to them as it never can come to children who have had religious home training, whose habits of belief and prayer have never been interrupted, and who, from earliest years, have been familiar with the Scriptures, and have constantly participated in public and social worship. Repentance to the man who has lived in sin, and whose thoughts have never been directed to the subject of religion, may well be a mighty convulsion and as the throes of an earthquake, while he who has been raised in the Church, and has lived in its light, comes into the conscious peace of faith with a quiet joy which scarcely stirs the outward demeanor. We may count people as converted sometimes when they are not, and it is well to discount most revival reports to some extent. But this was so under the preaching of the apostles and Wesley and Asbury, and other pioneers had occasion to lament over it. The true old-fashioned conversion was a conversion that reformed the man and led to a new and holy life. We have long ceased to judge of the genuineness of a conversion by the outward demonstrations of the occasion. We can point to good and exemplary Christians, some of whom went through a great and bitter agony, and others whose cup of wormwood and gall was not consciously so very bitter; to some who were overwhelmed with the wonderful light, and to others upon whom the day dawned sweetly and quietly, but not with a suddenly overpowering effulgence.

The fact may be assumed that the conversions of these days are as thorough, scriptural, and powerful as in the olden time. If the mere phenomena are not as violent, it is owing to the better training and greater privileges of those who throng our altars of prayer. For deep, intelligent experience in the things of God, it is questionable whether the average is not above what it was a half-century ago. We have not read better in the old Methodist books, tracts, and magazines than some we have heard from living Methodists within the last six months. We imagine the proportion of those going on to perfection, and of those who have attained it, is as great as it ever was.

Our administration of discipline may be less vigorous and vigilant than under our fathers. Preachers are perhaps not as careful in the reception of members, nor so justly severe in turning them out. Our people trench upon the rules concerning gold and costly apparel. This ought not to be, but then they give more to Christ than they used to do, and some allowance may be made on account of the altered circumstances and conditions of society.

We have not space to say much about the preachers. Our bishops do not live on sixty-four dollars a year, nor do they travel across the continent on horseback. Their labors are apostolic, notwithstanding, and mentally and physically more exhausting than those performed by McKendree and Roberts. The sacrifices made every year by the rank and file of the preachers are equal to any standard of heroism. The preaching is not inferior, either in unction or in mental power. We could institute comparisons between the leading pulpit men of this day and those of sixty years ago. This the reader can do himself, and, we are sure, not to the disadvantage of new Methodism.

We have reason enough to mend our ways in some respects, and to recall the past, but there is progress beyond the old and also beyond the new. We have little sympathy with that chronic discontent that is ever harping upon the old and drawing unfavorable contrasts. The fathers had their imperfections, and we have ours; but to say that ours are greater is more than truth. It is, at any rate, our privilege to gather up the wisdom of the past and the present, and to press on to a still nobler future.

ELIJAH'S MANTLE.

PAUL reminds us, in one place, that he owned a cloak. He had left it at Troas with Carpus, and from Rome he writes to Timothy to bring it, "and the books, but especially the parchments." This is all we know concerning an apostle's cloak. Whether it ever reached its owner, and what became of it, we cannot tell. If it had been Peter's cloak it would, beyond a doubt, have been preserved in the Vatican or somewhere else. Elijah's mantle comes down to us with its rich historical associations, and reference to it adorns our reflections upon the euthanasia of the great and good.

The prophet's mantle had seen hard and distinguished service. We first hear of it at Horeb, when, after the still small voice, "he wrapped his face in his mantle, and went out and stood at the entering in of the cave." It was with him, we may suppose, at the brook Cherith, at Zarephath, at Carmel, and his constant companion throughout his eventful career. The gray overcoat of Napoleon was not better known to the French army than was that mantle to Israel and to the court of Ahab. It seemed, from long use and association, to partake of the identity and personality of the wearer. As if invested with something sacred and supernatural, the prophet smote and divided the waters of Jordan with it, and after the translation Elisha wields it with like miraculous power. It had seen hard and distinguished service, but it was not worn out. It was a prize and a cherished legacy to the successor of Elijah. The mantles of the prophets, to be worth remembering and inheriting, must be of this sort. The service they have seen and the condition they are in when cast off are mainly important. It is not every man, nor even every good man, from whom a mantle of power falls when he is called away from his earthly course.

The prophet casts off his mantle as he enters the chariot. It fell from him. It gravitated to the earth, while the changed and spiritualized man ascended. The mantle had been the companion of his toils and sufferings, and had ministered to his comfort. So far as it was the type of his earthly ministry and activity, and so far as it witnessed to his bodily weakness and exposure, it was meet that it should be left. It was no longer needed for protection and comfort, and the ministry which it might represent was at an end. The prophet must leave his mantle. Flesh and blood can as easily inherit the kingdom of God as that the saint can take his mantle with him to heaven. His personal work and mission in this world are ended, and here he must leave them to be taken up by others, and, in the providence of God, to be perpetuated until the day of judgment.

Elijah had trained a man for the purpose, anointed him by divine command, and he was ready and qualified to take up the fallen mantle. Moses had his Joshua, Christ his apostles, Paul his Timothy. Martyrs and confessors and saints, as their mantles have dropped from them in death, have left their life-work to others of like heroism and devotion. As one generation throws off its mantle of labor and suffering it is taken up by another; and thus, while God translates his workmen, the work goes on. There are only a few in the roll of the centuries who stand out as preëminent, and who have impressed their individuality and personal greatness upon the world. Augustine, Luther, Calvin, Wesley, are almost alone in their eminence. Abraham, Moses, Elijah, Paul, tower above thousands of inferior note. The mantles of such men, in the hands of after gencrations and Churches, go on working moral miracles and smiting and parting the waters of the Jordan.

Elijah left his mantle—his work and ministry—to Elisha and the faithful of all time; but that which he could neither leave nor bestow was the vital thing. The spirit of Elijah was the Spirit of God, and God alone could give a "firstborn's" portion to him who sought it. The mantle had its glorious memories, and was a thing almost sacred; but it was a rag at best, and of little value without the more excellent gift. To attain to the power of Elijah's ministry, the spirit that moved and sanctified him must fall upon his successor. A succession of mantles is one thing; a succession in and of the Holy Ghost is quite another. The mantle of Church polity and ordinances, without spirituality, is a worthless shell. The mantle of a creed, worn without an inward life, is a cold and effete affair. Our denominational names and our pride in the memory and achievements of our founders are empty and absurd unless the Spirit accompanies. What is the cloak of Wesley worth, or that of Luther or Paul, unless the Spirit that blessed them and made them what they were inform and stir our souls? To see men strutting in the gowns of the apostles without the spirit of the apostles is as ludicrous as it is sacrilegious. The old fable of the conceited ass that invested himself with a lion's skin comes up in spite of us. The literal mantle, the clothing and millinery of a religious order, are in the line of a belittleing superstition. But all that is merely outward in forms, theologies, and symbols of faith, and the traditions of the fathers, are the embodiments of enervation without the higher and divine gift.

Nine hundred years after Elijah ascended a man appeared "in the spirit and power of Elijah." The main thing in John was "the Spirit and the power." Outwardly like the Tishbite, as became his peculiar mission—rugged, austere, and abstemious—mantled in the same ministry of a reformer, and with like outward conditions, that which made the Baptist an Elijah was that he came in the spirit and power of Elijah. The true prophetical ministry without the Spirit is an impossibility. Neither Elijah's mantle nor Paul's cloak can make a saint or a preacher unless a double portion of the Spirit—that of the first-born and heir —be poured upon him.

THE CAKE AND THE CRUSE.

THE food which the angel provided for Elijah under the juniper-tree was very simple, but most wonderfully nourishing. A cake baked on the coals and a cruse of water made up the frugal repast; but the prophet "went in the strength of that meat, forty days and forty nights, unto Horeb, the mount of God." In the case of Moses no note is found of any meat which prepared him for his forty days' fast in the mount, and in the case of Christ the angels ministered to him after his fasting and temptations were ended. All were alike miraculously sustained; but with Elijah there are means, although supernaturally given and invested with at least preternatural virtue. Moses and Christ were sustained directly by divine power; Elijah went in the strength of the meat which the angel supplied.

God had taken care of his servant at the brook Cherith by the ministry of ravens and the flowing streamlet. Again, he had provided for his daily wants in the house of the widow of Zarephath by multiplying the meal and oil as they were wanted. However strange and however miraculous, the supplies were daily, and suited to the habitual demands of nature. Here he eats, and by this single repast is made strong for a forty days' journey. The bread of one day had in it the nutriment which the bread of forty days ordinarily had. The miracle was not—as in the barrel of meal and the cruse of oil, or as in the Saviour's miracle of the loaves—in the multiplication of the quantity, but in the adequacy of this one repast to last through so long a period of abstinence. That one cake, kneaded by the hands of the angel and baked under his eye, had in it the nourishing properties of forty cakes ordinarily. The bulk was not increased, but the life-sustaining power was intensified. The manna of which the Israelites partook had to be eaten daily. The cake was not less miraculous than the manna in its creation, but it possessed this further miraculous property of sustentation long after it had been consumed.

In this respect it stands out in peculiar relief as something unique and to be distinguished from all that class of miracles which has some features in common with it. There was a virtue in that cake such as was not in the manna, and such as was not in the loaves and fishes. The prophet gathered no fragments, but he went in the strength of what he had eaten.

Beyond the lesson of providential care, the archetype of the letter may lie in things spiritual. There is the feeding of the discouraged and fainting soul, and the ever gracious and timely provisions which prepare the believer for unusual trials and dangerous and difficult undertakings. Often there is occasion for the girding up of the loins of the mind and for extraordinary manifestations of the divine power and goodness to give tone to faith, to quicken the spiritual apprehension, and to invigorate the courage and zeal. We imagine the transfiguration had something of this lasting and tonic influence upon the disciples. Long years afterward it is still fresh in the mind of Peter. It lingers in the apostle's memory as some scene of wondrous brightness, and he draws upon it for assurance and for the vindication of his faith. The majesty of Jesus, as it glowed there, is vivid and lustrous in his thought, and the voice which came from the "excellent glory" is clear and melodious, even as when he heard it in "the holy mount."

Some conversions, by reason of their sharply-drawn lines, are especially nutritious, while all are possessed of this quality of lasting virtue. When the soul is truly converted there is strength in the meat which, under conditions of faithfulness to the grace given, is not exhausted by the longest and most trying life. The frequency and aptitude with which Christians refer to their conversion indicate the consciousness of an experience whose impetus and blessedness are still felt. The stream which took its rise in the birth "from above" is, after many years, the same stream of life and assurance. We would throw no needless suspicion upon the faith of those whose conversion seems to require an almost annual renewal, nor are we to lose sight of that daily grace of which the manna may have been the type; but a genuine conversion is rarely evanescent. There is strength in that meat, and he who eats it will be likely to press forward and to surmount the obstacles which lie in the pathway of duty. There are passages in the religious life wherein the soul receives unwonted blessings, wherein, like Jacob at Peniel, some great victory is achieved, and there is a manifestation of truth and of God which marks a new era in the soul's history. The believer wakes up beneath the juniper-tree to find the cake and the cruse and heavenly ministries waiting. And from henceforth he is strong and uniform, and treads the high places of faith and labor with a triumphant step. In that nearer approach to God, that more perfect consecration, and that revelation of the Spirit, he has found an inspiration which warms his heart with a deeper joy, and gilds his subsequent life with a peculiar brightness.

There are means of grace, protracted and camp meetings, or hours of secret prayer, which make epochs in the history of souls—occasions in which the hungry heart receives a portion which invigorates it for years and even for a lifetime. Not all sermons have this quality of feeding the spiritual man. Dainty rhetoric, well-rounded periods, metaphysical speculations, and scientific apologies are not likely to give life to the fainting and weary. Crude and loose-jointed amplifications, soulless commonplaces, are a mockery. The real preaching of the gospel is strengthening meat. The cake and the cruse of water were very plain and frugal fare, but an angel provided them, and they were suited to the weary traveler's needs. We doubt not the cake had been turned and was well done, and that the homely cruse was filled to the brim with water pure and sparkling. There was no raw dough, no muddy water. If in Christ's name, and invested with a ministry higher than that of the angels, men are called to "feed the flock of God," they must look well to the cake and the cruse. It is food, it is strengthening meat, that the hearer wants, and not the vapid confections of light literature, and a gospel robbed of its power to awaken and save. We feel that we have been to *preaching*, and that we have heard a *sermon*, when the soul has been fed, and, when we go away in the strength of that meat, prepared afresh for the toils and cares of life. It is the sermon that follows us home, and rings in our ears all the week, and stirs up and quickens the conscience for a long time after we have heard it, that does us good.

We might do well upon the properties of God's word in this connection—how its promises, precepts, and declarations are nourishing and life-sustaining. A single promise suffices for the meditation of days, and the devout spirit finds food for weeks in a solitary passage. Not by bread alone, "but by every word that proceedeth out of the mouth of God," shall man live. And still further and most fittingly might we conclude these reflections by reference to Him who is "the bread of life," and the true bread which came down from heaven. Here is strengthening meat indeed. The cake and the cruse which met the prophet's surprised and bewildered gaze, by the laws of association, if by nothing more legitimate, bring us to Him whose flesh is meat indeed, and whose blood is drink indeed. He that feeds on Christ can go in the strength of that meat through the rugged wilderness, and beyond the heights and solitudes of Horeb, even to the heavenly Jerusalem.

LENTEN COOK-BOOKS.

WE have seen advertisements of them, but have not examined the books. We can only conjecture what their contents may be. We do not know that the use of them is prescribed by ecclesiastical authority, or that scriptural warrant is claimed for them. We suspect that some wide-awake publisher, appreciating the commercial value of the enterprise and seeing money in this new and unoccupied field, has of his own motion compiled the work. Ordinary cook-books contain descriptions of dishes that are innocent of meat, and that are sufficiently frugal and abstemious for the average ascetic. From them can be learned the most varied methods of preparing eggs, fish, vegetables, and of combining them in ways that shall gratify the palate without pampering the flesh. A cook-book just for Lent would seem to be a needless expense; but there is a sentimental, perhaps a devotional, demand for a book set apart for religious uses—one that has something devout in its title, and in which the type and paper are flavored with the taste of sacredness.

The announcement of lenten cook-books is, we fear, a bad sign. If people wish to fast they can certainly do it without any special recipes; and if they desire to eat very little, and that little very simple and plain, the more obvious course would be to lock up all cook-books, and banish them from the household and kitchen until the Easter bells shall sound their recall. Science and art can compound a most satisfactory menu, such as the gourmand would heartily enjoy, without so much as the smell of meat about it. The fasts of which we have account in Scripture were more heroic. That of the Master, from which we suppose the modern Quadragesima takes its designation, was something very different from this lenten fasting. This attempt to make things very nice is not in accord with the austerities, self-denial, and mortifications of the flesh which fasting or abstinence is supposed to imply. Elaborate cookery by book looks like an effort to disguise the bitter herbs and to find out some way of self-righteousness which shall require no sacrifice. The Pharisees did fast twice in the week honestly and severely, and, apart from its supposed justifying merit, their self-denial commands our respect; but what shall we think of a Pharisee's claim to righteousness while the ground of it is sugar-coated or altogether evaded? We have a genuine admiration for the rugged preacher who lived on locusts and wild honey. He was a voice crying in the wilderness, and a mighty voice. There was no pretense and no sham about him. His was a hard and self-denying life, with no elaborate cuisine connected with it.

Fasting is good, no doubt. Abstinence—a modified fasting—is also good for the body and for the soul. But this cook-book fasting and abstinence is at least open to suspicion. Our Romish and Anglican brethren have reason to be alarmed. Besides the excess of riot of the carnival and the unrestrained license that breaks out after Easter, the worldly and fleshly spirit, armed with its cook-books, has invaded Lent, and laid its profane and sensual hand upon its sacred austerities. As a period of special religious services and of private religious devotions, the lenten festival is most commendable. But there ought to be something of the salt of self-denial in it, and the mind should not be occupied and diverted by the study of a special literature for the kitchen. A protracted meeting of forty days, with temperate living in the meantime, cannot but do good; provided, of course, that it be not regarded as a penance for the dissipations which were suspended on Ash-Wednesday with the purpose of resuming them after Easter. How much of formality, self-righteousness, and will-worship there may be in the observance of Lent we do not know, but we may hope that, with due allowance for these abuses, there is a considerable gain of spirituality.

To those of us for whom Lent is without authority, ecclesiastical or scriptural, there is this danger: that we come to regard fasting as altogether an unspiritual thing, and that we come at length to neglect it, as being the figment of a superstitious and perverted asceticism. Because these travesties and abuses of a duty are pushed to the borders of absurdity, there is in this no reason why we should utterly neglect it. The old-time custom among Methodists of fasting on the Friday before quarterly meeting and on other special occasions, and private fasting or abstinence, has largely fallen into disuse. While fasting is not made prominent in the New Testament, and while the authority of an explicit precept can scarcely be claimed for it, still it has its uses and benefits when properly observed. If it induces a healthier habit of body, contributes to clearer thinking, promotes control of the appetites, and fits the heart for devout meditation and prayer, there is reason enough for it, even if it be not made obligatory by divine command. Privately, as Christ directs, each one may exercise himself herein, and discover for himself how much and of what kind is most beneficial for him. Our General Rules and our form of receiving preachers into full connection seem to contemplate the use of fasting as a means of grace, and, like praying, and religion generally, to be distributed according to each one's conscience and circumstances throughout the year. We are without a lenten season and without lenten cook-books, but we are not without the usage and custom of fasting. It is needless to say that we like our Methodist way best, and we would recall our people to its observance.

REVIVAL EXPEDIENTS.

The fact that the churches are deeply exercised on the question of saving the people is a most hopeful sign. It is a token for good that they are casting about for means to reach those who have drifted away from their pales and those who have never been brought within the immediate range of gospel influences. It must not, however, be concluded that the regular preaching and the usual organizations are failures. The basis of all is the Church, with its ministry, Sunday-schools, and its trained and disciplined agencies. Let it be remembered that the lay evangelists, the missionaries, and all extraordinary movements, issue from this center, flowing from it as from a fountain, and deriving their vigor and power from this great reserve of material support and spiritual force. The work of evangelists would not exist but for the churches, and the immediate fruits of their labor are greatly owing to the seed already sown by others. The results would not be permanent if there were no pastoral care and no organizations for the instruction and oversight of those who have been awakened and converted.

The expedients resorted to cast no unfavorable reflection

upon the old and tried methods of conserving and spreading the truth. Solid and doctrinal preaching to comparatively small congregations, pastoral visiting, and the careful instruction of the children, are as much as ever a necessity. Whatever may be effected by novel ways—by peculiar modes of presenting the gospel, by singing, and anecdotes, and tact in the manipulation of various means—there will always be need for the patient laborer and for those who work steadily in the old-time way. Many are doubtless tempted to ask: "What is the use of preparing and preaching sermons and of going through all the painstaking toil of the average pastor, when such men as Hammond, Moody, and Varley so far outstrip them in attracting and saving the people?" Their ministry is necessarily transient in its operations, passing rapidly from one field to another. It is not likely that their measures in any one place would command unabated interest if continued year after year. Their ministry is also incomplete, directed almost exclusively to the awakening and conversion of sinners, while the work of edification—the training and maturing of Christian character—is necessarily left to others. Pastoral care and Church discipline are needed to secure and perfect the fruits. Without these the results would be almost as inappreciable and evanescent as the morning dew.

They are not displacing nor doing the work of the regular ministry. Their expedients, however valuable for their special object, may not be as good for all purposes as those with which we are familiar. It is not unlikely that they would prove less enduring and effective in the long run. Our camp-meetings are exceedingly useful in arresting popular attention, in awakening sinners, and in quickening the spirituality of believers, but they are accessory and supplemental as related to our regular Church-work. The expedients for the awakening of sinners are attended by preaching specially adapted to the unconverted. Let us not fall into the habit of directing our efforts too exclusively in this one channel. The precepts and doctrines of the gospel are very largely addressed to Christians, and no inconsiderable part of the pastor's business is to feed the Saviour's sheep. Preachers must not neglect to feed the flock of God over which the Holy Ghost hath made them overseers. Christ's commission to Peter was, "Feed my lambs, feed my sheep." The life of the Church must be nourished and kept up. In our reaching out after the aliens we must at the same time give due attention to the household of faith. Under too much preaching to the unconverted the Church grows cold, and by our very attempts to raise the dead the living are killed. Warning and teaching go together, and in no other way can we present every man perfect in Christ Jesus. The most direct road to a revival of awakening power is through a deeper work of grace in the Church. A vigorous and healthy life here is sure to make itself felt in the conversion of souls. The wise housewife looks to the quality of her leaven as well as to the manner of its use. More spiritual preaching, the presentation and enforcement of personal consecration, and the necessity of holiness and communion with God, are needed.

It is a great mercy to a community already well stocked with churches, Sunday-schools, and preachers, for some flaming evangelist to come along with new and peculiar methods to stir the people and to draw them to Christ. But are we to depend upon these means? Cannot every preacher save souls, and cannot every Church have salt in itself? But few men can handle the popular expedients which are so effective in the hands of Moody and Sankey. They cannot tell anecdotes; they cannot sing much; they have not the wonderful tact, the histrionic art. Some are no doubt endowed and called to a special work, but surely every devoted man may be wise to win souls, and every Church may be the source and center of saving power. Churches and the religious people of a community wondering at the success of certain revivalists may be waiting for them and underrate their own means for awakening religious concern among the people. God is not dependent upon any class of measures or agents, and if we have the spirituality and the faith his abundant blessings will be showered upon us.

Withal, let us not lose sight of the fact that the measures of the modern evangelists are very much after the old Methodist way. Our field-preaching, experience-meetings, assurance, sudden conversions, direct and pungent appeal, the offer of a present salvation, and going out after the common people, are the things once roundly condemned but now being taken up by the Churches. We should be careful to keep up the primitive fire, and by all means hold on to the methods which have been so effective throughout our history. Revivals are going on in various quarters of our Southern Church—in Virginia and Georgia especially—of remarkable power. The whole Christian world is exercised and expectant. It is a time to look for a general refreshing. All our resources of prayer, all our efforts as Christians, all tried and lawful expedients, should now be brought to bear upon the great work of arousing the world and of seeking a Pentecostal baptism.

AN EFFECTUAL QUARANTINE.

The Bible tells us of one. Of the heavenly city it is written: "And there shall in nowise enter into it any thing that defileth, neither whatsoever worketh abomination, or maketh a lie." Sin, like earthly pestilence, must have had a spontaneous beginning. Cholera, and yellow fever, and other mortal plagues, are indigenous somewhere, and then they spread along the lines of travel and commerce by their contagious nature. Wherever the conditions are favorable, there they develop in an alarming degree, and sweep through communities as an epidemic. The first germ of sin was hatched in the will of some creature, how long ago and how far away we cannot tell. The beginning was among "the principalities and powers," and it spread until our earth was involved in the fearful calamity. As to us, sin is an imported disease; and yet it could have found no lodgment here if the human soul had not voluntarily opened the door for its admission. It is the peril—the necessary peril—of probation, both with angels and with men, that sin may befall them. Doubtless God used all means consistent with his moral government and the freedom of the creature to keep sin out of the universe, but a moral quarantine could not guarantee absolute security. In order to holiness there must be freedom, and along with freedom in probation there must also be liability to evil. Whatever the barriers were, sin got in. It is abroad in the universe and it is epidemic in our world. The law of God, the highest motives to obedience, the endowment of ability to stand, the walls of paradise, did not suffice to keep it out.

As prevalent in the earth, it has never as yet been confined to any particular locality. It is found in every community. Notwithstanding the watchfulness of parents, the most careful training, the antidotes of prayer and precept, its traces are found in every family, and those who are most completely isolated and separated from the social infection are touched by it, and sometimes destroyed. It has become the study and care of the good to protect society from the influence of base and obscene literature, and yet these fly-sheets of perdition and these pictorials of hell come through the lines to contaminate the minds and to debauch the imaginations of the young. In spite of efforts to lay an embargo on vice and to set on foot a blockade that shall keep out drunkenness and licentiousness, nearly every community is pervaded by crime and immorality. The attempts of churches to keep out sin have never been perfectly successful. The vows required are strong enough. The terms and conditions are discriminating, applying to goods as well as persons. In some cases the applicants must linger for a season in a sort of probationary quarantine-station, and in general they must give vouchers that they are free from contagion. There must be a clean bill of health. But there are some sinners in Zion notwithstanding. Here and there a goat is seen in the flock. There are some carnal persons among the spiritual, and sometimes these "roots of bitterness" smuggled in unawares spring up and trouble the society of the elect.

Our moral quarantines are even as ineffectual as the most of those which are established to protect communities against the inroads of pestilence. Both are justifiable, and are productive of some good. In regard to the latter we have our doubts. Some seasons, at any rate, the wasting disease seems to develop with wonderful spontaneity, and quarantines are no better than fences of straw. And at best there are so many avenues to guard, and the subtle germs may travel in so many ways—by sea, by land, and through the atmosphere—that no expedients can be regarded as absolutely effective. Sickness, death, and sin will always blight this lower world. Neither individuals nor communities can escape them.

The celestial city is the only place where the inhabitants shall not say that they are sick, where tears shall be wiped away from all faces, and where there shall be no more curse and no more death. There the bar against sin will be absolute and effectual. There will be a blockade that cannot be run, a quarantine that cannot be evaded. Without will be the deadly plague of sin, for it is written: "For without are dogs, and sorcerers, and whoremongers, and murderers, and idolaters, and whosoever loveth and maketh a lie." There will be no intercourse between the outer universe of evil and the city of God. Non-intercourse will be the established law. There will be no coming and going. The separation will be complete and eternal. "And beside all this, between us and you there is a great gulf fixed, so that they which would pass from hence to you cannot; neither can they pass to us that would come from thence." The good are thus shut in to their glorious and sinless home, while the wicked are shut out by an irrevocable decree of exclusion. Whether these restraints are of power or only such as are self-imposed by the character of the holy and the sinful, the fact is still explicit and clear. There is a great gulf fixed, and this may be needed in order to the security of the redeemed. Besides the strength and perfection of virtue and holiness acquired in the probationary trials of the present life and by the diligent improvement of the divine grace, it may be necessary further to guard the children of light by placing them beyond any possible contact with the wicked.

"Evil communications corrupt good manners," but across that "great gulf" no spores of infection can ever be wafted, and from the outer world of corruption no miasmatic exhalations can ever come. Security from sin is assured; and this is the assurance of all blessedness. There is this one obstruction that it cannot pass, this one inclosure it cannot enter. Along with a clearer understanding of how moral evil came into the universe, and how it obtained such disastrous sway in our world, will be the glad and rapturous assurance that sin can never touch us more. This sense of security will be one of the crowning elements of heavenly bliss. In spite of our quarantines here, we live in fear and trembling lest the fearful malady invade our homes and make our firesides desolate. In heaven there will be no fear.

THE END.

www.ingramcontent.com/pod-product-compliance
Lightning Source LLC
Chambersburg PA
CBHW051723300426

44115CB00007B/444